"Brimming with vivid characters and a deeply humanizing humor from the very first page, Kevin O'Hara's brilliant memoir of three decades spent among the "cider heap" of humanity—as one eloquent patient calls the psych ward—rolls along at a rollicking pace that makes it hard to put down. *Ins and Outs of a Locked Ward* is provocative, poignant and a genuine pleasure to read, even its grimmest moments."

> — Debby Applegate, winner of the Pulitzer Prize for biography and author of *Madam: The Biography of Polly Adler, Icon of the Jazz Age*

"Fans of O'Hara's radiant memoirs, *A Lucky Irish Lad* and *Last of the Donkey Pilgrims*, will love this account of his tumultuous years as a psychiatric nurse. He handled his patients the same way he treats his readers: with respect, a gentle sense of mischief and a subversive willingness to break the rules in the name of kindness and humanity. When they finally put me away in a locked ward, I'm going to call him out of retirement. What fun we'll have!"

> — Donald Morrison, author of *The Death of French Culture*, columnist at *The Berkshire Eagle*, podcaster at NPR's Robin Hood Radio, and former editor at *Time Magazine*

"In the best tradition of Ken Kesey's classic book *One Flew Over the Cuckoo's Nest*, this engaging journey through a psychiatric ward captures both the challenges and the humor of the human condition."

> —Donald Meichenbaum, Ph.D., Research Director of the Melissa Institute for Violence Prevention, Miami

D1606018

"I know of very few writers who find the truth to the stories of our lives like Kevin O'Hara does. If this was fiction I'd rate him up there with Twain and Thurber. But these stories are true. Red Smith once famously said, "Writing is easy . . . all you have to do is sit down and open your veins . . ." Well, O' Hara bypasses the veins and goes right to his own heart, which bleeds right into yours. This is a treat of a book."

— Matt Tannenbaum, owner, The Bookstore, Lenox, MA

"With this latest memoir, his third, this one as a longtime psychiatric nurse, Kevin O'Hara has done what few, if any, writers could do, which is to tell a tale that is both troubling and inspirational at the same time. Read it and reflect, and bring your heart, mind and soul."

— Eugene Christy, author of *The Isle of the Blest*

"At a time when we are facing a growing empathy gap, Kevin O'Hara's memoir helps fill that hole. His nursing tales are captivating, each one exemplifying concern, compassion, and caring. Having told us in *Last of the Donkey Pilgrims* about how his beloved donkey Missie gave him comfort during a yearlong sojourn around Ireland, O'Hara shows us that empathy in a caregiver is not just healing; it is human."

— Al DeCiccio, Ph.D., Professor of English, Salem State University

INS AND OUTS OF A LOCKED WARD

INS AND OUTS OF A LOCKED WARD

My Thirty Years as a Psychiatric Nurse

Kevin O'Hara

Apprentice
House Press
Loyola University Maryland

First Edition

Casebound ISBN: 978-1-62720-395-1
Paperback ISBN: 978-1-62720-396-8
Ebook ISBN: 978-1-62720-397-5

Printed in the United States of America

Design by Mikaela Fallon
Edited by Elle White
Promotion plan by Samantha Dickson
Author photo by Rick Popham

Published by Apprentice House Press

Apprentice
House Press
Loyola University Maryland

Apprentice House Press
Loyola University Maryland
4501 N. Charles Street
Baltimore, MD 21210
410.617.5265
www.ApprenticeHouse.com
info@ApprenticeHouse.com

To Belita,
Whose unfailing love and inspiration have made this book possible

Other books by Kevin O'Hara

Last of the Donkey Pilgrims
A Lucky Irish Lad
A Christmas Journey

Contents

Contents

Author's Note

The stories in this fictionalized memoir are based on true events. However, names and identifying characteristics have been changed to protect patient privacy. Conversations have also been reconstructed to the best of my recollection and, in some instances, I have compressed or expanded time, or otherwise altered events, while remaining faithful to the essential truth of the stories.

SUNDAY: THE BELL TOLLS

On a gull-gray December Sunday, I watched the dawning light filter through our bedroom blinds. Tossing restlessly in bed through a long hour, I rolled over to face the alarm clock once again, ready to silence its charmless chime before it woke my sleeping spouse, Belita.

I was a weekend charge nurse on Jones Three, a locked Psychiatric Intensive Care Unit of 15 beds at Berkshire Medical Center in Pittsfield, MA. Though faced with another arduous 16-hour double shift, I took solace in knowing that Sunday was generally easier than Saturday, given my familiarity with the patients on hand.

Staring up at my bedroom ceiling, I ran through the 12 clients currently in residence. Sadly, this Sunday wasn't going to be "eight on a plate," as staff called an easy single shift. More like "head on a plate."

Two tough patients, right out of Central Casting, were hell-bent on headlining our Monday morning debrief. First was Polly, a slim, 19-year old who numbered among her eating disorders a threat to eat a light bulb before the next meeting of her outpatient treatment team. Not an idle threat since she'd done it before, after being molested by a stepbrother, the incident which had triggered her disorders into play.

The other red-letter patient was Roy, an enraged detoxing alcoholic with a history of splitting human skulls with tire irons. He promised to take us out "systematically" if he wasn't released to watch his beloved New York Jets play that very day in the comfort of his own apartment. Unfortunately, Roy would be going nowhere, since a sheriff was coming in Tuesday morning to escort him for a 90-day stint at Bridgewater State Hospital for breaking probation. We wouldn't tell him, of course, for he'd likely end up in leathers after a brutal struggle.

Luckily, the weekend's staff was comprised of four of my favorite coworkers, with Nurse Hatchet* nowhere in sight, so it wasn't all bad. But, in truth, I was pretty spent. I had two more years until I could sign up early for Social Security and eke out a modest existence. A couple hundred more shifts, when I could barely face another day.

Far worse than the grind of three long decades on the locked ward, the mind games or patient threats, or even the badgering of Nurse Hatchet, were the deepening cracks in my emotional armor. I'd always been able to meet the desperate neediness of our charges with a jaunty sense that they were just like us, and we were all in this together. But, finally, my protective shield of humor had been breached by the battering of a thousand heartrending life stories.

(*Note: Nurse Hatchet—with a salute to Ken Kesey—is a collective pseudonym for colleagues with whom I didn't see eye to eye over the years. I call most of my coworkers by their real names, to give credit where it's due.)

Yes, for too long I'd been working the "cider heap" of humanity, as one intelligent patient described her kind: "We're all rejects—bruised, worm-infested, frostbitten—never to be picked for grocer's shelf or holiday basket, but just carried away by a merciless conveyer belt toward the cider press."

Belita woke moments before the designated minute of 6:10, and whispered into my ear. "One more day, Kev, and you'll be free for a week."

Yes, one more day.

I dragged myself from bed to the staircase banister, where I'd set out fresh clothes the night before. I would usually dress casually on Saturday, but always wore a shirt and tie on Sunday, to look the part of a charge nurse, and appear more presentable to visiting families and clergy.

Rallying myself to the task at hand, I left my house with a healthy stride, giving myself ample time to walk the hilly mile to the hospital. Walking in all weather was a habit I'd picked up on an eight-month, 1,800-mile perambulation of Ireland back in 1979, when I walked alongside a donkey and cart around its coastline. Another story, entirely.

Stopping first at O'Connell's Convenience, I bought a *New York Times* for our current events group, and a pack of community smokes, a practice that would set off Nurse Hatchet like a firecracker: "O'Hara, you've got to be the only RN in the world who buys cigarettes for patients!" No smoker myself, I didn't believe it made sense to withhold the one drug that offered our patients palpable relief, while the pills we dispensed left many drooling and twitching for years.

Purchases in hand, I arrived at the hospital entrance just before seven, where I paused to greet several employees as they rushed in. I made a private ritual of remembering my parents before going into work, saying a prayer, and listening for the seven o'clock church bells. My mother had been a psychiatric nurse in England and Wales during World War II, between leaving Ireland and arriving in America. She believed nursing to be a ministry and never entered the wards without saying a prayer "to guide my heart and hands." Those church bells also reminded me of my dad, who'd been caretaker and bell ringer for St. Charles Borromeo, our nearby parish church. I always found the bells a soothing tonic as I turned to face another day on the locked floor of human misery.

I was immediately approached by Security in the Main Lobby. "Hey Kev, that's a clip-on tie, right?"

Giving it a sheepish tug, I answered. "Aw shucks, Brian, I forgot."

Brian dismissed me with a friendly warning, "You know it's against hospital policy to wear a real tie on the psych units, right? Remember, we can't always be watching your back."

"Don't worry about me. They don't call me Kevlar for nothing."

Though my heart might be heavier than a sack of spuds, I'd always put on a jolly look as I approached Jones Three, like a clown about to enter the Big Top. And, believe me, many days were a three-ring circus. So, I painted a big smile on my face and opened the first of Jones's two secure doors, knowing I'd be pummeled all day long. Sixteen hours might well as be 16 rounds of a heavyweight bout. Roll with the punches, and hope to be standing at the end of it all.

Bracing myself, I unlocked the inner door, "Show time!"

At the barely discernible click of that lock, Clyde, Ling-Ling, and Uncle Rupert swarmed around me like bees to honey, and pursued me down the long hallway toward the nurses' station.

"Kev, you buy us house smokes?"

"Marlboro or Winston, right?"

"Not cheap generics, I hope?"

"And, please, don't say menthol."

I stopped to brush away my pestering trio: "Did you guys ever hear the expression, 'Never look a gift donkey in the mouth'?"

"C'mon, Kev, what did you buy?"

I stopped and smirked. "Eve 120s, long and thin, *very* elegant."

"C'mon, that's like smoking air. You bought Marlboros, didn't you?"

I pulled a pack of Sonomas from my coat pocket, a brand that had set me back $5.83.

"Ahh, well, they'll do. Can we go to the courtyard at 8:00?"

"8:30."

Clyde, a wild-whiskered chronic, threw his thick arm over me. "But it's the weekend, Kev."

I pirouetted out of his heavy grasp. "It's supposed to be 9:00 on weekends, remember? Jones Two goes down at 8:00. Now unhand me, you big oaf!"

Clyde believed I was Willie Wonka and often rummaged my pockets for a Wonka bar. Despite growing up like a weed in some forgotten garden, he had somehow amassed a wealth of knowledge about tropical fish, and took meticulous care of the ward's 80-gallon fish tank.

Ling-Ling, a pencil-thin redhead, got her nickname, as did so many regular denizens of our ward, from another patient, a frequent flyer named Sammy the Snit. She'd first been admitted to our floor with a black eye, the same day China gave that panda to the San Diego Zoo. Now, clear-eyed and rosy-cheeked, she sidled up to me. "I caught Sammy peeking into my room last night."

"No surprise there. You were twirling around him yesterday like a ballerina."

She punched my arm. "Was I that obvious?"

"Obvious! A blind man could see your intentions."

She stopped dead in her tracks: "Wait a minute! A blind man can't see anything!"

Ling-Ling played the coquette not only with Sammy, but also with me. One crisis worker, looking at her trend of Friday night admissions, asked her outright if she had a crush on me.

"Heavens, no," she laughed in her signature high-pitched cackle. "Kevin's cute in a weird kind of way, but no old graybeard is all that cute."

One thing I've learned about most chronics: they blurt out the truth like children.

Uncle Rupert was another unique specimen who defied any attempt at a precise diagnosis. He'd often wet a finger and lift it as if to check the direction of the wind, then stick his nose right up to yours, and inquire, "Are we having roast raccoon for dinner?"

Rupert's current admission was precipitated by the ingestion of a box of mothballs, or "Phoenix Stars," as he dubbed them. Severely ill for a week over in Medicine before landing with us, he explained when asked why, "I was going to bottle my camphor-scented farts in spray cans and sell them as air fresheners." We snickered, but Uncle Rupert truly believed he was onto a winner.

Now, self-disclosure was frowned upon for every nurse, especially psych nurses. But I took an antithetical approach, and became an open book. I brought my sons to visit the unit, and had taken scores of patients to visit my mom in her downtown apartment. Realizing I was no miracle worker, that empathy could go only so far, still I tried to normalize my relations with clients as much as possible.

Humor always seemed to help ease tension and create a bond, so I'd often work the house like a stand-up comic, full of pranks, antics, and general hijinks. Most patients responded in kind:

"Where did you get your nursing license, Walmart?"

"You're the one who should be taking my pills."

"Golly, the animals are running the zoo, and a patient is running the asylum!"

It was important for me to be one of them, rather than hiding behind the Lexan barrier of the nurses' station, where the Nurse Hatchets of the ward would hang out.

As I made way through the unit in the midst of my whimsical entourage, I caught a sidelong glimpse of Polly tucked into a corner, a bath blanket wrapped around her like a burrito. Her blank expression suggested that swallowing a light bulb might still be on her to-do list.

"Mornin' Polly," I said and casually moved on, not wanting to juice up her threat level another ten or twenty watts.

When our posse reached Roy's room, I peeked in to find the fearsome felon snoring away peacefully. I closed his door quietly, so our ruckus wouldn't wake him. "Let sleeping dogs lie," was an oft-whispered refrain on our ward.

I entered the nurses' station and quickly closed the door, lest my three faithful attendees tumble in at my heels.

"Mornin' guys, it's Li'l Kev."

Spencer glanced up at the wall clock—7:05. "You're

always late, Li'l Kev. Why's that?"

For some reason, I never told my mates about my custom with the church bells, but would instead fabricate a different harebrained story each time. Thumping down the Sunday *Times*, along with the DVD I'd brought from home, *Groundhog Day*, I made up my latest alibi.

"Get this. The guy in front of me was buying a dollar scratch ticket and laboriously counted out one quarter, two dimes, four nickels, and 35 blooming pennies from both his pant and coat pockets. Then he had to scratch the darn ticket right there. And guess what? He won a hundred bucks. Can you believe it?"

Ruth stood up to give me a hug: "No, we can't, but we love you anyway, don't we, guys?"

"Speak for yourself," joked Vinnie, our part-time weekend warrior.

I looked around. "Where's Bill?"

"Down in Dietary, rounding up breakfast."

Spencer handed me the day's packet of lab reports, recent histories, medication sheets, and day assignments, "Here you go, Charge Nurse extraordinaire, everything you need to look good for our on-call doc."

"Thanks, Spence. I'd be lost without you."

"No," my longtime colleague corrected, "without me, you'd be looking for a new job."

Spencer Trova and I were the last two nurses standing from the original Jones Two psych unit, which opened way back in 1974. Over the years, I had taken various junkets around the globe, but Spencer stuck with it, honing his skills by stints on the Cardiac and Intensive Care units. Thus for him, RN stood for "Real Nurse." On the other hand, I had little

Medical-Surgical experience and was totally hopeless during 'Mayday' situations, barely knowing the difference between a cardiac paddle and a ping-pong paddle. Of the many nicknames I had garnered over the years, Spencer's hit it right on the head: "Nurse Lite."

Ruth Tunnicliffe was another winner. A natural-born nurse, she was from Scotland by way of Africa, where her father had been a pathologist as she was growing up. He eventually came to BMC, and she followed in his medical footsteps. Ruth earned her own nickname of "Uptown Girl" by always dressing for work in style. Yet her meticulous attire betrayed no air of privilege, as she would often pass along her fine threads to the most woebegone of patients, dressing up our resident ragdolls. She was also a nurse to make Florence Nightingale proud, rolling up her sleeves to tackle the nastiest wounds, from ghastly burns to gruesome slashings.

Vinnie Coulehan, a gentle giant with a droll sense of humor, also worked for the Department of Children and Families with my younger sister, Anne Marie. On weekends, his towering presence kept many a hothead at bay. Lastly, there was Bill "Bingo" Lanoue, our go-to psych therapist, who kept watch over the floor and always put patients and their safety first. Yes, an all-star lineup without a crank on the crew.

After warm-up banter, we circled around the night nurse for morning report. Kathy Lane was another knowledgeable professional, whose invaluable insights on weekend summaries made me look good as I recorded them Sunday night for Monday's squad. Kathy always passed the baton cleanly on our never-ending race to nowhere.

"We had one admission early this morning, which brings our census to an unlucky thirteen," she began with a sigh.

"Sorry guys, he's a doozy, but let's start with those you know. No change in Theresa or Rupert, but both have routine blood work this morning. Polly, as you might suspect, didn't sleep a wink. That's three days now. Nor has she eaten. Same old game, scratching away, and I'm afraid you'll find her a handful. Sammy is Sammy, Reggie is Reggie, and Gilbert is Gilbert; you know the status quo there.

"Sorry again, but I had to get a 'Fall Risk' order for Henrietta. I know it's a pain, but I just got off the phone with her son, an obnoxious lawyer itching to sue the hospital if his dear mom happened to fracture a hip. I also made a judgment call and let Roy watch TV till 2, so maybe he'll wake up less of a bear. You owe me big time for that, Kev."

"Bless you, Kath."

Kathy shuffled through her notes: "Mr. Hyde continues to be a classic sundowner; sane by day, crazy by night. I read his day notes and said, 'Wow, what a sweetheart.' But then, at night, I take him to the bathroom, and he's ready to strangle me. Or I, him."

"Sundowning is so strange," Spencer shook his head. "You should've seen him yesterday, bouncing his grandkids on his knee like a gentle hobby horse."

"Yeah," Kathy snickered, "but if they rode with him into the sunset, they'd be riding one wild bronco."

Vinnie stood up and peered through our plexiglass window toward the kitchen. "What about Nellie?"

"No change. Says nothing, asks for nothing, does nothing. She may well be catatonic."

Nellie, 35, was an African-American from Raleigh, North Carolina, whom Sammy the Snit had nicknamed Tobacco Road. Confused by internal voices, she had boarded the wrong

Peter Pan bus and ended up in Pittsfield. Now she was sitting in a straight back chair, bent over with head tucked between her knees, sleeping soundly.

Ruth joined Vinnie at the window. "I've never seen anybody sleep so comfortably in such an awkward position. She's like a contortionist."

"Could be years of sleeping on park benches," Kathy surmised. "She does have family, though, and they're due here from Raleigh this afternoon to take her home. So better double-check her discharge paperwork.

"Now, we all know that Clyde and Ling-Ling were admitted Friday evening with threats of suicide. But, to no one's surprise, they've been model patients since boarding the Good Ship O'Hara."

Kathy turned and twinkled in my direction. "I'd love to be a fly on the wall when our mutual friend, Nurse Hatchet, hears of this tomorrow. As you know, Kev, she's been openly complaining that your weekends need more structure and less fun and games."

Spencer poked me with his pen. "I'd lie low for the next week if I were you."

I dropped my head to the desk with a stagy gesture. "Lie low? I need to run away."

"Dr. Carter's on call," Kathy continued, "but please take it easy on him. He was called in at 4 this morning to commit our dreaded patient #13, Nathan Cummings, our 32-year old roofer from Nashua, New Hampshire. I'm sorry to say, he makes our other patients look like cupcakes."

She summarized his Admission Note. "Nathan is diagnosed with religious grandiosity, believing that 'God the King' protects him from all bodily harm. To prove his invulnerability, he's totaled three cars in the past seventeen months, smacking into a tree, a telephone pole, and a bridge abutment—never leaving a skid mark."

"Anyone check his underwear?" Vinnie wisecracked.

"Miracle of airbags," shrugged Ruth.

"Not so. Two of his wrecks were old heaps without airbags. Had to be extracted from yesterday's crack-up by the Jaws of Life. Once he was medically cleared in the ED, he arrived on our floor like nothing had happened. Makes you shiver."

Spencer turned to me, "Kev, we're never going to Heaven, you know that?"

"Wow, that's cheerful chat. On a Sunday, no less."

"No, I mean it. Think of how many aspiring saints we've extinguished over the years with medication, simply because they were labeled with religious grandiosity. Imagine if Francis of Assisi were alive today. Here's a young man who talked to birds, gave away his possessions, and protested poverty by stripping naked. He'd be committed on a 20-day evaluation, and court-ordered to take monthly injections until his spiritual ambitions were squelched."

He paused, "But we've had saints on our floor, haven't we? Remember Grace of Krakow?"

"Remember?" I replied. "Not a Christmas goes by that I don't think of her."

"You've never told me her story," said Vinnie.

"Remind me, and I'll tell you later this afternoon in the courtyard."

I opened Nathan's chart. "This guy's history reads like a Stephen King novel. Why couldn't he have proven his invincibility closer to home?"

Vinnie growled, "What's the deal with him and cars,

anyway? He's a roofer, right? Why doesn't he just jump off a four-story building to prove that he's God's good buddy?"

"Remember the guy who tried to drown himself in Pontoosuc Lake last winter," Spencer recalled, "then changed his mind when he found the water too cold? Goes to show, you may want to die, but you want to do it on your own terms, have some control."

We heard the squeaking wheels of the food cart approaching the nurses' station, then stall abruptly. We looked out to see our marauding trio—Clyde, Ling-Ling, and Uncle Rupert—swoop down on its tray of donuts like squawking crows.

Bingo Bill shooed them off and escaped into the safety of the nurses' station. "Anyone want a bagel or donut before the rest get pawed over?"

I jumped from my seat: "Cinnamon, please. Thanks, Bill. By the way, could you whip up one of your signature bomblets for Roy when he wakes up? He's threatened to kick our butts, you know?"

Bill grinned: "Already on the menu."

"What's a bomblet?" asked Kathy.

"A bomblet," Bill explained, "is a megaton omelet, as powerful as any sedative in your med cabinet."

When exiting our station, Bill inadvertently left the door ajar, giving Sammy the Snit, a paunchy man in his 30's—dressed in his old high school football uniform—the chance to push through the doorway and shut off our nearest computer screen, proclaiming, "Guys, radiation kills!" before hightailing away.

Sammy had earned his moniker for the delight he took in ratting out fellow patients and staff for the slightest infractions. His multiple admissions were usually brought on by landlord evictions, when Sammy would shut off oil furnaces in the dead of a winter's night. In fact, he had waged war on all electrical appliances but the TV, which he could watch unblinkingly for hours on end.

Sammy also had an inexhaustible penchant for nicknames, baptizing half our clients over the long years.

"Why do you call Theresa, Parmesan Head?" I recently asked him.

"Why?" he blustered. "Because she's got a super-bad case of dandruff, that's why!"

A hard whack on our Lexan window catapulted the five of us from our chairs. It was Clyde who mashed his face against the pane in a hideous contortion. He then held up two fingers, motioning for a cigarette, and pointed to the clock. Out on the floor, we could see Polly, still enshrouded in her blanket, circling around as aimlessly as a tiger fish in our aquarium. At that moment, Dennis, our night aide, popped in through the side door. "Hey, guys, I hate to break up this fiesta, but I need some help out here. Old Mr. Hyde has been playing with his feces again, and I don't think you want me to pull Bingo Bill away from buttering the English muffins."

Vinnie snapped on a pair of latex gloves, muttering, "We really need to buy Mr. Hyde a box of kiddie finger paints."

Kathy reclaimed our attention. "Now, can we please get back to our problem child? This is all fun and games, but I really do have a home to go to."

As if on cue, Nathan made his first appearance, a beefed-up Samson in a sleeveless jersey, lumbering into view with a Bible in his meaty claw.

"Dang, he's cut like Waterford crystal," I whispered. "Look at those carotids, thick as Alaskan pipelines."

Kathy pointed to his labs, in addition to his abs. "That's it, Kev, you pinned the tail on the donkey. Positive for steroids."

"Maybe a little 'roid rage to fuel his delusions?"

Kathy looked him over with a clinical eye. "Could be. But I'd warn Bill to secure any knife he might have out there. Think about it—angry, psychotic male feeling trapped and persecuted, sees Bill cutting onions with a sharp knife, wrestles the knife away and starts slicing and dicing—not onions, but you or me or any of us."

I put an arm around her. "Gee, Kath, I thought I was crispy. Time for a sabbatical, do you think?"

"Nurses don't get sabbaticals, a real pet peeve of mine. I'm just saying. But who listens to a night nurse, conjuring phantoms out of the dark? No one. Still, that knife is there for the taking."

"Maybe we should get Bill to cut his veggies in here, off the unit."

"Duh, you think?"

Bill happened in at that moment, with his sharp knife securely tucked away.

"What's up with our new friend Nathan?" I asked.

"He's got an angry edge, for sure. Pounding back orange juice like there's no tomorrow. Can you offer anything to calm him down?"

Kathy thumbed through the Med Kardex. "Just PRN Haldol and Ativan, but he's already refused those. Oh, one last caveat. His parents are visiting this afternoon, and it's reported that he has a volatile relationship with his step-mom."

"Peachy," groaned Ruth.

"Well, crew," said Kathy, wrapping up her report, "I hate to spoil the party, but I have to go. Any last questions?"

"Yes," I begged, "take us with you?"

When Kathy and Dennis had signed off, the five of us huddled together, like a football team facing an impossible third and long.

I barked out the play: "Guys, same Sunday game plan: bomblets, courtyard, current events, *Groundhog Day*. After lunch: courtyard, visiting hours, football. We know the headliners—Polly, Roy, and newbie Nathan. Any questions?"

"Should we let Polly scratch away?"

"No real choice, as she'd just up the ante. Better scratching with a paperclip than chewing on glass."

"Can she get hold of any light bulbs?"

"Engineering removed all the nightlights on Friday," assured Ruth, "so I think we're safe."

"Well, let's stay vigilant," I emphasized. "Remember that suicidal girl a while back with the severe peanut allergy who won a three-pack of Peanut Butter Cups at Bingo? If she'd eaten 'em and croaked, her story would've hit the tabloids with my name attached to it. Not the kind of press I'm looking for at the heel of my day."

"Heel of your day?" Vinnie snorted. "You're gonna be carried out of here."

"Two more years, Vin, and I'm counting down the shifts like it was my last week in 'Nam." I looked around at my trusty mates. "Okay, crew, let's row this dinghy safely to shore. Keep a hand on the tiller and an eye out for storms, because I aim to reach the safe harbor of Patrick's Pub at midnight for my well-deserved pint of black grog."

* * *

We broke from the nurses' station toward our respective duties. Ruth led a brittle Henrietta by the hand for a refreshing bath. Spencer, our data man, was scanning recent labs and Radiology results. Vinnie was supervising Clyde's shave, having deposited Mr. Hyde, bathed and dressed, into a chair where he gazed out our windows at cooing pigeons on the sill. Meanwhile, indefatigable Bill filled the kitchen with an intoxicating aroma of peppers and onions.

As charge nurse, I'd double-task by handing out meds. This kept me up to speed when the on-call doctor, rotated each weekend, asked about medication efficacy, current dosages, and side effects. Medication was now almost invariably our go-to treatment, replacing most traditional modes of therapy.

I was heading for the Med Room when Sammy the Snit started the first ruckus of the day. He was watching television with a few other patients, as he did at every opportunity. "Hey, everyone, look! Gilbert's on TV! They're calling him a sexual predator!"

Sure enough, the local cable station was posting mug shots of community sex offenders, and there was a grim black & white photo of Gil on the screen. Seeing himself, Gil fled to the sanctuary of his room, while I backtracked and grabbed the remote.

Sammy flailed his arms in protest. "You can't do that! That's public information! Residents have the right to know that Gillie's a perv!"

I politely advised Sam to shut his yap, but he blathered on like a barker at a sideshow. "Hey, everybody, now we know why Gillie's so fat. He eats all his own Halloween candy, because the law won't let him hand out his treats to little kiddies."

I grabbed Sammy by the arm and escorted him to his room

for a "voluntary" timeout. There he threw himself onto the bed, and kicked up his feet like a whiny brat in a supermarket.

Ready to read him the riot act, I tried to reason with him. "Gil's never caused you any problems, so why call him out like that?"

Sammy jeered back. "Because it's *funny*! Did you hear the music playing in the background? Unbelievable! It was *You're Never Gonna Get It* by En Vogue? Can you top that? And ain't it the truth! 'Never gonna get it . . . never gonna get it!' The guy's so simple, it kills me."

He paused and looked up, waiting for me to get the joke and crack a smile. It wasn't happening.

"C'mon, Kev, you *know* it's funny."

"Funny? You think Gil thinks it's funny?"

Like a kid with a stern parent, Sammy suddenly realized who was keeper of the keys. He sat up and tugged at his frayed football pants. "Okay, okay, I was wrong. But I still want to have a good day, Kev. Can I, Kev? Can I have a good day? How about I stay in my room for one hour and then apologize to Gil when I come out?" He grinned with the confidence of a successful wheedler, perhaps a secret bond between us. "C'mon, Kev, what'd you say?"

"One hour," I warned him before exiting his room, "but one misstep, and you'll be in here the whole day."

I found Gil in his bed, rocking back and forth beneath a heap of blankets. "Sorry, Gil. Sam was way out of line there."

Gil continued his habitual rocking, nuzzling deeper beneath the covers. According to his own story, he'd been urinating behind a dumpster when he heard footsteps, and turned to find a young girl passing by, thus exposing himself. I was inclined to give him the benefit of the doubt. We'd housed many sex offenders over the years, tough birds many of them, but Gilbert wasn't like that. Essentially a kind soul, his life may well have been shattered by a simple piss. The ensuing charges of public urination, lewd behavior, and exposing himself to a minor had introduced him to an unending world of heartache.

His rocking slowed, and he finally peeked out from the covers. "Aw, Sammy's just being Sammy, doing mean things to everybody. You should've seen him at Friday night Bingo, messing up Reggie's winning card before Bingo Bill could call back the winning numbers."

Tears stained Gil's cheeks. "It's that picture I hate most. They picked the worst of 'em, to make me look bad. I smiled for the first one, but one cop shouted, 'Hey, jerko, this ain't no passport photo, because you ain't ever going nowhere!'"

The thought of it made him burrow back into the covers. I tried to lure him out. "You going down to the courtyard? We got house smokes."

I barely heard his muffled response. "Naw, I'll just stay here 'til breakfast."

Gil had often told staff that if he could live that one moment over again, he would've gladly wet his pants.

As I resumed my mission to the Med Room, I noticed seven of our thirteen patients standing at the back door as they awaited their first smoke of the day. So the first meds I passed were the pack of Sonomas to Ruth and Vinnie, on their way to lead the eager group down the stairwell three floors to our locked courtyard.

Granting the deleterious effects of nicotine, it was the only drug in our arsenal that could calm an irate patient or lift one from the doldrums. Said one patient defending his smoking habit, "Why do you think a cigarette is a convict's last request when facing a firing squad?"

On my way, I passed Nathan sitting before the TV, his black leather Bible tight in his grip. Superficial cuts marked his hands and face, but he showed few other signs of his catastrophic crack-up. I approached him for the first time. "Good morning, Nathan. My name is Kevin O'Hara. I'm the charge nurse here on weekends, and I'll also be working with you today. Would you like to join the others for a smoke or a little fresh air?"

He thumped his fist against the Bible, as if pounding a baseball mitt, "Now that's some contradiction. Smoke or fresh air? Gotta be one or the other, can't have both. Do you know second-hand smoke kills, or hasn't that news reached this hick town yet?"

I acknowledged his argument, but tried to mollify his anger.

"You've got a point, but the courtyard is quite airy. There's a basketball court if you want exercise."

He looked away.

"I hear your parents are visiting."

He glared at me. "No, *not* my parents, just my father. He left my mother for a dingbat, and she's as far from my mother as Hades is to Zion."

"Well, when they arrive, we can all meet with Dr. Carter and see where to go from here. Any questions or concerns that I can help you with right now?"

"Yeah, get me the hell outta this loony bin."

"That's our goal. But, for now, you might want some breakfast. You're in luck, because we have quite the spread on Sunday. Fresh fruit, omelets, bagels . . ."

He waved me off like a pestering fly. "I'll pass."

Spencer caught me shortly down the hallway. "Any luck with the new guy?"

"Whiffed on three straight pitches, I'm afraid."

With the majority of folk in the courtyard and relative peace restored, I was preparing pills in the Med Room when I heard a knock at the door. "Kevin, it's me, Sherry from Housekeeping."

Sherry was top-notch, working our floor every other weekend and tackling the most menial chores with energy and resolve.

"Kevin, remember the donkey I was telling you about, the thirty-year-old jenny in Savoy?"

"Molly, right?"

"No, Moxie. Last night she was killed by lightning, the second donkey in two years."

"Oh, that's a shame."

"Yes, it's quite a coincidence, but I know how much you care about donkeys."

Sherry had read my book on traveling around Ireland with my donkey, Missie, and took every opportunity to talk about our shared love of the breed. In the flush of my mini-celebrity after the book came out, after decades of gestation, she asked what I intended to write next, and I brashly replied, "My two-week notice." Five years later, I was still sorting pills and trying to cope with the likes of Roy, Polly, and now Nathan.

But, in truth, my donkey remained my guide. I had fashioned my nursing practice in imitation of her, trying to be a humble and gentle beast. As we sought shelter each night in Ireland, Missie would sometimes be pastured with highstrung thoroughbreds. At first, I was concerned for her safety— that she'd be kicked or bitten—but soon realized she had a unique ability to calm down the hair-trigger reactions of even racehorses.

A horseman in Cork informed me that donkeys were commonly used as protectors of the herd, as well as mates for more skittish horses, to settle them down. Never threatening or competitive, they're simply meek creatures going about their own business.

"Remember," he told me, "equines are social animals, like ourselves, and who wouldn't want a pasture buddy like your loveable nut-brown mare there?"

And it was true. I'd sometimes put Missie in a paddock with other horses bucking and whinnying, and come back a while later to find all the animals peacefully cropping grass side by side.

When I returned to the hospital after my two-year hiatus, our unit was experiencing the necessity for the use of physical and chemical restraints, so I asked and received permission from my boss, Eileen Myers, to do my best imitation of Missie. With a reduced caseload, I stayed in the milieu for extended periods simply as a benevolent presence, and was able to soon break down an embattled "us versus them" mentality.

In mixing with the herd, I was happy to play "Good Donkey" to Nurse Hatchet's "Bad Ass." I spoke the language of the patients rather than of psychiatry, heavy on humor and helpfulness, light on rules and demands, and emphasizing mutual respect. Each year after that, our Restraints and Seclusions declined until our unit was cited as the least restrictive in the Commonwealth by the Department of Mental Health, a distinction I prized above all.

So for years, the donkey nurse grazed contentedly amongst wild colts, fierce stallions, frisky or broken-down mares, and jackasses of every description, trying to do no harm and keep the peace.

When I emerged from the Med Room that morning, I found the floor as peaceful as any Irish meadow. Contented smokers were up from the courtyard, a Debussy prelude piped in sweetly from WAMC, and the *Times* was scattered hither and yon, with the aroma of percolating coffee pervading all. Polly's scowl had softened into something that could be taken for a smile. Even Roy seemed passably amiable, loosening his belt as he tried to polish off Bill's humongous bomblet.

Only Nathan and Nellie remained detached from the group: The Gift of God immersed in the Gospels, and Tobacco Road still folded up like a lawn chair.

With the atmosphere just mellow enough for tomfoolery, I announced, "Medication time, everyone. Come one, come all. And good news, I haven't made a med error in three days, might be a new record."

"Oh, great!" Sammy shouted out, sharing a table with Gil like old pals. "So you're gonna make one today?"

"I'm just saying," I shrugged. "So you best know your shapes, sizes, and colors."

Ling-Ling piped up: "Hey, Bearded Nurse, you giving out any high drops today?"

"You mean eye drops?" Clyde asked.

"No, high drops! That's when Kevin gets up on a chair and plops them into your eyeballs like a mad bombardier."

"Yeah, but don't worry," Polly slipped from her bath blanket and uttered her first words of the day, "Kevin's saline drops usually bounce off your forehead and run down your nose."

I passed out the pills quickly, in my own maverick fashion, stacking cups labeled with patients' names, and doling them out to the intended recipients. This was against hospital policy, but I was a one-trick pony—er, donkey—and over my career, this 'stack 'em high' system had worked like a charm.

Bingo Bill, in turn, working faster than a one-armed cook at a truck stop, called out. "Hey, Nellie, what would you like in your omelet?"

Amazingly, Nellie lifted her head from her tucked position, glanced at the food laid out in abundance, and answered in a Southern slow-as-molasses drawl. "Two eggs, please."

Sammy bolted from his chair, laughing hysterically. "Two eggs? An omelet is an egg, you ninny! Bingo Bill wants to know what you want inside of them!"

Startled by Sammy's outburst, Nellie slipped her head back between her knees, like a turtle retreating into its shell. Ling-Ling rushed to her side, running her fingers along Nellie's long braids while scolding her secret heartthrob. "Nice going, bozo!"

Ling-Ling was finally able to coax her roommate to sit at her table. Who was this sweet Southern transient grazing in our grassy field, I wondered.

Overall, the bounteous brunch seemed to put everyone in their best frame of mind. Several of the women pitched in to assist Bill with the cleanup. Even Polly made a gesture of help before wrapping herself back in her blanket and resuming her scratching. In turn, Bill's bomblet had sent Roy to bed in a stupor, with nary a thought of his beloved Jets.

Soon everyone, even Nathan, was watching *Groundhog Day*, a comic story of multiple do-overs that always seemed to engage and uplift our patients, and the rest of the morning passed without incident.

The peaceful spell was broken at the special Sunday

noontime dinner, when the metal lid from Uncle Rupert's tray went flying across the kitchen like a Frisbee.

"What's this?" he growled, looking at the relatively sumptuous plate of chicken and potatoes. "I asked for roast raccoon!"

I rushed to his table. "Rup, Rup, calm down. Roast raccoon isn't on the bill of fare, believe me. Can I order you something else?"

He lifted his index finger into the air, smacked his lips, and rubbed his greasy nose up against mine. "Two hot dogs, please, and hold the pickle."

"Got it!"

I returned to the nurses' station to call Dietary.

"Not to play devil's advocate," cautioned Ruth, "but we had a meeting during the week with Dietary, coordinated by your longtime foe, and both sides agreed that patients can no longer change menus once their trays arrive."

I objected to Ruth's warning: "Thanks, Ruth, I got the memo. But Nurse Hatchet failed to make an exception for patients who can neither read nor write, like our dear Uncle Rupert."

Ruth shrugged, "I'm just trying to keep you out of hot water."

I dialed Dietary: "Hi Krystal, it's Kev. Li'l Kev. You know, the funny gray-bearded guy you put a restraining order on a while back?"

Laughter: "What now, Li'l Kev?"

"I heard about Wednesday's meeting about menus and all, but here's the thing: if Uncle Rupert doesn't get two hot dogs for lunch, he'll go over the edge and take me with him. So what do you say, be a lifesaver? You'll do it? Really? Oh, thank you, thank you! You're the bomb. No, you're a peach, unless you want to be a bomb. Ten minutes. Great! I'll let him know they're sizzling on the grill."

I slid open the nurses' window and called out. "Rupert, your dogs will be here in ten minutes."

Spencer shook his head. "I don't know how you do it."

Ruth reached over and mussed my hair. "It's that peeping leprechaun voice. 'Hi, Krystal, it's Li'l Kev.' Bloody sickening, it is."

"Do for the patients, and you'll never get stung. That's been my motto, you know."

I looked out to see a smiling Rupert offer his chicken dinner to Henrietta's visiting husband, maybe one of the few things he's ever had to offer anyone.

The visitors' telephone rang at 1 p.m. sharp.

Spencer answered. "Yep, be right down."

He hung up and turned to the crew. "Man your stations, everyone. Nathan's parents have arrived."

Ruth picked up a walkie-talkie, our hotline to Security. "Should I call the Blue Coats?"

"Yes, but just put them on alert," I decided. "Nathan's been okay, so no sense in setting the stage for a confrontation."

Over the years, we'd often call Security and gear up for showdowns that never materialized, though sometimes their presence could actually incite a conflict. But if we did need their assistance, it could take a few precious minutes for them to arrive at our end of the hospital.

I hurried down to greet the Cummings couple, as Vinnie went to inform Nathan of their arrival. Our team had earlier agreed that the family should meet in the main conference room, a safe distance from the patient population.

At the front door, I found Mr. Cummings distraught and

road-weary, standing alongside his fashionable younger wife. His handshake was weak and tremulous, and I could only imagine his heartbreak over the dark of night call from our Emergency Department.

"We'll have you visit your son for a few minutes alone, if you like," I proposed, "and then Dr. Carter and I will join you. Sound okay?"

He nodded. "How is he?"

"Physically, he's miraculously in one piece. He hasn't given us any trouble, but he's a bit withdrawn, sticking to himself." I tugged at my knit tie. "Any concern he might get aggressive with either of you?"

Mr. Cummings shook his head in firm denial. "No, he's never been violent. Just to himself."

As Nathan sauntered down the hall toward us, without a hitch in his gait, it was hard to believe that barely half a day had passed since this muscular roofer had been extracted by the Jaws of Life from a twisted ball of metal. Tears flowed as father and son embraced, but Nathan totally ignored his stepmother.

I led them into the conference room and pulled the door partially closed, while I hovered outside, listening for trouble that might warrant an intervention, more or less standard practice for staff in volatile family situations.

"Why, son? Why do you want to hurt yourself?"

"I don't want to hurt myself, Dad. I just want to prove something."

"Prove what, Nathan?"

"That God is great, and He is my shield."

Mrs. Cummings spoke: "That's true, son, God is great."

"Don't ever call me son, you redheaded bitch."

I edged closer to the door.

"Please, Nathan, be kind," she answered. "We all believe that God has the answer to your problems."

"Now, Martha, let's not get into that."

"But your son needs to know how much I care. Nathan, dear, your father and I just spent a glorious week in Rome, and we brought back something especially for you."

I peered around the corner and saw her go into her purse for some sort of vial, draw it forth, then reach across toward Nathan, saying, "For the Lord's protection." She was trying to make the Sign of the Cross on his forehead with her oily thumb.

I entered the room just as Nathan slapped her hand away. He wiped the oil from his brow and shouted, "Don't ever touch me, you Whore of Babylon!"

He turned to me: "I gotta take a shower and get this gunk off me. Now!"

As he ran toward the bathroom, I leaned out to sound the alarm. "Bill, grab some soap and towels for Nathan, and tell Spencer to call Security, stat!"

Stepping in front of his indignant wife, Mr. Cummings struggled to explain, "It was only holy oil. From Rome. For Nathan. Nothing more."

I began to guide the pair out of the room, "It will probably be better if you see Dr. Carter down on Jones Two and let the situation here cool down. I'll get someone to escort you, and I'll join you and the doctor as soon as I can, with an update."

I was shooing them toward the exit, but when passing the bathroom, Nathan flew out the door, still fully-clothed, and hurled a wad of towels at Mrs. Cummings. He next came charging at her, but I stepped in between them, raising my hands in a pacifying manner, "Nathan, please, they're leaving. Let them go."

But Nathan lunged forward, and I suddenly found myself airborne in the roofer's powerful arms before being slammed to the floor like a bundle of shingles. Shocked and writhing in pain, the wind knocked out of me, I lay on my back, gasping to regain my breath. As in a waking nightmare, I saw Nathan looming over me like Samson, ready to tear me apart, limb by limb. My bell truly rung, I closed my eyes and waited for the inevitable second blow that would be my death knell.

However, rather than following up on the mayhem, Nathan had frozen above me, as if stupefied by the blow he had dealt. In quick response, Spencer and Vinnie escorted him to the Quiet Room without a struggle, while his horrified parents were ushered safely off the floor.

Meanwhile, Ruth and Bill had corralled the other patients into the kitchen area, closing the heavy wooden doors behind them. Our practice was to "modulate" the unit, to isolate the common areas from any crisis, lest commotion multiply. Bedlam has a notorious knack of turning contagious.

Jones Two staff came running up the stairs after hearing the loud thump above them. "It was like someone dropped a piano," they reported. Dr. Carter was next at the scene. He knelt down beside me to assess my condition. Despite his evident concern, he quipped, "Nothing here a pint of Guinness can't fix, good buddy."

I tried to smile, but couldn't.

The Blue Coats were quick to follow, huffing and puffing after their mad dash up three flights of stairs. Then the first responder MET Team, led by Sue Earle, our weekend nursing supervisor, with whom I had weathered many a storm over the years. "Relax, Kevin, we'll take care of you." Sue brushed her hand over my brow, a nurse's touch.

Seeing the concern in her eyes, I admitted, "I'm really hurt, Sue."

She turned to the MET team: "We need a fracture board, stat!"

"Sorry, don't have one in-house."

"Then call 911, and have an ambulance bring one here immediately!"

I stared up at the ceiling, certain that things weren't copacetic when a hospital needed to call 911.

During the lull, the crew took turns offering me comfort and assurance, though their pained expressions reflected my condition. Ruth slipped a pillow behind my head, her eyes full of tears.

"How are the patients?" I asked her.

She smiled wearily. "Always wearing your cap, aren't you? They're fine, and Polly has promised not to hurt herself in any way."

I winced as a surge of electricity seared down my left leg. "Don't believe her," I panted, "she might take this as an opportunity."

"I don't believe so," said Ruth, "she's terribly shook."

Within minutes, two rugged EMTs wheeled their stretcher on to the ward, where I still lay flattened. The no-nonsense pair promptly fitted a cervical collar around my neck, and positioned a thin plastic fracture board to my starboard side.

"We're going to slide the board gently beneath you and then transfer you onto the stretcher. Now try and relax, and we'll do the rest."

No zenned-out yogi on a bed of nails, I froze up and

braced for a jolt. Yep, a thousand volts.

Once I was aboard, they raised the gurney, and Sue directed them toward the hallway elevator. But instead, they wheeled me toward the far exit.

Sue called after them. "Where are you going? It's quicker to the ED from here."

"Sorry, ma'am," one of the EMTs grunted. "He's our patient now, and protocol is to transport him to the ED by ambulance. If we don't, it's not a run, and insurance won't reimburse us."

Sue rolled her eyes. "Now I've heard it all. You actually mean to drive a seriously injured man around the block to the ED, rather than going directly by this elevator?"

He shrugged his shoulders impassively. "Ain't my rules, ma'am."

Sue wasn't having it. "As acting supervisor, I command you to use this elevator. If not, I assure you your company's contract will be scrutinized before its next renewal."

She led the disgruntled pair down the elevator, and across the complex to the ED. At every threshold where the carpet met tile, another jolt pierced me. As I was wheeled down the hallways, I could make out the whispered exclamations of passing staff. "My God, that's Kevin from the Jones Wing."

As my stretcher zeroed in on the ED, Sue received a stat emergency call, leaving me to the mercy of the irritated EMTs. Most unfortunate. Informing no one, they whisked me through the Emergency Room doors, rolled me into a vacant cubicle, transferred me from gurney to stretcher, drew the curtain, and disappeared.

Alone and forgotten, with a broken back that screamed bloody murder, I tried to call for help, but I couldn't draw the necessary breath. I tried again, but my pathetic rasp was drowned out by the incessant wail of a nearby infant. After long minutes, an unfamiliar employee poked her head around the curtain, clipboard in hand, "Hi, I'm Melvina from Admitting. What's your medical coverage?"

I thought I had died and gone to Hospital Hades. Cutting through the torment, I managed to squeak out, "Melvina, please, I'm really hurt. What docs are on today? Rich Dodge? Mike Coyne? Ged Deering?"

"No, none of them."

"How about nurses—Joe Amuso? Kelly Melle? Mary Benoit?"

"Nope, haven't seen them, either."

Hearing this, I felt like Lazarus being told that Jesus was out of town.

"Please," I begged her, "I can tell that it's awfully busy here, but could you tell someone, anyone, that the patient in Cubicle 7 has a pain level of 10 times 10 to the 20th power. Thank you, thank you so much!"

Seemingly unmoved by my plight, she exited the cubicle with a firm tug of the curtain.

Just as I felt myself descending into the depths of indifference, a vision of mercy appeared. It was the lovely aide Paris Roosa, daughter of Ceil, our weekday charge nurse. "Hi, Kevin, I'm your guardian angel."

My, was she ever!

In a flash, Paris had covered me with a warm blanket, taken my vitals, and gently slipped off my shoes. She apologized for the delay, saying a nasty motorcycle accident had just preceded my arrival.

"A motorcycle accident in mid-December," I moaned.

"Must be one of our own."

"Maybe so," said Paris. "State Police believe he took dead aim at a large tree."

Shortly, Dr. Fred Landes entered the cubicle and shook my limp hand. "Sue Earle just called down to tell us how you saved a visitor from a violent attack. Good work."

"Thank you," I moaned.

He proceeded to examine me and run down a checklist of questions, the most relevant of which was "What's your pain level?"

"Ten," I answered with emphasis.

"Are you allergic to morphine?"

"No, doctor."

"So you've had it before?"

"Yes, in Vietnam, years ago."

"We'll give you four milligrams to start and run an IV per Trauma Protocol, just in case anything unforeseen happens. Transport will be in to get you down to Radiology for some x-rays." He patted my shoulder, "Now try and relax. We'll have you feeling more comfortable in no time."

"I guess if I were still in 'Nam, I'd be getting a Purple Heart."

Paris piped up: "I can get you a purple lollipop!"

Just as I was feeling back in the care of friends, I was rudely returned to the nether regions of medical hell by an impersonal traveling nurse. He set up my morphine drip with all the sentiment of a state trooper issuing a ticket, "There you go, that should do it."

He departed without further word, then stuck his head in a few minutes later, "Any relief?"

"Still at ten. Might do better with a shot of Jameson."

"Maybe you just got a crush on Molly Morphine."

"No," I shot back irritably at his crass response. "Maybe Miss Molly *just* isn't cutting it."

After he repeated my initial dose, I went off on a wild train of thought, imagining that this guy was a traveling junkie, stealing my morphine and replacing it with a useless saline solution for off-duty fun and games.

When I returned from Radiology, I found Spencer pacing back and forth in my small cubicle.

"How you doing, Kev?"

"Not sure, but probably rib and spine fractures."

He gave me an appraising look, "You're really hurt, huh?"

"Oh yeah, and morphine isn't all it's cracked up to be."

"We're all sorry, Kev, the whole team. I hope you know that. Bill and I were helping Mr. Hyde in the far bathroom. It happened so fast."

"There was nothing anyone could've done," I assured my longtime buddy. "It was like someone running a red light. Bam! So enough about it. What's he up to, anyway?"

"Nathan? Still in the Quiet Room with two Blue Coats, no further trouble."

Spencer let out a chuckle. "He keeps telling them that the female nurse with the beard attacked him first."

I was in no position to laugh, even though I was inclined to.

"Sammy witnessed the whole thing, and he's painting you up to be a real hero," Spence continued. "He thinks Mrs. Cummings would've been a goner if you hadn't intervened."

"Intervened? I just got in the way." It hurt my ribs just to think about it. "What's up with the others?"

"Polly's been a peach, surprisingly. I guess crisis brings

out the best in her. In honor of you, Sammy pledged not to unplug anything for 24 hours, and Krystal sent up a tub of ice cream with all the trimmings to help settle the troops. So there's our Theresa pouring gobs of chocolate syrup over her three humongous scoops of ice cream and says, 'I wish Kevin got body-slammed every day.'"

"Nice to be loved," I moaned. "Nellie get off okay?"

"Nope, spending another night. Her mother and aunt, both in their seventies, arrived from North Carolina after a twenty-hour bus ride, and were set to turn right around and take her back. Can you imagine? So I got a hold of our old buddy, Sean Jennings, and he used his leverage as our new veep to get them a free night at the Crowne Plaza. You would've loved 'em, Kev. Desperately poor, but so sweet. They even brought in homemade cookies for the gang."

"Nice of you and Sean. Did Roy go on a rampage over his Jets?"

"Nope, Bill's bomblet finished him off for the day. Oh, here, the patients sent you these." He handed me a fistful of homemade Get Well cards. "You'll especially like the one from your girlfriend, Ling-Ling."

Her card showed a stick figure grasshopper held in an open hand, with the caption, *"Hop, hop, to a quick recovery!"* With a smile, I opened it and read, *"Dear Kevin, I hope you're not dead yet. If you are, I did have a crush on you. But if you're not dead, don't get any funny ideas when your back gets better. X's and O's, Ling-Ling."*

I laughed through my pain, "Best come on I've had in years."

"Speaking of which, does Belita know what's up?"

"No, not yet. Paris wanted to call her, but I told her to hold off till I get all my results back. No sense putting her through this waiting game."

Spencer stood to leave. "Well, I better get back to our charges. We're all rooting for you, Nurse Lite."

"I know that."

"Think on the bright side. You'll actually be able to enjoy this Christmas in peace."

"Yeah, that's one consolation," I conceded, waving my good old friend goodbye.

I might've felt neglected when I first arrived in the ED, but that turned around at the 3:30 shift change when I found myself visited by a stream of hospital buddies. Despite HIPAA confidentiality, my injury was "the shot heard 'round the wards," and so many of my colleagues stopped in to check on me that I felt very well cared for indeed. And, please, let me exonerate that traveling nurse. Despite the depth charges of pain that continued to detonate in my lower back, I was absolutely looped.

I heard a voice from behind the curtain, "Hi Kev, it's Chris. Can I come in?"

I welcomed my current boss and old college pal, Chris Doyle. "Chris, I thought you had tickets for the Colonial Theater tonight?"

Taking a seat on a stool beside me, he gave my shoulder a reassuring tap. "I'm not going anywhere until I check in on my friend. Pretty banged up, huh?"

"Heard my bones snap, for what that tells you."

"Ouch!"

Chris and I had graduated together from UMASS in Amherst, and his mother, Anna, had been an inspiration to me early in my career. In the thirty years since, Chris's over-all smarts and superior nursing skills had lifted him up the managerial ladder, until he was the nursing supervisor for our entire psych department of 150 strong.

Paris peeked through the curtain: "Kevin, two policemen are here to see you. Should I bring them in?"

"I guess, sure." I turned to Chris. "What's up?"

"They're probably here to see if you're going to press criminal charges."

"On Nathan? I'd be a hypocrite to press charges."

"You don't think his attack was deliberate?"

"I don't know, but the guy's totally deluded."

Chris stood. "Let me go out and talk with them, give you a little time to think about it."

My head fell deep into the pillow. I knew some of my colleagues, notably Nurse Hatchet, would argue that the mentally ill should be held accountable for their actions, their anger fueled by a recent spate of assaults against workers in mental institutions nationwide.

"Time in the brig, like any other felon," she would rail. "Letting them off with a slap only encourages them further."

Even at BMC a month ago, a coworker had his nose busted and pressed charges against his assailant, cheered on by Nurse Hatchet. But that assailant was a sociopath with a long rap sheet, definitely a bad egg. My guy was authentically out of his mind, with a textbook diagnosis—psychotic disorder with religious grandiosity.

My antagonist would call me a minimizer, an enabler, a coward. But after thirty years of working with the mentally ill, I'd be a fraud to call the cops on a guy who made a practice of cracking up cars at full speed. He might be invincible, and I decidedly not, but I didn't want to see him gavelled into submission.

I thought of a story my mother told about her being attacked by a patient at St. Andrew's Hospital, back in England during the war. The patient had pulled Mom's hair so severely that she had to soak her head in a basin of antiseptic for three days. Back on duty, she had the choice of returning to the same ward or of going elsewhere to avoid her assailant. Mom answered, "I'll go back to my ward since it was Miss Piggott's illness giving out, not herself." Seven decades later, I felt the same way.

When Chris reentered my cubicle with the officers, I told them of my decision and signed off on papers to that effect. The sergeant handed me a copy but warned me saying, "Your decision will be a moot point if your x-rays show fractures. In that case, we're mandated by law to press A&B charges against him."

"What would happen then?" asked Chris.

"Round the clock guards until we can arrange transfer to another facility, probably Bridgewater. There he'll probably do a few months, get medicated per court order, and be back on the streets by February."

"Just in time to buy another car during the President's Day Sale," snorted the junior officer.

Dr. Landes joined us and confirmed what I suspected all along. Multiple fractures. The sergeant closed his clipboard with a snap. "That's all we needed to hear, doc." He turned to Chris. "Mr. Cummings is now in our custody. Our officers will replace hospital security until he gets transferred."

He tapped my hand before leaving. "Sir, enjoy your time off."

After the police left, Dr. Landes was more specific. "Kevin, your images show multiple right-side rib fractures, also lumbar

spine 1, 2, and 3. We're going to admit you to Neuro to sta-
bilize your back, control your pain, and keep an eye out for
complications."

"Like what, doctor?"

"There's always a chance of internal bleeding after such
a blow. Your vitals are stable, but we won't take any chances."

"Doctor, what do you think in the long run?" I looked up
at the baby-faced physician. "I mean, will I ever play a good
game of golf again?"

He smiled: "Did you ever play a good game before?"

Chris laughed, having seen me out on the links.

"Seriously," the doctor foretold, "your ribs will heal of
their own accord in six to eight weeks, but your lower back is
a trickier matter. Your transverse processes are fractured, yes,
but not displaced. Forgive the pun when I say you caught a
break there. Barring any setbacks, you should be back to your
old self in six months."

Thanking the good doctor for his honest and hopeful
prognosis, I encouraged Chris to go ahead with his evening
plans. Now alone and swooning from opiates, I was happy to
hold no grudge against my assailant. I might think differently
down the road if I could no longer mow my lawn, or line up a
putt. But not for now. Whatever my shortcomings, I was truly
able to turn the other cheek.

I pulled the heated blanket to my chin, sure that such for-
giveness would speed my recovery. I stared at the glowing lamp
above me, and felt enveloped in a veil of goodwill. In my gran-
diose state, I felt a kinship to Pope John Paul II, who'd visited
his would-be assassin in prison and had forgiven him. Yes, a
humble donkey nurse, after all.

I emerged from a heady snooze and blearily made out a

figure standing in the light above me.

"Belita?"

My dear, tearful wife was there, with our younger son, Brendan, who still lived with us. Spencer had filled them in, but Belita still cried over her "white as a ghost" husband, laid out with a cervical collar and dripping IV. She clutched my hand as tightly as if I were hanging off the edge of a precipice.

Brendan asked if he could help in any way, and I pointed to the empty Styrofoam cup on the nearby stand. "They won't let me have water, so could you ask for more ice chips? The pain meds have made me so thirsty that I could murder a pint of Guinness right now."

He smiled, reassured that his father was far from dead.

Stroking my forehead, Belita spoon-fed me the ice chips, bringing to mind a memorable winter's night thirty years earlier and one floor above, after she'd given birth to our elder son Eamonn. After her cesarean, I'd sneaked into her room in the wee hours and fed her ice chips. Now, she was returning the favor.

Another friendly nurse, Shannon McKeever, appeared through the curtain. "Good news, Kevin, your bed is finally ready up in Neuro. Before the transfer, I have orders to give you 15 milligrams of IV Toradol, which, by the way, is more effective than morphine."

After the infusion, Shannon turned to Belita and Bren. "The medication will soon put Kevin to sleep, so you might want to say your goodbyes for now. But please, feel free to call the Neuro Unit at any time, day or night."

I held Belita's hand tightly as I slipped into a troubled slumber of tolling bells, dead donkeys, and a voice intoning, "You're gonna be carried out of here."

MONDAY: ANALGESIC MUSINGS

An ivory-robed goddess hovered over me as I awoke. Or was it an angel addressing me?

"Would you like to give it another go?"

"Please?" I groggily rose to semi-consciousness.

She tenderly brushed the hair off my damp forehead, her breath warm and sweet. "How long has it been?"

I smiled secretly at the prospect of heavenly delights. "Too long," I murmured.

She produced a plastic urinal, as my drug-induced fantasy collapsed like a game of Topple.

I reined in my bawdy thoughts and gaped blearily at my surroundings: a maze of IV poles and beeping monitors. A jab of pain solved the puzzle of where I was and why. It was morning on the Neuro Unit, and I'd gone from Sunday nurse to Monday patient in an eye blink, falling through the looking glass as I fell to the concrete floor of Jones Three.

"O-oh, that? How long? Just before I got clobbered."

With a gesture of infinite grace, my charming nurse Candace handed me the urinal. "I'll raise the head of your bed, nice and slow."

Curtains closed, I tried to urinate, but my riveting pain blocked the flow. Of all the times for my plumbing to fail, why now? Imagine, I quickly computed, I'd peed approximately six times a day times 60 years, which amounted to 132,000 piddles in my life without a hitch. Now, I'd mysteriously acquired a shut-off valve that can only be opened by a 14-inch rubber catheter snaking its way through my urethral canal to my bladder, an incredible voyage I wanted no part of.

Candace called from outside the curtain. "Any luck?"

"Not yet. Can you give me another minute?"

She left, but returned shortly with a portable bladder scanner. "Opiates play havoc with smooth muscle like the bladder wall," she explained. "You received two liters of Normal Saline in the ED last night, so you must be distended."

She lifted my johnny top and rubbed the cold jellied wand over my surprisingly protuberant belly. "Congratulations, you're in your second trimester," she smiled. "No really, you've got a whopping 1200 cc's in there."

I tried to calculate the volume, but my brain was mush. "Is that a lot?"

Candace rolled her eyes. "I'll need to call a doctor and get an orderly to straight-cath you for urinary retention. You don't need any more complications."

I groaned. "Is Scott working?"

She gave me a wink. "Yes. Do you prefer him for your plumbing work?"

"No, wise guy. I just want someone with experience, not some rookie who'll give me a urinary tract infection. Last thing I need now is some greenhorn working on my shorthorn."

Candace left with a giggle. "I can see why you've worked on the Jones Wing all these years—crazy suits you. Oh, you're due for your next dose of Toradol. What's your pain level?"

Her question brought my ugly reality back to me, and after another spasm, I truthfully raised ten fingers.

Minutes after I received my injection, Scott sat at my bedside, genuinely upset. "Sorry, Kev, this whole thing is wrong, real wrong."

"I can ask for Jim or Eric, if it bothers you."

He threw the cath kit on the bed. "Naw, it's not that. But why you? You're one of the good guys."

"Thanks, Scott, but everybody's number comes up."

"You don't seem very angry."

"The guy's a sick pup. Besides, with the medicine I just got, I'm softer than a toasted marshmallow."

Scott palpated my bloated bladder. "Ooh, you must be uncomfortable."

"Not as much as you'd think. All those pints of Guinness probably stretched it some."

He opened the kit. "I'm sure you inserted dozens of catheters during your orderly days. So you know it's not too bad, just a slight burning sensation."

"Yeah, but I hear payback's a bitch."

He prepared his sterile field. "When were you an orderly?"

"Between '71 and '74, when I was going through nursing school."

"Damn," he chortled, "I was still in diapers." His gloved hands lubricated the catheter tip. "Now, think pleasant thoughts. But, please, not too pleasant."

I squeezed my eyes shut as I felt the initial chill of the numbing agent. Thankfully, the powerful effects of Toradol eased the discomfort. They also sent my mind reeling back to my early days as a night orderly.

One long-ago winter's night, I reported to work at 11 p.m., and warmed myself in the cozy confines of the nursing lounge, adjacent to the Emergency Room. There I sat with our friendly ER crew: nurses Marie Evans and Kay Shaw, with supervisor Mary Jane Marcinczyk. Over coffee, Mary Jane gave us a brief rundown of the house, and a more detailed account of a recent transfer from a Vermont hospital—a 20-year-old quadriplegic named Timothy Quail.

"Poor kid," tenderhearted Kay exclaimed. "So young to be so hurt."

"How did it happen?" asked Marie, pouring creamer into her coffee.

"He fell backwards into a shallow area of Lake Champlain this summer, and broke his neck on some rocks," Mary Jane explained. "C3 and C4, I believe."

"Why the transfer?"

"He apparently asked a male housekeeper to suffocate him with a pillow, so his doctors thought a change of scenery might improve his mood. He was a sophomore at St. Michael's College in Burlington, and perhaps couldn't bear the visits from his healthy friends."

"What a pity," sighed Kay. "Last year the same thing happened to that lovely girl who dove into a ravine over in New York State."

"Tiffany Jacobs," Marie replied factually. "I was on duty the night she came in. Did you know she died at home soon after her discharge? Police suspect that her sister drowned her in their bathtub, but it was never proven."

Mary Jane patted my knee. "Kevin, could you stop by and cheer him up a bit during your rounds? He's in Jones Rehab, 102."

"Sure, but what do I talk about?"

"What do you talk about!" scoffed Marie. "Tell him the same crackpot stories you tell us every night."

"But you guys are easy to talk to. No need to watch my p's and q's. You've seen and heard it all."

Kay reached over and pulled me smartly by the ear. "Are you insinuating we're a jaded bunch of old biddies, you young whippersnapper?"

I broke free of her grasp. "I'm just saying."

"Give it a try," Mary Jane advised in a motherly tone. "He's your age and, if nothing else, won't it pass a little time for both of you?"

"Okay, I'll do my best." I grabbed an oatmeal cookie on my way out the door. "After all, that's why they pay us orderlies the big bucks."

"Good lad, yourself," lilted Kay, putting a second cookie into my hand.

It was midnight when I called on Timothy Quail—a clean-cut, sandy-haired kid whose slim body lay lifeless beneath the blankets. Only his head, dotted with ice-blue eyes, rolled restlessly from side to side.

After my clumsy introduction, he immediately criticized the threadbare cardigan I wore over my orderly garb. "Time you burnt that old sweater, don't you think?"

I was taken aback by his gruffness, but chirped up rather than taking flight. "Not after I almost lost it in Hong Kong."

His blue eyes went from cold to hot, and burned into me like an acetylene torch. "Hong Kong? How the hell did you ever get to Hong Kong?"

I fought hard not to show any emotion. "My R&R from Vietnam, almost two years ago this December." I reached forward to give him a better look at my worn sleeves. "This sweater was a family hand-me-down, and pretty much worn when I got it. But it's got a history."

"It oughta be history."

"I suppose, but you don't understand its sentimental value. I gave it to my high school sweetheart, Lily, and she gave it back to me the night before I left for boot camp, after she'd worn it every day for a month. When we said our goodbyes, I promised her I'd wear it as often as I could, as if she were still wrapping her arms around me."

"A die-hard romantic," Tim grunted.

I sat in the chair next to him and picked lint off my pilled but prized cardigan. "Oh, yes. Even after Lily broke up with me while I was stationed in Texas, I stayed true to my word and took the sweater to Vietnam. I even packed it up with my civilian clothes when I went to Hong Kong."

"What was Hong Kong like?" Tim betrayed a glimmer of interest.

"Pretty cool. Imagine, after eight months sleeping in a stifling, screen-and-plywood hooch, I woke up at the luxurious Luk Kwok Hotel, looking over Victoria Harbor dotted with colorful Chinese junks. Not to mention droves of pretty Chinese women.

"But that first night," I continued, "I was so dazzled by 'The Pearl of the Orient,' that I left this sweater behind on the Star Ferry—a steamer that plies the waters between Hong Kong Island and the mainland of Kowloon—and I didn't notice it missing till the next morning."

Tim rolled his eyes mockingly, "You must have freaked."

"Freaked!" I blustered. "It was like the Vatican misplacing the Shroud of Turin! So I ran down to the harbor and waited for the steamer. There I learned that the Star Ferry operated four identical boats, carrying hundreds of passengers across the harbor every eight minutes. Imagine the thousands of people who might have spotted my sweater, on whichever of the four steamers it was on."

"Well, you're wearing it now, so I already know how this story ends. Get on with it, and tell me how you found your old rag."

"I boarded the first ferry that docked—Twinkling Star— I'll never forget. Amidst the blare of foghorns and the rush of commuters, I fought my way to the bow of the upper deck. And there, holy bejaysus, was my beloved blue cardigan, draped over the selfsame bench where I'd left it the night before."

I paused and took a deep breath. "By God, Tim, I couldn't have been more surprised if Suzie Wong were wearing it, or lovely Lily herself! I mean, what are the chances?"

Tim cracked a smile. "No surprise there. Who else would want it? You're just lucky somebody didn't toss it overboard!"

I pretended to be offended. "Oh, you're real nice."

"I'm just saying. You couldn't give that rag away to Goodwill."

I examined my sweater with due reverence: "I know it's all frayed and gone at the elbows, but I just can't let the memories of this old garment go."

Rosemarie, the floor's charge nurse, came hurrying to the door. "Kevin, you're wanted on Five North, stat."

Running off, I called back to Tim. "Look, gotta go. I'll stop in some other night."

He shook his head back and forth. "Yeah, yeah, that's what they all say."

I was back on Rehab the following night, and found Tim

staring blankly at the ceiling, not that he had many other options. His was a textbook example of a shattered life, but I mustered the energy to make a stand-up comic's entrance. "Hey, I'm back, the guy with the moth-eaten sweater."

I was greeted by a wafer-thin smile. "What'd you know, a guy who actually keeps his word."

With the ice starting to thaw a bit, I told him more of my stories, and eventually he told me a few of his own. At one point I was bold enough to ask, "Any girlfriends?"

Tim looked at me a long moment, eyes unblinking, and I figured I'd stuck my foot in my mouth. Not so. He motioned for his ginger ale and took a long sip, before candidly addressing the delicate issue I'd raised.

"I'd been dating Audrey Nolan for ten months before my accident, and I was head over heels for her from the start. My first true love. She was a bit of a party girl, though, and would always call me a stick in the mud. Pretty prophetic, huh?

"She visited me every day for weeks after the accident, but then stopped coming round. Not even a proper goodbye. Maybe I'd have done the same if I were in her shoes.

"Shoes," he hollowly repeated, "think about that. I'll never buy another pair, wear another pair, or tie another pair. Ain't that a royal kick in the ass. Can't do that, either—kick!"

His head began to rock in agitation. "Once I realized she wasn't coming back, I asked a cleaning guy to snuff me out with my pillow. Sort of half-joking, like he'd actually say, 'Sure, kid, no problem.' Did you hear about that?"

I nodded. "It must have been so difficult for you in so many ways."

He bit his lower lip, something he could still feel. "Next thing I know they transfer me down here, saying a change of scenery might do me some good." He let out a snort. "Change of scenery. Yeah, like going from one white ceiling to another is going to improve my mood. I'd love to send those bastards up in Vermont a blank postcard!"

His eyes filled with tears, but as I reached for a tissue, a swift turn of his head halted my actions.

"Listen, I know you're trying to help and everything, but right now I need to be alone."

I watched a tear trace its uninterrupted course down his face. "Sure, but we'll catch up some other night, okay?"

"Whatever." He dismissed me with a snap of his head.

A few nights later I worked Tim into my rounds again, when he had a scheduled catheter change. I went bouncing into his room, with a quip at the ready, when I stopped dead in my tracks. "Whoa, I'll be back in a bit."

"Hey, wait. I'm due for a new catheter. What's the hold-up?"

"I think you have a pole holding up your Big Top." I pointed to his sheets. "Looks like the circus is in town."

"Circus?"

"Yep, I say you're sporting an erection, mate."

Tim blushed. "I can't feel it, you know, or anything else down there. It must have a mind of its own."

"Don't they all?" I exited with a laugh.

Returning a few minutes later, I closed the door behind me and took a peek under the covers.

"Any change?" Tim asked.

"Nope. Looks like you're holding a weekend jamboree. I know you're happy to see me, but this is nuts, literally."

He cracked a welcoming smile: "You're a bastard, O'Hara, you know that?"

"Me?" I chuckled, delighted to find him in a better mood. "You're just lucky I don't *penile-ize* you for delay of game."

I quickly removed the old catheter and proceeded to open the fresh catheter kit.

Tim struggled to lift his head. "What're you doing? You gonna put in a new catheter while I still have a hard-on?"

I snapped on my sterile gloves: "I have places to go, people to see. Plus, I think I know how to drop this bad boy."

He eyed me dubiously, and gulped, "How?"

I picked up the new catheter and made an elaborate show of tying a knot in its length. Then, before his goggling eyes, I proceeded to apply lubricant to its narrow tip and took aim at his wagging appendage. "Maybe this will do the trick?"

Tim shut his eyes, but from sheer self-protection, his errant member ran down the flag. I untied the knot, and inserted the catheter effortlessly.

"Did it work?"

"Like a charm. You can now open your eyes."

Job done, I disposed of my kit and gloves. "Now I need to report my remarkable findings to the New England Journal of Medicine."

"What? You're going to write a paper about my erection?"

"Why not?" I winked. "I even have a working title: *'Dropping Tim's Bad Boy: A Clinical Study.'*"

Tim cracked another smile: "O'Hara, you're truly the king of the disorderlies."

During the ensuing weeks, I visited Tim on a nightly basis. I'd assist Rosemarie in turning him every two hours to avoid bedsores, and freshening him up a bit. One night, after she'd left the room, Tim whispered, "You know what I think about every time I see her?"

"What a good nurse she is?"

"No, though she's nice enough. She makes me think of my Uncle Will. He fought alongside my dad in Italy during World War Two. They both made it home all right, but while my dad never talked about those years, my uncle came back a man obsessed. You know how some guys come home shell-shocked? Well, Uncle Will came home titty-shocked."

I laughed. "I hope he didn't try to collect disability. But what does that have to do with Rosemarie?"

"That's just it, her name. My uncle was so blown away by Italian women, that he had two naked images tattooed on his forearms, Rosa and Maria. What babes! You could get aroused just looking at them." His eyes took on a faraway look.

"Listen, Tim, you get aroused at a catheter change, so that's not saying a whole lot."

Snapping back, he countered, "You're lucky I'm a quad, O'Hara, or right now you'd be one stand-up comic laying flat on his back."

"I'm sure you could do it." I pretended to cower as I left the room.

One night, out of the blue, Tim asked if I ever got injured in Vietnam.

"Yep, once."

"You okay to talk about it?"

"Sure, I'm good."

I flopped down in the chair beside him and stretched my weary, ward-hopping legs. "I had three days left to go at Cam Ranh Bay when I learned the guys at the South Station were planning to throw me a going-away party. But I begged them not to."

"Why not?"

"Bad karma, for starters, and I didn't want to jinx myself. It seemed like every sad story out of 'Nam was of guys getting killed or wounded at the beginning or end of their tours. All I wanted was to wake up on my 365th morning and board my 707 Freedom Bird for home. That's it. No fanfare, no fond farewells, nothing. But despite my wishes, they threw me a party anyway. Any excuse for a celebration, I guess."

"What was your bash like?"

"Like all the others—stale pretzels and Schlitz beer—while swapping our favorite war stories. Rather than the Airman's Club, they held the party in my crew chief's hooch, while his Akai reel-to-reel cranked out The Moody Blues, non-stop. Heck, if I had a dollar for every time I heard *Nights in White Satin* that year, I'd have come home a millionaire."

"Any pot?"

"Yeah, but I rarely smoked since it always left me craving for my mom's nut-fudge brownies. Anyway, it was pitch black when my shindig broke up, but for the yellow flares that lit up our perimeter. I headed for the shower stalls, pleasantly drunk, wearing only boxers and flip-flops, carrying my towel and shaving kit. A few weeks before, an old sarge from our squadron was bitten by a water rat, and ended up delirious with rat-bite fever. So rather than walk the wooden planks laid out over the dunes like I always did, I took extra precaution by walking on top of the revetments."

"Revetments?"

"Four-foot high retaining walls filled with sandbags that helped protect our flimsy hooches. I was only thirty yards from the stalls when I heard these blistering explosions jarring the night. Incoming rockets, right? So I jumped into a revetment for cover, and landed on an upright nail."

"Ouch!"

"You can say that again. Somehow I managed to hobble through the night to the nearest infirmary where the medic on duty gave me a shot of morphine, and had my foot soaking in a basin of green antiseptic before I could say 'lickety-split.' I'll tell ya, Tim, the combination of beer and morphine knocked me for a loop. Then I must've dozed off, because when I woke, my foot was neatly bandaged, and the medic was measuring me out for crutches."

"Were you still under attack?"

"Nope. It seemed the barrage had stopped as quickly as it began. Just the eerie silence that followed every attack, like the air had been momentarily sucked out from the sky. Charlie always lobbed a few mortars at us every month, just to remind us he was still out there.

"Anyhow, I asked the medic why the crutches. And he tells me that my foot was going to cramp up something awful, like I'd stepped on a punji stick, a crude implement the enemy used to slow down our troops in the field. By this time, the morphine had sent my head into the stratosphere, and the thought of a Purple Heart suddenly popped up. I mean, why not? A Purple Heart gave you extra leave time, as well as life-long respect from civilians and military personnel alike."

"Sounds reasonable enough."

"I thought so, too. So I cleared my throat and said, 'Hey, doc, I've been working the flightline for months, and I've seen hundreds of soldiers being loaded onto AirVacs for home with all sorts of terrible wounds. But I wonder, even though my injury is petty in comparison . . . well, you know, I wonder if you might recommend me for the Purple Heart?'

"'Purple Heart?' he questioned. 'Tell me again, what

happened?"

"So I told him how I was walking the revetments to avoid the rats, and jumped on an upright nail when I heard the incoming rounds. But rather than digging out the necessary paperwork, the medic splits a gut, like it's the funniest thing he's heard since it was rumored how Bob Hope favored Phyllis Diller over Raquel Welch at the USO shows.

"'Incoming rounds?' he roared. 'Hey, man, they weren't incoming rounds! That was the Navy side blowing up old munitions. Didn't you read the memo?'"

Tim muffled a laugh. "Let me guess. No Purple Heart?"

"Nope. Just a pair of bamboo crutches to carry my sorry ass home."

"Well, at least you made it, unlike fifty-thousand other poor souls."

I stood up from the chair and gave Tim's head a friendly rub. "Amen, to that."

A week before Christmas, Mary Jane asked me to accompany her down to the main kitchen. "Kevin, good news. Tim's being transferred to Mass General tomorrow for more intensive rehab."

"Really? He didn't say anything to me about it last night."

She pulled a bunch of keys from around her waist and opened the door to Dietary. "We only got word this morning. If nothing else, it's a step in the right direction, as his family lives in the Boston area."

Mary Jane led me into the kitchen's walk-in cooler. "You told me that Tim was fond of tapioca pudding, so I've squirreled some away."

She handed me a large covered bowl. "Here you go, for his last night here. Hope he enjoys it."

"Thanks, MJ. That's very kind."

"Rosemarie tells me you've been a big help."

"Easy duty, he's a good guy."

At the stroke of midnight, I entered J102 with a rat-a-tat-tat to the door, and a bowl of pudding in my hands.

"What's this?"

"We hear you're off in the morning, so Mary Jane had me bring you a midnight snack."

"Not tapioca?"

"Yep."

He raised his eyes to the ceiling. "There really is a God!"

He watched hungrily as I removed the plastic wrap from the bowl. "Darn, I forgot a spoon."

"There's one in my top drawer." He turned his head, and took delight in helping me with the search. "There, there, see it, right beside the small flashlight!"

"Got it."

I cranked up his bed to a sitting position. "So I hear you're leaving us tomorrow?"

He smacked his lips as I lifted the first spoonful of the unexpected treat, and smiled after swallowing. "Yep, another white ceiling to ponder the mysteries of the universe. Intensive rehab, too. What a joke, huh? What are they going to accomplish? Find out that three pillows under my knees are better than two?"

I loaded up another spoonful and looped it around his head like the old Maypo TV commercial. "But you're excited about the move, aren't you?"

"I guess. Supposedly they've got this cervical specialist who's promised he'll have me home in six months. If that's true, it'll be one year on the button since my accident. Hey, did I tell you how my brother Tommy is reading up on teleportation?"

"Sci-fi stuff? Or do you mean more like meditation?"

"Sort of, but even better. Once you get the hang of it, you can leave your body and go anywhere. Tommy thinks I'm an excellent candidate. He's a super brother, you know, says he'll do anything for me. He's always telling me, 'Better to have a mind without a body than a body without a mind.' That makes sense, doesn't it?"

"Perfect sense," I agreed.

"Once I get the knack of it, do you know where I'm going first?"

"Back to Burlington."

"Nope, Hong Kong. There I'm going to board the Twinkling Star and see the place where my good friend O'Hara beat all odds, and showed that miracles can truly happen."

He opened up for another bite, the metal spoon scraping against his lower teeth.

"Tim," I braved, "can I ask you something?" I broached a question long on my mind.

"Shoot."

"What do you think about when you stare up at that blank ceiling?"

"Sports, mostly," he answered without hesitation. "I told you how I played baseball and basketball in high school, right? I visualize myself at-bat in the major leagues. I've hit home runs off every star pitcher in the bigs, often a grand slam with two outs in the bottom of the ninth. I love to follow the trajectory of my towering, gravity-defying shots."

"Wow, a real Hall of Famer!"

"Wait, I've got another visual mantra that I replay over and over to myself. It's the NCAA Finals. St. Mike's, which would've been my alma mater, versus Kentucky for the national title. Down by one with two seconds to play, my brother Tommy passes me the ball. As I drain the winning 30-foot jumper at the buzzer, I get knocked out of bounds. But instead of whacking the back of my head against the hardwood floor, I fall into the arms of the prettiest St. Mike's cheerleader of them all, Audrey Nolan."

He paused. "Sounds foolish, I know, but you can't imagine how many times I've played that movie in my head, to lift my spirits. Or to escape embarrassing moments, like when a female aide is cleaning me up after I've literally shit the bed."

"Sounds like a great diversion."

"Here's another. My social worker, Mary Green, has introduced me to books on tape. Right now, I'm listening to *Lonesome Dove*. She's even got me into classical music. Me, strictly a rock 'n' roll guy! For the past month, I've been listening to Franz Liszt's *Transcendental Etudes*, to get me in the mood for teleportation."

"Listen to you, a regular maestro."

On the whole, Tim seemed upbeat about his impending transfer, and increasingly philosophical about his condition. "While I was up in Vermont, the hospital chaplain told me I should offer up my suffering for the less fortunate in the world. 'Less fortunate!' What a joke, I thought, and here I can't even blow my own nose without assistance. But, you know, that chaplain was onto something. Even though I'm little more than a talking head, I'm not bad off. Think about it. I'm fed, cleaned and sheltered, and in no physical pain."

He let out a sigh, his blue eyes scanning the ceiling as if it were the universe. "Hard to believe, but even in my sorry state, I'm better off than a third of the world's population who still live in extreme poverty. Imagine, literally two billion people are worse off than I am. Me, a lifeless quad! Now, how's that for a staggering statistic? So lately I've been taking the chaplain's advice, and offering up my condition for all those millions who suffer in this suffering world. And guess what? It helps me, and it might even help all those poor folks, too."

Rosemarie came knocking at the door. "Sorry, Kevin, but Two South just called for the third time."

I looked down at Tim: "Well, guy, gotta go."

"Wait, man," he struggled to find the words. "I just want to thank you for putting up with me and my moods, especially in the early going."

I gave his ear a good pull. "No problem. We had ourselves a few good laughs, didn't we?"

His eyes lit up. "I'll say."

"Remember, Tim, always keep your chin up."

I winced at my last verbal blunder, but he didn't seem to mind. "It's all I can do, but at least it's something, isn't it?"

I gave Tim a final rub to his head before walking out the door, never to see or hear from him again.

The following night, during my Rehab rounds, I asked Rosemarie if Tim got off okay.

"Without a wrinkle, I'm glad to report. In like a lion, out like a lamb. He should be a reminder for all of us to enjoy every healthy moment God gives us. Isn't that so?"

"It is," I wholeheartedly agreed.

Before I left the unit, I ventured into Tim's unoccupied room, and sat down on his bed. Somehow I knew he was thinking of me at that very moment, as I him. I imagined the aides at Mass General attending to him now. First the bed bath, then the application of Sween Cream to his elbows, hips, knees and ankles. Especially his coccyx region, most susceptible to breakdown. They might make a few wisecracks, or gag at first exposure to his soiled sheets. Then they'd remake his occupied bed, rolling him from side to side, "like a rolling pin," as Tim would say.

It might be another humiliating ordeal, but Tim would be teleported elsewhere. Yes, he'd only be hearing the thump of the ball, the roar of the crowd, the squeak of sneakers, and the slap of bodies in the paint. Then Tommy's crisp outlet pass, followed by his long winning jumper at the buzzer, only to fall again and again into Audrey Nolan's outstretched and loving arms.

* * *

Passing from Tim's evaporating dream into my own present reality in Neuro, I heard Scott the orderly call out, "Thar she blows!"

I felt an inner pop as Scott's rubber catheter breached my bladder neck, sending a torrent of urine splashing into a plastic catch basin, like waves crashing up against a seawall.

"Oh, damn!"

I lifted my head. "Anything wrong?"

"Blood in the urine."

"A lot?"

Scott continued to direct the catheter's stream into the basin. "Hard to tell. Even a little looks like a lot. It's pretty red, though."

Once my bladder was drained, Scott showed me the container of dark-reddish urine. "Jeez, looks like I've been eating nothing but beets for a month." I wanted to laugh it off, but it looked ominous.

Scott tried to ease my anxiety. "This kind of thing happens a lot after blunt trauma, and usually clears up on its own. I also know that marathon runners get it from time to time."

"Yeah, but I just didn't run 26 miles. What happens now?"

"We'll send a spec to the Lab, just to be sure. Then your doc will probably order a CT scan to check your kidneys, along with an indwelling catheter till it clears up."

"Oh, great," I groaned. "I'm going from the frying pan to the fire."

Scott snapped off his gloves after the cleanup. "Don't worry, Dr. DeMarco will take good care of you."

"Dr. Bill DeMarco?"

"Says so on your chart. Nothing but the best for our ward hero."

Long before Dr. DeMarco became BMC's Chief Hospitalist, he was my primary doctor. Besides being the best at his job, he was a known quantity to me. My mood began to lift—if anyone could get me back on my feet, it'd be this guy, hands down.

Years earlier, when I was seeing him for my annual physical, he was always baffled by my refusal to take the Hepatitis B vaccine. He'd argue, "Kev, you work on a locked psych unit where sick patients are known to bite, spit, and scratch. Not to mention your chances of getting stuck by a needle. So please, stop your pigheadedness, and get the vaccine."

"Sorry, Doc," I'd answer flippantly. "Do you think Mother Teresa ever bothers with a Hep B shot while working the gutters of Calcutta?"

He'd raise his eyes to the heavens, and say, "I hate to break the news, Kev, but you're no Mother Teresa." With that frank clarification, I took the shot, and we'd gotten along famously ever since.

Despite the pain medication, my first day in Neuro passed in fractured agony, until Dr. DeMarco arrived at my bedside, accompanied by a cadre of white-coated interns. Dr. Bill introduced them, "Kev, these are the King's Men, and we're here to put you back together again." To combat my immediate pain, he ordered a stat dose of Dilaudid, a powerful analgesic that lit up my synapses like a pinball machine.

Next, he sent me on a bone-jarring ride to Radiology for a CT scan, in which an invasive dye cruised through miles of veins before showing up in my kidneys. The procedure gave me hot flashes, and a more intimate appreciation of female menopausal woes. A lingering metallic taste made me feel like Dorothy's Tin Man.

Back in Neuro in a thoroughly groggy state, I felt a warm hand cover my own. "Kev, it's Alex. How you doing, chief?"

The pieces fell together, slowly. Where I was and who this was—my ultimate boss, Dr. Alex Sabo, chairman of Behavioral Sciences at BMC. Dr. Sabo called everyone chief, though he was the real chief, and a good one. I'd heard he had visited me in the ED yesterday, only to find me conked out.

"I'm okay, Alex, but I'm afraid I won't make for good company. I've been heavily . . . "

I dozed off mid-sentence, though I remained vaguely cognizant of his presence.

Dr. Sabo was one of the BMC's brightest stars, coming to us after running the prestigious McLean's Hospital outside Boston. Not only a Massachusetts Psychiatrist of the Year, but Alex was also on a perennially contending Triathlon team in Berkshire County's signature sporting event, the Josh Billings

RunAground. His special mission was to reduce Berkshire County's suicide rate, and he was tireless in that effort. Now he was looking out for Nurse Lite, making sure every angle of my case was being covered.

After a rocky start, Alex and I had gotten along great over the years. He credited me with working the good side of every patient, and I respected all that he had accomplished. Now I came awake enough to formulate a sentence, "Alex, remember your first visit to Jones Three, when I thought you were going to fire me?"

"I was never going to fire you, chief," he smiled. "I just didn't know what to make of you at first, that's all."

My heavy eyes closed again, and I drifted back to our first memorable meeting years before . . .

Back in the day, I used to treat the recording of my week-end summaries as if it were an audition tape for *Saturday Night Live*. Tending to be a little punch-drunk while taping late Sunday night, I tried to give the Monday crew all the relevant facts, but also a few laughs.

One Sunday, I'd laid down a good track, given our colorful cast of in-house characters. I might have been a bit loopier than usual, having worked back-to-back double shifts, and knowing I was scheduled to fill in again the next day.

Early that Monday morning, I relished the chance to eavesdrop as the day staff assembled in the conference room to hear my routine. I was all set to bask in the sound of appreciative laughter when something decidedly unfunny happened.

Onto the unit, walked our ballyhooed new boss, Dr. Alexander Sabo, arriving unannounced and asking to sit in on the morning report.

Ceil Roosa, the charge nurse, abruptly contracted a bad

case of Porky-speak. "W-w-why, yes, d-doctor." She knew as well as I that my comedy reel would not be the best introduction for our esteemed new chief.

Peeking into the room, I could see the crew fidgeting nervously in their seats, as Ceil hit the play button on our small Sony cassette player. With a crackle, on came the oh-so-mellifluous voice of yours truly.

"Hi guys, it's Li'l Kev, giving you the weekend report. Our current census is ten, so let's start with our three most recent admissions, shall we? All of them are season ticket holders that I'm sure you'll recognize.

"First up is our beloved Jackie, or Whackie, as she insists on being called, known only by her first name, like Cher or Madonna. You may recall how she claims to be the long-lost love child of Betty Crocker and Mr. Rogers, found abandoned in a schoolyard in Biloxi. Her reason for admission this time is that the Whopper went up a nickel at Burger King. Now, guys, let's do the math here. It's costing the state $880 a day to house Whackie because the Whopper went up a Jeff. Bad odds for the taxpayer, don't you think?

"Next up is Dicky Sommers, known to us fondly as Mr. Malaprop, who's back with us following a dispute with his slum—er—landlord. You'll remember him as the fellow who hails from the Canadian city of 'Winnebago,' yearns to visit the Vatican's 'Sixteenth Chapel,' and often complains that his remarks are taken 'out of contest.' However, his religious beliefs remain steadfast, as when he proclaims, 'We're all God's children, that's why we're born with biblical cords.'"

One of the crew stifled a laugh, and cast a guilty glance at Dr. Sabo.

"Then we've got Luckless Lou, who spent nine hundred

bucks last month on 900 numbers. For the uninitiated out there, 900 numbers are porn lines. You might recall how Sammy the Snit once summed up Lou's ill-luck: 'If Luckless Lou fell into a bucket of rubber nipples, he'd come up sucking his thumb.'"

On and on I went, zanier and worse. Of course my jive-talk was interspersed with pertinent information, but not enough, I'm afraid, to balance the scales for our new chief.

Too afraid to take another peek into the room, I listened by the doorway, hoping for a cannonade of laughter that would break the stifling silence surrounding the droning on of my snickering voice. But not a titter did I hear at my trench humor, that, even to me, began to sound inappropriate and uncaring.

My report concluded: "So guys, that ends my Sunday night rap, but there's no need to be glum, because Kevlar will be right outside the door to greet you at the conclusion of this report. *Adios* from the guy everybody loves to hate, or hates to love. Your braying donkey friend, Li'l Kev."

The Sony machine finally clicked off, as I heard the clearing of throats and scraping of chairs.

I fled into the small laundry room before a word was spoken, and sneaked a peep as the crew emerged from the conference room. Ceil was the first to walk by, her face flushed with embarrassment. JoJo caught a glimpse of me in my hidey-hole and quickened her pace. Rob gave me a glance and ran his index finger across his throat. Even my good buddy, Charlie, stuck his head into where I had cowered between washer and dryer, to offer the kindly advice, "I'd find a better hiding place if I were you."

I followed Charlie's quickened pace to the linen closet,

while looking back to see Dr. Sabo enter the nurses' station.

"Charlie, how bad was it?"

Charlie pulled fresh sheets from the top shelf. "How bad? Let's just say, a bucket of nipples bad."

"Eek, really?"

He turned to me. "Think about it, Kev. You're a senior nurse here, whereas our new director, straight out of the Who's Who of Psychiatry, begins his chairmanship by listening to your midnight rant at the Improv."

I must've turned green, because Charlie tried to buck me up some.

"Kev, we all know your quirky ways, and good intentions—to know Kev is to love Kev—but Dr. Sabo doesn't know you from Adam."

"How did he react as he listened?"

"Who knows? We were too afraid to look at him."

"Did you hear him laugh? Even a little?"

Charlie looked at me in disbelief. "Oh, yeah! He really split a gut over your comment about biblical cords. And you're the guy who's always bellyaching about never winning Nurse of the Year. I gotta tell you, Kev, with those goofy reports, you'll never even be in the running."

Charlie turned to go about his business, leaving me to stew in my solitude. I knew I couldn't hide all day, and would eventually have to face Dr. Sabo, so I popped out of my rabbit hole, braving fox or snare. Spotting the doctor standing alone in the hallway, I approached him thinking to myself, "If a new broom sweeps clean, I'm destined for the dust bin."

"H-hello, Dr. Sabo," I stumbled. "M-my name is Kevin O'Hara, a longtime nurse here. I'm afraid you'll recognize me as the one giving the report this morning. Looking back, I realize it wasn't all that professional."

He shook my hand cordially. "Nice to meet you, Kevin, and I agree about your report. In fact, in all my years of psychiatry, I've never heard anything quite like it."

I hung my head, waiting for the axe to fall. But, instead, I felt his hand on my shoulder. "But, I must tell you, chief, it was very funny."

And that right there was, as Bogie told Claude Rains, "the beginning of a beautiful friendship."

I smiled in my sleep, and woke again to find Dr. Sabo gone. But I wasn't alone for long, visited by family members in the ten minutes allotted at the top of each hour. A lunch tray soon appeared, but I was too doped up to lift its lid. I seem to recall a flurry of nursing students chirping around me like hedge sparrows. A deep snooze. A dinner tray left untouched. A trip to Radiology for an MRI where a jackhammer pulsated through my head. Once I ventured a sip of ginger ale, but its bubbling effervescence tickled my nostrils and stimulated a sneeze that rocked my world like an earthquake.

Eric Dickhaus popped up like the Mad Hatter, wanting to check my indwelling catheter.

"Haven't got one yet," I told him.

"Yeah, you do," Eric laughed. "I put one in two hours ago." Then he was gone, and so was I.

Coming awake again, I glanced up blurrily at the wall clock. Nine o'clock? Nine in the morning, or nine at night? What day was it? My tongue parched, I reached for water on my bed stand, but found a stack of magazines instead.

A voice cut through the haze. "Your brother from Boston left those."

"Left what?"

"Those magazines. Says you like astronomy."

I cautiously turned to see a racked-up redheaded guy in his late forties talking to me from the next bed, hooked up to every medical contraption invented since the Iron Lung. I later learned he was the motorcycle dude who'd caused yesterday's bottleneck in the ED.

"Oh, my younger brother, Dermot."

"Said he'd be back tomorrow."

"Thanks. By the way, I'm Kevin."

"I got that. What a flood of people you have looking in at you! You the mayor, or something?"

"Nope, just a longtime worker here. Sorry, your name again?"

"Oliver. But friends, when I had 'em, called me Ollie or Ols."

"Nice to meet you, Ollie, though we could've picked a better place, say a tavern?"

"Got that right," he answered flatly. "Nurses keep telling me I'm lucky to be alive, but I'm not feeling it yet. I've got a punctured lung, a busted leg, and a few unhappy organs."

He paused when his Pleur-evac chest tube kicked in, sucking excess fluid from his left lung. "How about you? What's your damage?"

"Rib and spine fractures. And now, bloody urine."

He glanced down at the catheter bag dangling from my bedside. "I heard you got your ass kicked?"

"It wasn't a fair fight," I tried to make light of it. "I didn't even have the chance to raise my dukes."

Ollie went silent, and I thought he was done. In his pulverized state, I couldn't believe he still had the strength to speak at all. After a spell, he was back at it. "You and your brother are close, huh?"

"Like two coats of paint," I acknowledged. "How'd you know?"

He looked directly at me, through his pain and into my own. "I could feel his concern, how much he cared."

I was struck by Ollie's openness, and summoned the energy to respond in kind. "We grew up together in the middle of eight kids, and shared the same bed for 14 years. We even worked here at the hospital together. First as orderlies, then as psych nurses."

His bloodshot eyes widened. "Two male nurses in one brood. What's the chances?"

"I guess it's a family thing, since our mom and two aunts were also psych nurses. Derm always joked that we had to become nurses. If not, our only Irish alternative was to become male nuns."

"Now, that's a scary thought," Ollie chuckled. "You two must have loads of stories from the nut ward."

"Oh, quite a few," I agreed. "I only hope I have a few more in store, and my career hasn't come to a crashing end."

Before Ollie could reply, his assigned nurse came around and closed his curtain for a dressing change. In turn, I picked up a *Sky & Telescope* magazine, and thumbed through Hubble images of luminous star clusters. While stargazing through the pages, I dozed off and found myself skyrocketing back to the '70s, towards a Jones Two space odyssey with Dermot . . .

"Derm, it's the perfect night to take patients to Springside Observatory. On Fridays, it's open to the public. There's no moon, and it's clear as can be. C'mon, it'll be a blast."

My younger brother, sitting behind the nurses' station, closed a patient's chart and looked up at me with one eye cocked.

"I don't know, Kev. I hear the Astronomy Club also meets there on Friday, and they might be a little too stuffy for our gang."

"But that's the point," I argued. "It's our job as psych nurses to stamp out stigma, right? Didn't Dr. James Cattell tell us that our main mission is to assimilate patients back into the community? That's why they're closing Northampton State, and every other state institution. Don't you remember our Stamp-Out Stigma softball game last summer?"

Dermot eyed me wryly: "'Stamp-Out Stigma?' I think we stamped it in, for good."

Yes, that Saturday in July had been a total disaster. In that cracked brainstorm of mine and a few peers, we proposed to mix patients and staff into two teams for a softball game at Clapp Park, a nearby public ball field. Unfortunately, a local newspaper made mention of the event, which brought out scores of curious spectators.

Our hope of having patients blend into normal society wavered in the very first inning, when Ernie Olds smashed his bat to the ground after striking out—and he, a staff member. If that didn't get the fans stomping their feet, more action was coming. The next batter was a chronic patient with an intermittent explosive disorder, nicknamed Cherry Bomb. The first pitch actually hit him in the batter's box, and patients and staff alike braced themselves for his inevitable eruption. All exhaled in relief when he calmly trotted to first base.

However, with the very next pitch, a called strike, Cherry Bomb went bolting around the bases, plowing into every player in the infield, and charging into home plate like a Mack truck, sending our catcher halfway up the backstop.

Raucous fans roared from the bleachers, hollering

"Welcome to Looney Bin Baseball!" along with other half-witty catcalls.

Undaunted by their chorus of jeers, my squad batted in the bottom of the first. Erin Go Braless reached base on an error, Nancy Nurse walked, and Smokin' Joe tripled to deep left center. But rather than scoring, Erin threw on the brakes at third, joined there by Nancy, with Joe bringing up the rear, all three halted at the sight of Cherry Bomb guarding home plate like a hungry convict over his bowl of stew.

In short order, the bases were literally loaded—our entire team of nine, three to each bag—with no one left to bat. With that impasse, our game degenerated into name-calling and temper tantrums. The crowd was merrily stomping their feet and egging everyone on. The staff had to acknowledge that our honorable effort to integrate our charges into the mainstream had failed miserably, and wisely called the game on account of sunshine.

"C'mon, Derm, that softball game is long past and forgotten. Tonight at the Observatory will go a whole lot better. Mark my word, Dr. Cattell will praise both of us at the next Grand Rounds for such innovative psych nursing."

Dermot gave me a well-practiced look of skepticism, but I grabbed his wrist and whispered, "I'm also thinking of joining the Astronomy Club, and this will give me a look-see on hospital time."

Once Dermot reluctantly caved in to his elder sibling, I canvassed the unit and rounded up four space cadets to shoot for the heavens. With the group chosen, I ran it past my good buddy, Spencer Trova, the charge nurse on duty.

"Spence, Derm and I have four patients eager to go stargazing at Springside Park; Rebecca, Zoe, Dicky and Buster.

What do you say?"

Spencer screwed up his face. "I'm not too sure, Kev. A lot could go wrong with that bunch."

"Like what?"

"Like what!" Spencer removed his glasses and rubbed his eyes deeply. "Did you just ask me, 'Like what?' What if Dick spots a cat along the way, or Rebecca morphs into a thumb-sucking brat? What will people make of Zoe conversing with Zippy? And, if you're crazy enough to take Buster, better stick a few Thorazine in your pocket in case he has a meltdown."

"That sounds like a yes, right?"

Spencer dropped his head into his hands. "I must be crazy to take charge nurse for a measly 25 cents more an hour."

I thanked Spence profusely, and set off to gather my crew.

Dick Whittington, let's call him, was the first to arrive at the nurses' station, dressed in gaudy "SAHC" orange inmate scrubs, from his previous abode, the San Antonio House of Correction. He flipped the pen like a switchblade before scratching his name across the sign-out sheet.

"Dick, you got anything else to wear besides those prison togs?"

"Nope, just these," he snarled, "and I don't give a twinkly fart what people think of me wearing 'em."

Dick's troubles had begun around the time of Woodstock in '69, as he sat outside the Hot Dog Ranch on Linden Street in Pittsfield, smearing relish on his wieners. There, to hear him tell it, a Calico cat walked up and talked to him, convincing our Dicky to pack his bags and move to Texas, where he'd find his "San Antonio Rose." As instructed by that fount of female wisdom, Dick boarded a Greyhound bus, and in short order, he was eating enchiladas across from the Alamo, searching bars and bordellos for his destined sweetheart.

But things rarely end favorably for people who heed a stray cat's suggestion, and Dick's "Rose" turned out to be one prickly thorn bush from Abilene. There followed a contentious divorce, two psych committals, and three incarcerations, the last for animal cruelty. More specifically, cat abuse, since Dicky had pledged to kick the "pink-puckered asses" of every cat that ever crossed his path, whether they spoke to him or not. Dick concluded his seven-year Texas odyssey back at the Hot Dog Ranch, owning nothing but the prison garb on his back.

Next up, Zoe, a chunky, sandy-haired girl, who took the pen cautiously from Dick's hand, and propped up on the counter a large shocking-purple monkey, her longtime pal Zippy. Years ago, at Newberry's Five & Dime, the stuffed monkey had called out to her from a high shelf of toys, "Zoe, my name is Zippy. Take me home, please."

Zoe was smitten—who wouldn't be, by this purple charmer?—and after a trip to the cash register, the pair pledged their undying commitment to each other. Zippy's mouth was permanently stained from drinking, or attempting to drink, his favorite soda pop, Orange Crush.

Many patients had favorite stuffed animals for comfort, but Zoe's was different. Way different. She handled Zippy as skillfully as a ventriloquist with his dummy. Zippy could nod his head, shrug his shoulders, or give you a sharp poke, if given cause. Roommates of Zippy claimed to have heard him burp, sneeze, and even fart on occasion.

Though psychiatry tells us not to play into a patient's delusions, hospital workers doted on Zippy. It wasn't uncommon to see a dietary aide offer him a scoop of ice cream, or a phlebotomist pretend to draw his blood, while a nervous Zoe held out his little arm. Zippy even wore a newborn's blue wristband, courtesy of Admitting!

I gently suggested to Zoe that she might leave Zippy in her room, in case he might catch a cold, though I was certain of her answer in advance.

"Not a chance," she scowled, buttoning Zippy's little coat to his stained chin. "Where I go, Zippy goes. And where Zippy goes, I go. Got it?"

"Got it."

Rebecca came next, another young woman who looked a lot like Raggedy Ann, long red pigtails and all. She had a penchant for morphing into a churlish child quicker than the stooge Moe could poke Curly in the eye. I took note of her signature as she signed out, looking for any hint of a childish scrawl—a warning sign of imminent transformation to a bratty she-devil worse than any Tasmanian creature.

"Rebecca, you feeling okay?" I inquired, the picture of therapeutic concern.

"Yes, fine. Why?"

"Well, it's comforting to know that you're you, and not about to become somebody else."

She smiled a reassuring smile. "No, I'm good, Kevin. Really."

Not long before, intrepidly or perhaps foolishly, I'd taken her to nearby Morningside Bakery, where she suddenly turned into a tiny tornado, laying waste to a stack of cupcakes, before demolishing a three-tier wedding cake headed for a reception that same afternoon. Not my finest hour as a therapist, I assure you.

"Rebecca, you doubly sure?"

She took a deep breath, like a diver poised on the high

board, and sprang: "Why even ask me to go out and see your dumb stars if you're so worried about me? I never switch unless I feel threatened, and right now you're threatening me. So bug off, before Rebecca becomes Becky the Bitch!"

Tugging the pen free of her clenched fist, I handed it to Buster, thankful that Spencer was out of earshot. With these rumblings, he might put a total kibosh on our whole excursion.

Buster was a handsome, middle-aged man, but the sickest of the four. If his widowed father hadn't been a tireless advocate for him, Buster still would have been wasting away in the back wards of Northampton State. He earned his nickname from the silent movie star, Buster Keaton, since he rarely spoke and his hefty daily dose of Thorazine left him stone-faced, incapable of cracking a smile.

Daft as the others, Dermot and I were the guides for this night's celestial junket—two starry-eyed Irish longhairs still searching for our pot of gold.

When he heard the exit door buzz, Spencer shouted, "Be back in an hour, not a minute more!"

"Sure thing, Spence," Derm and I flashed him a thumbs up, and jovially shepherded our flock into the clear, chilly night dotted with stars.

Free of the ward's confines, the six of us tramped the half-mile to Springside Park in happy disorder, then up the rutted path to our rendezvous with the stars. Rebecca and Zoe led the way, singing, *"Star light, star bright, first star I see tonight."* We soon arrived at the observatory, situated on a sloping hillside facing away from the glare of city lights.

Mustering our forces, we entered the smallish cabin, where we saw a large telescope peeking through a hole in the roof—the big eye in the sky. A half dozen members of the

Astronomy Club milled about the cramped quarters, tossing around names of comets and nebulae as if chatting about their grandkids.

Suddenly, a prickly nausea came over me. I had made a big mistake, because a few members gave us cold, unwelcoming looks. My charges shuffled uncomfortably into the refuge of a dark corner, away from the all-seeing eyes of these seasoned stargazers.

Packed into this recess, Zippy gave me a sharp jab to the ribs, and an uneasy Dermot whispered into my ear, "Nice going, Kev."

I stood speechless, realizing my selfish folly, as I looked around at our four patients. Rebecca was fidgeting, on the verge of jamming her thumb into her gob; Dick was scanning the floor for a cat to kick; Zoe was hanging on to Zippy for dear life, and Buster stood as lifeless as a statue on Easter Island.

I tried to buck up my troops. "Don't worry, guys," I whispered, "we're in for a real treat."

"I hope so," muttered Dick, "because right now I feel like Uranus, and mine."

The program commenced, with everyone taking turns at the telescope, our group the last to be called. We each quickly peered through the eyepiece of the impressive telescope, and shuffled back to our corner without comment. But as club members took their successive turns, expressions of awe and sighs of fascination escaped their lips.

"My God," gasped one dapper gent, "have you ever seen the westerly spread of Ophiuchus in such splendor?"

Dick grumbled into my ear: "Damn, you'd think these dickwads were watching a peep show."

In fairness, the presiding professor was accommodating to our party, no doubt guessing our current residence, and took time to point the telescope toward Jupiter's moons and Saturn's rings; mere door knockers to the infinite heavens. When Zoe lifted Zippy to the eyepiece for his first look, titters escaped the club members. However, Zippy's sharp turn and dead stare put a quick halt to their amusement.

At the program's conclusion, the professor looked our way and asked, "Since this is your first visit to our observatory, I wonder if there's something particular you'd like to see before we close for the night?"

The six of us gulped collectively, not having a clue what to request, my own limited knowledge of astronomy suddenly falling into a black hole.

One club member, who'd observed us disapprovingly since our arrival, spoke up with a snooty air, "Maybe you'd like to view Vega in our North American Nebula?"

Another chortled, "Or perhaps the Veil Nebula on the southern edge of Cygnus?"

"Enough!" The professor gave the pair a withering glance. "But may I suggest . . . "

"Ex-x-cuse me!"

Dermot and I turned in disbelief to see Buster's hand held aloft. From a man of so few words, this singular utterance was more astonishing than the starry spread of the Great Rift above.

"Yes?" the professor responded encouragingly.

Buster fidgeted in his shoes, dug his hands deep into pockets, and rasped, "I don't know about anybody else here tonight, but I'd sure like to see Cleveland, Ohio in that thing."

There followed a moment of uncomprehending silence,

as hushed as the Milky Way itself. But then an eruption of laughter rang through the cosmos.

Baffled by the club members' ensuing hilarity, Buster scratched his head and shouted above the din, "My grandmother, Mary Rooney, lives there!"

Well, that was it, wasn't it? Amid their rising mirth, we hastily took our leave, scuttling swiftly out the narrow entry, with Zippy's tail tucked well between his legs.

"Nice going, Kev," muttered Dermot again, as we walked down the park's rough path toward the hospital. "I can't wait to see how you're going to write this one up for Dr. Cattell."

I gulped: "The patients seemed to enjoy it."

"Oh, yeah, look at 'em. They're over the moon."

I couldn't look at first, sorry for the shame I had exposed them to, taking this vulnerable quartet out of their comfort zone for my own selfish purposes. But then Derm pulled me by the sleeve, and we silently surveyed our charges.

Dick was taking a long look skyward and contemplating the star fields, maybe for the first time. "You know," he said, "it's amazing there are people smart enough to know the names of every star in the sky."

Rebecca wrapped her thick red pigtails around her. "We're so infinitesimal, it's frightening. No wonder I regress into my tiny, terrible tantrums."

Buster was gawking upward too, his thoughts all a muddle, perhaps trying to comprehend how a telescope could make Jupiter's moons visible at 500 million miles, but not a well-lit American city just 500 miles to our west.

Zoe and Zippy led our troupe with lighthearted steps, but suddenly fell back into the long grass to gaze deeply into the firmament. Urged to follow suit, we all joined the pair, and looked up in silent contemplation at the vast, mysterious universe.

"Well, my little man," sighed Zoe, giving Zippy a heartfelt squeeze, "did you enjoy your night in the heavens?"

To the merriment of all, Zippy rubbed his stained nose up against Zoe's, and nodded his little head, yes.

TUESDAY: ROOMIES
AND ROAD BUDDIES

I awoke from dreams of heavenly splendor into the hellish reality of the Neuro Unit, and of my own pain. But I was soon medicated and wheeled over to Neuro Stepdown, where I could gaze out the window at the Taconic Range, the same view of hills I had as a schoolboy at St. Charles School atop Nobility Hill, just a half mile away.

My spirits were lifted by the transfer, reduced from red to yellow on the triage level. But I was still in the dark about my overall prognosis; namely bloody urine, rib fractures, and three busted vertebrae that continued to send sniper shots down my left leg.

Despite my physical woes, I took great interest in the duties of the medical floor nurses that morning, finding their tasks very different from my own on Jones Three. Psychiatry is a science in which medication now rules, and where seasoned nurses address situations with keen interventions and soothing banter. But Three West was Technoland, and I marveled at these smart nurses who performed a variety of complex and perplexing procedures.

For instance, the IVAC attached to my right arm, which

had given me fits to operate on Jones, was like spreading butter to these young, computer-savvy wizards. While my 20-something-year-old nurse was effortlessly calibrating my IV, I caught sight of my reflection in the window—a slightly-built gray-bearded gent—which offered a stunning portrait of what I'd become after 30-odd years of nursing: a blooming dinosaur.

Dr. DeMarco and his posse of white coats circled my bed once again. "Kev, as we suspected, your CT scan has revealed blunt trauma to your right kidney as the cause of your hematuria—resulting from the impact of your fall, not a nick from your fractured ribs."

I fell back against my pillow dispiritedly. "What now, Doctor?"

"We'll do daily blood draws to check your hemoglobin and hematocrit, and set up a Urology consult just to keep a close eye on it. Fortunately, such injuries usually heal by themselves. But I do have some good news. The neurosurgeon who just read your MRI, says you won't need surgery on your lower back." Dr. Bill patted my shoulder. "So you've escaped the knife, old pal. All told, I'd say you'll be playing golf again next summer."

Thanking the good doctor and his crew as they filed out, I found myself clinging to his hopeful vision of swinging a club again. Not the greatest golfer, but I've been an enthusiast for the game since caddying as a kid. For me, nothing was more enjoyable than an evening nine, followed up with a beer or two. Sometimes I wonder if I truly love the game, or simply play it to work up a thirst.

After lunch, Ollie from Neuro was wheeled into my room. He was hooked up to so much tubing that he looked like a manatee entangled in a fishing net. As the stretcher was positioned between our two beds, he reached out wincing to shake my hand.

"We meet again. Looks like we're in this thing together."

I also winced, returning his grasp. "Fellow travelers on the road to recovery."

"I wonder how long that road is gonna be?" Ollie groaned.

"With any luck, I hope to be walking again by Christmas."

"Not me," he gasped. "I'm afraid my punctured lung has let all the air out of this Christmas, not that it would've been much of a holiday, anyway."

"Hey," I offered, "before you get situated, you want the window?"

"Nah, I'm good. You gotta remember you're not a nurse anymore, just a banged-up patient like me. Besides," he snickered, bracing himself for the transfer, "I'll get a better view of passing nurses from the door."

Ollie let out a yowl as he was shifted from gurney to bed, attached lines trailing behind. A big, burly guy, long red hair and a beard were his most prominent features. Back in Neuro, I gathered that besides his crushed leg and collapsed lung, he had an abdominal bleed that was a big concern. I'm no expert in internal medicine, but I guessed he was looking at a year of rehab, with the actual trauma probably knocking a few years off his natural life.

Settled into his bed, Ollie was able to wheeze, "Don't know when I'll get out of here. Just hope it ain't feet first."

Trying graveyard humor, I replied, "Don't worry, I know all the undertakers in town—Dery, Dwyer, and Devanny—so if I see any of them loitering outside, I'll shoo them away."

"Dery, Dwyer and Devanny," Ollie repeated with a cough. "Sounds like an old Irish ditty."

He was surprisingly cordial for a man in his condition, and right from the start, I noticed how cooperative and appreciative he was with his caretakers when back in Neuro, despite his physical discomfort. So I was very glad to have Ollie as a roommate, even though his bleeping equipment could keep a narcoleptic awake.

That afternoon, while Ollie was deep in sedation, Dr. Jerry Carter, chief of the Primary Care Outreach Team, and the same doc who'd come to my aid on Jones Three, appeared above me once again. We bantered for a bit, but then he turned serious and peered at me questioningly, "You angry about all this?"

"You billing me for a psych assessment, Jerry?"

"No, purely pro bono."

"I'm a hurtin' turkey, but I'm not angry. Besides, I've learned over the years that anger impedes recovery."

He pulled up a chair beside me. "True enough, that."

"What's Nathan up to, anyway?"

"He's been a model patient since the attack. Helps when you have two police officers watching his every move."

"Still referring to me as a bearded woman?"

"Oh, yes," Jerry chuckled. "In fact, I've got to ask him if he thinks you're a hottie."

I raised my fist as if to bop him one: "That's special, doc. Top shelf."

Despite his light tone, Jerry surveyed my wounded body and turned somber. "We're all pulling for you, Kev, you know that?"

"Thanks, Jer, I know." I swept my arm to take in the roomful of flowers. "I mean, look, there might even be a bouquet from Nurse Hatchet in the bunch. Lots of solidarity here in the hospital."

After glancing at the sleeping Oliver, Jerry leaned in and whispered, "Nursing is concerned that your roommate is still actively suicidal, and wants me to write an order for round-the-clock sitters. What's your take?"

"I don't know, doc. I can't even figure out what I'm thinking about half the time, let alone Ollie."

"Even flat on your back, you're still a lifetime psych nurse. You must have some impression. Does he seem suicidal to you? The state police seem certain that his accident was intentional."

"Maybe so, Jerry. But I think his fever has passed for the moment, and sitters would only aggravate him. He's also future-oriented, looking forward to meeting his pulmonologist, Dr. Dan Doyle, tomorrow. Besides, there isn't much he can do in his present condition."

"Please let me know if anything changes."

"Sure thing. But, tell me, did you and Sue Earle bunk us together on purpose?"

"Medicine doesn't assign rooms the way you guys do it up on Jones. It was just the luck of the draw. Now get some rest, good buddy, and I'll call in on you both tomorrow."

After Jerry left, I drifted off into reflection on how we handled room assignments on our psych ward. There are fifteen beds on Jones Three, six double rooms and three singles. Also, two Quiet Rooms reserved primarily for emergency situations. These QR's, fitted with cushioned walls, ceiling mirrors, and one-way windows from the nurses' station, were usually anything but quiet when occupied.

When a new patient was admitted to our floor, the charge nurse would study the Floor Board like a jigsaw puzzle, to determine where this new piece might fit in. A bad placement could ruin the whole picture, and set off problems in every direction.

Some guidelines for choosing roommates were simple enough: never put two suicidal patients together, lest they form an alliance and try to go out in tandem; never put two psychopaths together, lest they form a pack and go on a rampage; never put a pyromaniac in with a paper hoarder, lest the whole floor goes up in flames.

Single rooms were usually reserved for elderly patients with medical conditions, or clients with flamboyant behaviors. During my thirty-odd years on the ward, we'd seen them all. And housed every sort, every age from 16 to 99, every quirk and fear, every sexual orientation and habit, every mental capacity, every state from comatose to hyper, quiet to loud, and the full spectrum of human types from near-saints to hardcore sociopaths. How do you fit that together, into a pretty, or at least coherent, picture?

Upon arrival, new patients were escorted into a QR, and asked to change into a johnny top and hospital pants, per floor protocol, so staff could search their civilian clothes for contraband. Sharps, such as knives, razors, needles, and nail files, were of highest priority and duly confiscated when found. Over the years, we've found sharps concealed in barrettes, pant cuffs, shirt collars, and even tampons. Searches have gotten more difficult over the years with street apparel offering more and more zippered enclosures. Don't get me started on cargo pants, which have more pockets than a mob of kangaroos.

I rarely dealt with female patients, but typical male pocket items included matches, lighters, bus stubs, loose change, pills, keys, worthless Scratch tickets, cigarette butts, stubby pencils,

Keno receipts, rabbit's feet, religious medals, and AA coins for varying days of sobriety. I once excavated an old condom from a wallet, which by brand and appearance, seemed to date from the Trojan War. "Always travel hopefully," the owner sheepishly confided.

All tobacco products, along with matches and lighters, were labeled with the patient's name, and were placed in our cigarette bin, accessible during scheduled smoking breaks. We had four such courtyard breaks on weekdays, six on weekends. One time I confiscated a tin of Kodiak menthol tobacco chew that the patient begged to keep at his bedside. When I explained floor policy, he kissed the tin respectfully, and explained that it contained his mother's ashes.

"Okay, keep it, but tuck it away safely," I warned him, "in case someone tries to steal a pinch."

Search complete, staff would encourage patients to send valuables, especially cash and jewelry, to the hospital vault, since many prized articles had vanished over the years. This involved the tedious but necessary process of filling out Possession Forms. Though we'd harbored plenty of thieves in that time, the most amazing disputes over property arose from sheer misunderstanding. Many of our folks were demented or delusional, and could easily swipe a roommate's apparel and immediately form the conviction that it was their own.

"Dorothy," I recently confronted one patient, "Sally wants her sweater back."

Dorothy bared her yellow teeth: "Say what?"

"That plum-colored sweater you're wearing belongs to Sally. We have it listed on her Possession Form. Could you please give it back to her?"

Dorothy folded her arms in defiance: "Hand it back? If it's

not mine, why does it fit me so perfectly?"

"Duh! Because you both wear Medium."

One morning, an addled oldster named Frederick strolled out from his room, sporting his young roomie's favorite band garb: a Korn cap and Slipknot hoodie. Needless to say, our resident metal head popped a bolt at seeing his sacred garment stained by a drivel of porridge, and came screaming to staff. "That old creep you stuck me in with is wearing my cap and hoodie!"

I went to Frederick and delicately asked him to return the belongings.

"Give 'em up? Why?" the befuddled octogenarian protested. "They're mine!"

The headbanger fumed, "If they're yours, old geezer, name me one Slipknot song. Just one!"

Searching his depleted memory bank for a lyric title, Frederick came up with Robert Frost, another old-timer. Fearlessly looking into the kid's bulging eyes, he uttered, *"The Road Not Taken,"* before hobbling away in triumph.

We had one patient who earned the nickname Mr. Potato Head, in reference to his penchant for appropriating anything that could be attached to one's face, such as eyeglasses, wigs, or hearing aids. He coveted false teeth above all, like a poacher his elephant tusks, and stalked any patient he spotted with a tube of Polident in their hand. He was totally enamored by Beatrice Tarr, an elderly patient whose ill-fitting uppers were the size of Domino tiles.

One morning, I noticed Mr. Potato Head's jaw writhing uncomfortably at the kitchen table. Worrying that he might be showing symptoms of tardive dyskinesia, a common side effect of Haldol, I was about to draw up a syringe of Cogentin, its antidote, when I heard an unusual clacking in his mouth. Asking him to open wide, I found Beatrice's missing lowers rattling above his own.

As a community-based psych unit, many of our patients were well-known to the system, seasonal repeaters whom staff thought of as "easy hits," with their quirks familiar and mannerisms manageable. Their return to Jones Three often seemed like a homecoming of sorts, brought on by heightened symptoms, but occasionally just for a break from their mundane existence.

These "easy hits" tended to be comfortable with us as well, and would arrive with armloads of cherished possessions. Mildred, for example, never left her residence without her entourage of colorful doll clowns, from Weary Willie of Ringling Brothers fame to the Bim Bom duo from the Moscow Circus. On weekends, she'd call us into her room to watch her clowns perform.

Turning off the lights, and instructing someone to beam a flashlight across the dark floor, she'd have Weary Willie, armed with a tiny mop, comically chase the moving spill of light. Clever, indeed!

Dotty never failed to bring her menagerie of stuffed dogs, from Corgi's to French poodles. Not to be outshone by Mildred, she'd hold her own Westminster Dog Show, asking staff and patients to judge her preening pooches as she guided them around her imaginary green carpet.

Skittles, nicknamed for her tie-dye psychedelic wardrobe, would arrive with three trash bags stuffed with colorful attire. Glad rags in Glad bags, ironically speaking. She'd change into a dozen outfits a day, each time looking like a refugee from Woodstock. Sadly, this pretty hippie maiden was ravaged with schizophrenia, and looked much older than her 26 years.

Vanessa, an ex-librarian, carried in so many books you'd think she had been exiled to Saint Helena. She'd laze about in bed all day like Cleopatra on her barge, immersed in dusty old novels. When invited to attend a non-mandatory group, Vanessa would peek over the top of her book and reply, "Really? Put down *Anna Karenina* to paste magazine pictures onto poster board? I don't think so!"

Marnie brought in so many religious items that her room resembled the gift shop at the Marian Fathers in nearby Stockbridge. Being a good Catholic lad, my right knee would reflexively buckle in genuflection upon entering her room. Above her bed hung a large wooden crucifix that, were it brandished, would make a most formidable weapon.

Staff like Nurse Hatchet were strict gatekeepers and limited a patient's incoming possessions to mere essentials, sending the bulk back with their outpatient workers. "We don't want to make them too comfortable," these staffers might complain. "They're here for the short term, that's it." But most staff were happy enough to let our easy hits spend a week or so with us, as long as we had spare beds, and our well-known guests were calm and cooperative.

Possession Forms complete, we'd follow up with a lengthy Nursing Assessment, from vital signs to current medications. That done, we'd show our new admit around the unit, and introduce them to their roommates. Many patients knew each other from prior admissions, or from their limited social orbits of outpatient clinics, shelters, AA meetings, and local soup kitchens.

Sometimes a patient would vehemently reject a new roomie, either due to past conflicts or just a bad first impression, sending us back to the puzzle board. Remarkably, given our wide array of extreme characters, pairings generally worked out. We seldom had to deal with racial issues, either, though frankly the Berkshires are rather monochrome. The ward created its own commonality, and a makeshift community resulted.

Unforeseen conflicts could, of course, break out on that first night, as old habits and behaviors bumped up against each other. David, for instance, needed the window open, summer or winter, as he suffered hot flashes from his medication. Cheryl needed her overhead light on to prevent childhood nightmares. Jane slept beneath her bed, to shield her sexual fantasies from other prying minds. Gordon slept crouched up in his closet, which made his roommates a tad uncomfortable. Ronald's nocturnal rituals would make a porn star blush. Jimmy swept a flashlight to all four corners of the room, searching for something he'd never find.

Snorers, teeth grinders, sleepwalkers, and **C-PAP**-wearing patients who suffered from sleep apnea, could also set off spats. Other residents were slobs, plain and simple, their rooms piled high with soiled, mildewed clothes. Tracy, a retired fisherman from the Maritimes, belched like a foghorn off the Grand Banks. Others might fart through the night, the most notorious nicknamed Crop Duster, who could clear a room quicker than mustard gas on the Western Front.

Level Three sex offenders, deemed high-risk or predatory, could complicate room arrangements even further. Our most infamous inmate wore a gray woolen cap shaped like a condom, receptacle tip and all. He could not control himself in the presence of a female form—moth to flame—and had to be monitored constantly. He boasted of being able to sniff out a woman's menses without fail, and did so with frightening accuracy.

Other males were just your typical randy roosters, who might risk everything—okay, a cigarette break—for a stolen kiss from the fairer sex. Conjugal acts were forbidden, of course, though I'm certain a few couples had succeeded in doing "the giddy-up" in one of our three co-ed bathrooms.

Sammy the Snit was one of our long-term repeat guests. Besides dispensing nicknames to nearly everyone, he earned the reputation of being our resident Sex-Buster, having blown the whistle on many an aspiring Romeo and Juliet. Roaming the unit like a Roomba, he'd root out dirt wherever he could, not just illicit liaisons but any infraction, however slight. Spying a violator, he'd run and bang on our nurses' window, as if the ward were aflame, frantically waving a Patient Handbook. "Hey, guys, I just saw Wilbur sneak a bag of chips into his bedroom! Look, it says right here, *Rule # 6: Absolutely no food in your bedroom.* You gotta bust him, and bust him bad!"

Nobody escaped Sammy's scrutiny. He was the ultimate stickler, as well as a heckler. To him, the law was the law, like bricks to a mason. He reminded me of the storied Pittsfield cop who actually issued a parking ticket to his mother-in-law on Christmas Eve. Yes, Christmas Eve. One of our patients complained astutely, "If Sammy the Snit had sat with Jesus at the Last Supper, Judas Iscariot would've gone down in history as a good guy."

Needless to say, no one wanted to room with Sammy, and that suited him dandy. So we usually tried to put him in a single room, where he'd bellow through his high-screened windows at unsuspecting pedestrians on the sidewalks below.

"Hey, they're planning to give me a lobotomy, and I haven't

passed my GED's yet!"

* * *

My ruminations on roommates, there on Neuro Stepdown, were broken up by visits from a steady stream of co-workers during shift-change, who offered sympathy and support. Meanwhile, Ollie was surrounded by a fresh flock of medical students who pecked, poked, and prodded him from head to toe. Ollie was a ten-in-one patient, true enough, so it seemed that every medical student, regardless of rotation—Medical, Surgical, Orthopedic—was assigned to pay him a visit.

When the last gaggle waddled off, Ollie turned to me and grumbled. "If I have to share my history with one more turkey, I'm gonna bust out of here and buy myself a hunting license."

I looked across at my banged-up roomie, his right leg strung up to a Balkan frame.

"Good luck with that. But remember we're a teaching hospital, and you're an instructive case, you've got to admit. How else are these new docs going to learn?"

"Learn? Half of 'em can't even speak English."

"Now, now, Ollie, diversity is a good thing, and these foreign students can be very helpful. In fact, they represent the best and brightest of their countries. Think Olympians here."

He let out a sigh and sank deeper into his bed, unconvinced.

"No? You don't think so? Let me tell you a story. There was a woman who came into the ED not long ago with severe seizures, but no past history. Not one attending doctor had a clue, until a Thai intern noticed small pierce marks on her back that resembled snake bites from back home. He asked her husband if they'd been to Thailand; the answer was no, but the wife had just bought a coat made there. When the suspected coat was brought in, the intern took a scalpel to its lining and discovered a nest of minuscule snakes. The woman was given the needed antidote and discharged the next day. So hold your tongue, my man, because one of these interns just might save your butt."

Ollie remained unimpressed: "I don't have some exotic mystery disease, just a racked-up body. I hope you didn't put your patients through all this Q and A bullshit?"

"I'm afraid so. Filling out questionnaires is a big part of the job, the essence of our diagnostic method. For example, we have a Substance Abuse form that has to be filled out on every patient, whether it's a refugee from a methadone clinic sporting a 'Born to be Bad' tattoo, or some Grandma Moses look-alike."

"That'd really tick me off," Ollie asserted with some finality, before nodding off again.

Our back-and-forth sent me once again on a well-medicated train of thought, as I recalled a recent Substance Abuse assessment I'd done on an entertaining old codger, Paddy O'Looney.

I approached Paddy cautiously one fine midsummer's morning, having been warned of his thunderous moods. His admission diagnosis—Agitated Depression; Rule Out Trans Ischemic Attacks—simply meant he was a crusty old crank, thrown off-kilter by a few mini-strokes. He'd been brought in two days earlier by his wife and three old-maid daughters, who reported that loveable Dad had become moody and potty-mouthed at home, and not the least bit loveable.

The patient in question was dressed in a red flannel shirt and brown corduroys, a lanky, sinewy old bird with a scowl that would send the friendliest mutt scurrying for cover. Undaunted, I expected to find common ground in our ancestry, so I extended my hand and introduced myself with emphasis.

"Good morning, Mr. O'Looney. Kevin O'Hara is my name, and I wonder if I could sit with you privately, to ask a few questions? Well, to tell the truth, quite a few questions."

He leaped off his chair like a Kilkenny cat, both fists raised in defiance: "What, again?"

I backpedaled, fearing a blow from the rangy boxer. "Sorry, sir, but this is a nursing assessment, quite different from your initial intake with Dr. Dorothea Schuetz-Mueller."

Cursing to the four winds, my charge reluctantly followed me to the Sensory Room, where he plopped himself down on our old wicker rocker.

"Let's get on with this bullshit," he fumed, eyeing me irritably as I set up a laptop computer between us.

Ready to commence, I told him the first section dealt with Substance Abuse.

"Substance abuse? What's that got to do with the price of fish? I'm here because I'm a grumpy old coot, not a drug fiend."

I tried to explain: "It's not just illegal drugs, sir, but all substances. Like caffeine."

"Caffeine! What's wrong with a cup of coffee?"

"Nothing, sir, but we've had patients go through caffeine withdrawal in the past, and it's not very pleasant. In fact, we recently had a patient who drank eight pots of coffee a day and, boy, did he end up with one walloping migraine!"

"Eight pots! He must've spent his whole day hovering over a piss pot. Myself, I drink a cup, maybe two, each morning."

"Okay, got that. How about nicotine?"

"You mean cigarettes?"

"Yes, or a pipe, or cigars. Even snuff or chewing tobacco."

"I smoked a pack a day for 37 years but gave 'em up a while back, after my nagging daughters made me smoke out on the porch. Second-hand smoke kills, they kept telling me. Now, ain't that some ripe new bullshit. The way I figure, if you die from second-hand smoke, you weren't long for this world anyway."

"What about alcohol? Any history there?"

He lurched forward, digging the rockers' ends angrily into the carpet. "Are you asking me because I'm Irish?"

"No, I ask everybody. It's a standard question."

He leaned back a bit. "It just rankles the piss out of me how every detox center is named after an Irishman—Doyle, McGee, O'Reilly—like we're the only nationality who enjoys a drink. Why not Bradley Detox? Or Smith? Or Quadrozzi? I've even heard they're selling a new non-alcoholic beer called No Drool's."

I laughed, but caught myself: "O'Doul's."

He shot me a glance that declared he was having none of it.

I scrunched back behind the keyboard: "Mr. O'Looney, when did you start drinking?"

"Seventy-seven years ago, at age seven."

My chin dropped.

"Don't go shitting a tree stump! My dad would fill a shot glass of Piels at dinner on a Sunday, so I could feel like a big man at the table. He enjoyed his beer, and would read the newspaper's obits like other dads would read the sports pages. When he'd find an Irish wake to attend, he'd smack his lips and say, 'You know you're truly Irish when the sight of a casket makes you thirsty.' And when giving a toast, he'd raise his glass and often say, 'The liver is a terrible organ. It needs to be punished.'"

"Would you say he was an alcoholic?"

"Heavens, no! But his brother was, my Uncle Joe. He'd get all juiced up doing the morning crosswords."

"How much alcohol do you drink on a daily basis?"

"One or two beers a night."

"Week nights?"

"Yep."

"How about weekends?"

He looked at me sharply, swinging his leg as if aching to boot me through a distant goal post. "Three or four."

"I'm sorry, but we need to be accurate here. I don't want you to go into withdrawal, you know, the Irish jigs."

I cringed in disbelief as the defamation escaped my lips, definitely not a joke for this company.

His eyes cut me to ribbons: "Listen, bucko, every Saturday I go to Rita's Package Store and get a dollar for my returns. Five cents times twenty equals a dollar, don't it? That's less than three beers a day."

"Still tough on the old liver," I suggested, aware that my own weekly intake rivaled his own. "You might consider a daily B supplement, or Milk Thistle. Anything to help with those slivers in your liver."

He wagged a threatening finger in my face. "You're beginning to sound like my bullying wife."

"Sorry, but I wouldn't be doing my job if I didn't offer some advice."

He looked down at his scuffed shoes, and then his face rose up all soft and soapy, as if in remorse. "You know, I've lately heeded my wife's warning on this drinking business, and quit altogether. And, bless her dear heart, I already feel the benefits."

"Really?" I asked in all innocence.

"Since my abstinence," he nodded, "I wake up clear-headed, feel stronger, and have my appetite back. Yep, after years of poisoning myself with that toxic tonic, I've finally found peace in sobriety."

"Good for you, Mr. O'Looney! How long have you been sober?"

He slapped his knee, and roared, "Since coming into your goddamn nut house, two days ago!"

Having been duped but good, Nurse Lite proceeded more cautiously. "Have you ever used or abused benzodiazepines, pills like Valium, Ativan, Klonopin?"

"Never took a happy pill in my life. Never will."

"Cocaine or heroin use?"

He looked out the window, feigning deafness.

"So that's a no. Opiates or methadone?"

He continued to look out the window.

"Mr. O'Looney, I know these questions don't necessarily pertain to you, but this computer program won't allow me to bypass any box without entering an answer. Here's another: Have you ever smoked marijuana?"

He had a ready answer for this one. "Remember how President Clinton said he never inhaled? Well, I had the opposite problem. I never exhaled!"

"Good one, that," I chuckled. "What about LSD or Ecstasy?"

"Nope."

"Okay, last question on this part. Mushrooms?"

He smacked his lips. "Yep, morels, tastiest mushrooms in the world. Pick 'em myself in the woods back home."

Having completed the substance abuse section, I rolled up Paddy's sleeve and took his blood pressure.

"Your BP's a tad high; a buck-sixty over a hundred."

"Why wouldn't it be high sitting through this shit detail."

"No meds for that, either?"

"Devil a one! Old Doc Potts kept pushing 'em on me, though, but I told him I came into this world a high-revved engine, and I was going out the same way. I'm not letting anybody tinker with my natural timing, nobody no-how."

"Better than a blown gasket. I can tell you at this rate you're four times more likely to have a stroke than someone with a benchmark blood pressure of 120 over 80."

He dismissed my stats with a bugling fart that lifted him clear off his rocker. "Well, whoop de do! The way I figure, if I get one of those one-sided strokes, it'll give me time to get back to my stamp collection."

"You collect stamps?"

"Yep. First-day issues."

"Any stamps from Ireland?"

"Nope. Never been, either. Must be a reason why my grandparents left the place."

"It's beautiful, you know."

"So ain't the Berkshires."

"True enough." I retreated to the computer screen. "You mentioned Dr. Potts, but I don't see him listed here."

"Old Potts croaked ten years back. Here he goes preaching to me about hypertension, and the poor bugger drops dead on a golf course."

"How?"

"Seems he got stuck in one of those sand bunkers and never came out. Stroke, stroke, stroke, 'til he got the big one."

"As a golfer myself, I guess there are worse ways to go."

"His replacement was another pill-pushing jackass, Doc Wiggins. You got his name there?"

"Nope."

"Saw him a while back, after I passed blood."

"In your urine?"

"Where else?"

"Had you eaten beets or rhubarb beforehand?"

"Nope, damndest thing. My good buddy Walter Whitby got a way with words, like that poet Shakespeare. One night at Young's Roadhouse, he pointed out some stuck-up asshole at the bar and said, 'That guy thinks he pisses port wine.' You jotting this down?"

Fingers poised over the keyboard, I looked up. "Some of it."

"So that evening, after I knocked back a few beers, I hit the jacks and, Holy Toledo, don't I go pissing bright red. So I knock back another beer just to clear the pipes, and whaddya know, it's redder still!

"Spooked, I go home and dumbly blurt out my condition to the wife and three kittens. Well, don't they go into conniptions, like I'm going to bleed out on the kitchen floor. Next morning, they posse me down to see Doc Wiggins, who wants to inject dye into my kidneys."

"An intravenous pyelogram to check your kidneys for stones, tumors, that kind of thing."

He waved off my explanation. "After that, he wanted me to see another doc—a pecker specialist—to go jamming a tube up my peter to take pictures inside my bladder."

"A cystoscopy," I nodded. "Did you follow up with either recommendation?"

Paddy looked at me like I had two heads. "And go dribbling in my undies till my dying day! Just what my wife needs to find in her Monday laundry basket, ain't it? Not only that, but he also wanted to roto-rooter my arsehole!"

"A colonoscopy," I deduced.

"Yeah, a freaking trifecta! So I pledged then and there to never mention another health matter to my family again, even if a tomcat comes jumping out of my ass!"

I muffled a laugh as he continued to rant.

"So I storm out of his office, leaving mama and the three kitties caterwauling, and go see my mechanic friend Hank Lawless, the smartest guy I know. There I show him my stack of appointments and he cracks me open a suds, and says, 'Paddy, you'd be a fool to stand for these abominations, because it's all about the power of suggestion. Didn't you say yourself it was the port wine comment that got you pissing blood? Myself, I wouldn't give it another thought unless you go pissing it again. Meanwhile, take an iron pill. Geritol's the ticket for that sort of thing. As far as roto-rootering your bunghole, did I tell you what I'm going to have inscribed on my tombstone? Here lies Hank Lawless, dead at 93, who never had a colonoscopy.'"

"That's quite the epitaph."

"Then, over a second beer, Hank summed it all up for me: 'The way I figure, our brains have internal regulators, much like gasoline engines. Everything runs smoothly 'til some son-of-a-bitching quack mucks things up.' Now ain't I lucky to have a wise old friend like Hank?"

"Maybe so, but have you passed blood since then?"

"Devil a drop. And if I do, so be it! At my age, even those

bastards at Sears have stopped trying to sell me warranties."

Paddy took a deep breath. "Now, back to this blood pressure bullshit. What a hoax! Think about it! You can never get an accurate reading in a doctor's office."

"White coat hypertension," I agreed.

"No, johnny-top hypertension!" Paddy looked like a cartoon character with steam shooting out of his ears. "First, they dress you up like a babbling buffoon, with your arse hanging out like two bread loaves for all the world to see. Then a pretty nurse goes snickering by while the doc starts pumping up your arm. All this time, you're staring down at a rubber glove and a tube of jelly laying in wait for the grand finale. The dreaded 'thumb up the bum' to check your prostrate."

"Prostate."

"That's what I said, prostrate. You got beeswax in your ears?"

Paddy's engine was now racing at 100 miles an hour, and his spark plugs were firing red hot. So I thought it was a good idea to wave the yellow flag. "Mr. O'Looney, why don't we finish up after lunch?"

"Hey, you wanted my medical history, and I'm giving it to you, once and for all. See this here?" He leaned into the window's light and pointed to the right side of his nose.

"What, that little wart?"

"Yep, before I swore off doctors for good, I was in one's office for some reason or another, and instead of listening to my actual complaint, the doc went straight for my nose and told me I had a *squeamish* cell carcinoma, one of the deadliest skin tumors of all. I told him just to freeze it off, like a wart off a knuckle, but he rolled his eyes like that was the dumbest thing anybody has ever said since Colonel Custer told his cavalry to saddle up. So he sent me to a swank plastic surgeon named Dr. Face, believe it or not, over in Albany, or All Bananas as I came to call it.

"His whole operation was mainly about making titties. Now, I ain't saying that's not beneficial to mankind, but you wish a doc blessed with such God-given hands might fix a poor kid's cleft lip from time to time.

"Anyway, the doc examines my little wart, and goes all serious, telling me that I likely have a two-centimeter melanoma growing beneath my bump that will only get larger, with a 70 percent chance of it being malignant. He then wipes his brow, as if shook by the sight of it, and says I need to make an immediate appointment for a two-hour procedure.

"'Whoa, slow down,' I tell him. 'Talk to me straight, doc. What's two centimeters? Dime-sized? Quarter-sized? Size of a Denny's pancake?' He tells me nickel-sized, a small thing but a big risk. I tell him it's something I've had for years, without any growth, and my mother had the same thing on her nose and lived to be 97, God bless her heart. He says she didn't have a melanoma like mine—like he personally examined her fifty-seven years ago.

"I keep trying to get out of his examining chair, but the doc is not taking no for an answer. So he calls in the big guns, which were on the chest of his assistant, Daisy. She had a pair of his house specials, something to behold, the size of cantaloupes. Hubba Hubba was all I could say as she leaned over to offer me encouragement. What a view of the Grand Tetons, the magnificent Continental Divide, did Miss Colorado show me."

He winked: "Catch my drift, son?"

"Oh, I get what you're saying, Mr. O'Looney, but let's get

back to your medical history, shall we?"

"Well, I finally got Dr. Face out of my face by saying I'd think it over and call back in a day or two. Next morning I go over to Hank's and take the magnifying glass I use on my stamps with me. He checks out my wart with his mechanic's eye and says he has a tool to touch up my hood ornament if I ever feel the need. So I call Miss Colorado and tell her I'm betting on the 30 percent chance of my nose bump being be-nine. That, my son, was ten years ago. And my little growth hasn't grown a smidgen since, thank the Lord."

Mr. O'Looney was so pleased with himself, and with the chance to tell his story, that his mood had improved markedly. I hit the Save button on the assessment questionnaire and closed the laptop, and just listened to what he had to say. Not only was I amused, but I also tended to see the matter his way. Despite his comic belligerence, he was one of those supposedly crazy patients who, over the years, made more sense to me than some by-the-book medical professionals.

He suddenly jumped off his rocker, and stood to attention like a cadet. "So here I stand before you at a healthy 84, despite what my wife and daughters, or any doctor in the world, may think. Not bad, hey kiddo?"

"Not bad at all," I agreed. "I hope I'm as fit at your age."

He leaned toward me: "Wanna know my recipe for life-long good health?"

"Sure, I guess."

"Plenty of water! Plenty of walking! And plenty of—I'll give you a hint. It begins with the letter S," he said with his gray eyes dancing.

"Sex?" I ventured.

"Sex? Are you mad, son? It's spitting!"

"Spitting?"

"Sure, spitting. I once had a ball of phlegm in my throat, thought it would be my death plug. For three agonizing days I hovered over a steaming lobster pot, hoping to dislodge it. Just when I thought I was going to meet my Maker, I finally hocked up the cough-ball. Since then, I've made a point of keeping my passages clear. I drink plenty of water, walk a mile or two every day, and spit in the high grass along the way."

"My, that's a novel health regimen."

"It works, son! Now, are we finished here, because right now I could eat the horse pulling a meat wagon."

"That's a wrap, Mr. O'Looney, and thank you."

"Join me for lunch?" he asked with a twinkle in his eye.

"Be glad to."

Marveling at his transformation from anger to animation, I fell in step as Patrick O'Looney led the way to the kitchen, whistling an air as lovely as Danny Boy, his threatening visage and cloudy prospect having broken, for the moment, at least, into an inexplicable burst of sunshine.

It made me smile to think of it, and in that mellow mood, I joined my roommate in drifting off to sleep.

* * *

By the time dinner came around, my bed was encircled with so many bouquets that I felt I was awake at my own wake. Ollie, in contrast, could have been a blow-in from Burma, with nary a card, call, or visitor. When I apologized to him for all the interruptions and comings and goings, he shrugged it off in good humor. "Forget it, Kev. I've always been the odd man out."

After visiting hours, Ollie and I shared our first real back and forth, confirming we would be a good match as roommates. He'd been an Army brat, an only child, born at Camp Drum in New York, but had moved all over the country during his father's military career, which included an early stint in Vietnam. His many uprootings played havoc with his education, and his ability to form lasting friendships.

"I'd have a school buddy for half a year," he confided to me, "and the next thing I know, his dad or my dad gets posted elsewhere. After a while, it was easier to stay a loner."

Following his father's discharge, the family settled in Tucson, but both parents passed away when Ollie was still in his twenties—Mom to cancer, Dad to alcoholism. Ollie briefly mentioned his son, Davy, but never alluded to a wife or girlfriend. When I asked what brought him from the sunny Southwest to the snowy Berkshires on a Harley-Davidson in December, he mumbled into his chest, "Trying to outrun my demons."

Though Ollie, in his shattered state, struck me as a friendly and gentle character, he was clearly a man of sorrows. His face was etched in misery; the dark swollen pouches beneath his eyes looked like reservoirs of unshed tears.

Our conversation was interrupted by our eagerly-anticipated med nurse.

"What's your pain level, Kevin?"

"Still at ten, I'm afraid."

"Sounds like two milligrams to me." She drew up a bolus of Dilaudid.

I turned gingerly onto my side to take the shot in my butt, and caught sight of my catheter bag, whose contents remained as red as a Vermont barn.

"Whatever you're giving him," Ollie coughed, "I'll take a double!" Despite his severe pain, the collapsed lung meant that his treatment team had to be more cautious with his meds, due to the risk of further respiratory complications. In truth, his battered condition warranted more time in Neuro, but a three-car pile-up on the Mass Pike had bumped him down to Neuro Stepdown.

In a matter of minutes, I had conked out, as if kayoed by Mike Tyson. The next thing I recall is a terrifying dream, dizzyingly powered by the narcotic. I was riding on a dazzling carousel, gripping the pole of a shimmering pony, going up and down, round and round, on the verge of a nauseous swoon. Instead of a prized brass ring to reach for, I circled past a spinning sequence of grinning psychedelic faces, which I recognized as caricatures of Jones Three patients! Too much, too much, too much!

A distant voice jerked me off my steed. "Hey, man, you okay over there?"

I woke up to find myself rattling my side rails. "Say what?"

"You've been whimpering like a frightened old dog over there."

I looked across at Ollie, whose unruly red hair, lit up eerily by the green luminance of his IVAC screen, made him look like a drowned Viking covered in seaweed.

I squeezed my eyes shut, trying to rein in my runaway thoughts. "Wow, Ollie, I was tripping on a whirling carousel."

"Better not tell the nurses, or they'll lower your dose."

I tried to shake off the lingering vision. "I don't know. It wasn't very pleasant. What time is it, anyway?"

"Coming on 1 a.m., or oh-one-hundred, as my dad used to say. One more hour till your next carnival ride."

I reached out shakily for my water, as my hallucinations dissipated into spots and splotches. "Strange, Ols, but my carousel pony kept sweeping past these crazy faces—like that Munch painting *'The Scream,'* you know?—representing patients on our ward who'd once roomed together: Ling-Ling with Tobacco Road, Diesel Dan with Pencil Man, Crop Duster with Uncle Rupert . . . "

"Hold it!" Ollie piped up. "You actually put that farting machine in with a roommate?"

"Wait. How do you know about Crop Duster?" My eyes went wide with surprise.

He laughed: "How? Because you told me."

I looked up at the ceiling, still pie-eyed. "I did?"

"Man, are you ever looped. But you never mentioned Diesel Dan and Pencil Man. They come with a story?"

"Yep, a long, winding one."

"Well, let's hear it, because neither of us is gonna get any shut-eye until our med nurse comes 'round. And it's a story about roommates, right? Roomies like you and me. Two buddies in it for the long haul."

"You got that right about this pair, for sure."

Still floating in a narcotic cloud, I launched pleasantly into my tale.

"Diesel Dan was a guy pushing sixty, unmarried and working the New York racetrack circuit—Black Rock, Watkins Glen, and Lebanon Valley Speedway—just over the mountain from here. It was there he suffered a severe stroke, a real bleeder, that left him with left-side paralysis. In the blink of an eye, Diesel Dan went from cruising around in his candy apple red '67 Mustang, to being pushed around in a black and silver Everett and Jennings wheelchair."

Ollie cleared his throat. "Damn near happened to us."

"But for the grace of God," I agreed. "After his stroke, Dan ended up in a nursing home that he called Hell's Lobby. After developing deep bedsores in his buttocks among other woes, he tried to strangle himself by tying a wet sheet around his bedpost. That attempt on his life was how he wound up on Jones Three."

I looked over at Ollie to check on his reaction, but he seemed wrapped up in the story, so I continued. "When he came to us, I asked him what triggered his suicide attempt, and he just waved his good hand down the lifeless left side of his body and said, 'You're joking, right?'

"On our floor, he'd sit all day in the doldrums, his only comfort coming off the back end of a lit cigarette. When we'd ask how he was doing, he'd look up at us, eyes unblinking, like two dead pumpkinseed fish in a pool of stagnant water. 'Doing? I'm doing great! Just sitting here waiting to fill my pants.'

"Charlie and Bingo Bill, our recreational guys, tried their best to pep him up some. They brought in car magazines and even helped him build a Revell model of his Mustang. But it was easier to pull a wool sock over a wet foot than to get him to smile. Stroke took away his taste buds, too."

"Damn, O'Hara, this is one cheerful story."

"Sorry, Ols. I can stop if you like."

"Naw, I'm a big boy. Go on."

"Oddly, there was one talent his stroke left him—he could mimic the sounds of any combustion engine from a VW Bug to an Alfa Romeo. His specialty was a Greyhound bus, where he could emit a perfect diesel roar from the right side of his mouth. When he was first admitted, he'd often do it to entertain the other patients down in the yard. But the novelty soon wore off, and he stopped doing it altogether."

"Too bad you couldn't get him on one of those so-called talent shows they've got on TV these days—ol' Dan sounds like a sure winner."

"Got that right. Anyhow, two weeks into his admission, we're positioning him in bed after packing his deep bedsores with moist dressings. But on this night he's all chatty and upbeat. Good to see, yes, but sometimes a sudden spike in mood is a bad clinical sign for a prospective suicide."

"How do you figure?"

"It could mean that the patient finally has a plan, as well as the strength and courage to pull it off. When I gave his pillow a second flip that night, I happened to feel a lump inside the pillowcase. Sure enough, I found a sandwich bag half-filled with chewed-up Tylenol that he must've squirreled away since his nursing home days. Enough to do the trick, too.

"He cursed me to hell when I found it, and begged us to just let him go. At that point, we had little choice but to move him to 78-1, across from the nurses' station, and put him on close five-minute checks. But the staff knew it was just a matter of time. Over the years, we've had people like Diesel Dan, who were hell-bent on ending it all, and no earthly intervention could change their minds. Depression is as deadly as any cancer."

"Seems to me he'd be better off dead."

Again I looked over at Ollie, but he appeared to be deep in Dan's story, and not thinking about his own, so I proceeded with my tale.

"You'd think. But here the story takes an unexpected turn. Who gets admitted but his unlikely savior—Pencil Man—a tall, lanky, long-distance trucker, a real son of the lone prairie, whose sharp facial features belonged in a shaving commercial. Tough as nails, too. All sinew and no bullshit. When we learned he was a trucker, it was a no-brainer to room him in with Diesel Dan."

"How'd he happen to enroll in your Laughing Academy?"

"State troopers stopped him for erratic driving at the Pike's Lee Interchange, and found him fry-o-lated on amphetamines. His driver log books showed he'd been transporting fresh produce from Fresno to Providence in 60 hours flat, snorting speed for octane. Pencil Man's lettuce was crisp, all right, but Pencil Man himself was crispier than the Colonel's fried chicken."

Ollie tried to whistle, but couldn't summon the air from his punctured lung: "Sixty hours. That's some trucking."

"I'll say. Anyhow, the court immediately sent him to us on a 20-day forensic evaluation. But before he hits our floor, he starts seizing in the ED and ends up in ICU. For the next week it's touch and go—Grand mals, arrhythmias, the works. Damn near checked out before he dried out."

"So why Pencil Man? Let me guess, always bragging about having lead in his pencil?"

"Nope. He got the nickname from Sammy the Snit, from a story our rawhide trucker told us that first morning when he was healthy enough to take a break in the yard. He was wearing a black cowboy hat with matching boots, looking a lot like Hopalong Cassidy, silver hair and all, and talking in a prairie twang that I'll do my best to imitate."

"Let's hear it."

"Okay, here goes: 'I stopped to bunk at a truck stop north of Albuquerque this one night, and found the surrounding hills covered in a weird swirl of snow and cloud, so things were eerie from the get-go. I'm back from my shower and ready to hit the rack, when a stranger knocks on my cab and asks me for a cig. So I pull a Marlboro from my pack when, boy howdy, he's got a knife pinching my windpipe, demanding my wallet and a sexual favor to boot. Not inclined to oblige with either request, I picked up a pencil and quick as lightning jabbed it into his ear. Right through his eardrum and into his cauliflower brain like a ramrod.'"

"Damn," gasped Ollie. "True story?"

"Didn't know at the time, but he told it so convincingly, there were inch-long ashes dangling on undragged cigarettes, something I'd never seen before on our unit. He even demonstrated his move by snatching a pen from Charlie's breast pocket, and darting it through his loose fist with the heel of his other hand. Like something out of a martial arts movie."

"Bruce Lee, baby!"

"Sammy, always on the scene and always ready to pop off, asked if our bad-ass cowboy did time for killing the guy, or got off on self-defense?

"The cowboy lifted his hat off his sun-baked brow, and drawled, 'Time, son? I'll only do time if the Good Lord sees fit. But I felt so dang sorry for that dingbat after killing him, that I brought him back to life in a jiffy.'

"'How so?'—we wanted to know, and he told us right off.

"'Easy as falling off a log, you morons. I killed him with my pencil, didn't I? So I just jammed the eraser end into his other ear, and bim-bam-boom, up he hopped, good as new.'

"Diesel Dan laughed straight away, but it took the others a few seconds for the coin to drop.

"'Fooled you fools, didn't I?' Pencil Man boasted as he

offered his Marlboros around to the group. 'But just so you know, if any of you jamokes come bothering me or my roomie here with any untoward advances, I'll turn your sorry asses into pencil holders.'

"This time, everyone laughed straight away, and Diesel Dan looked up at Pencil Man with eyes brighter than halogen lamps. But more surprising was the way the tough cowboy-trucker returned Dan's gaze; this time, it was his cig dangling from his mouth. You could tell some special bond was being forged, but its nature remained mysterious."

"What do you think it was?"

"Hadn't a clue at the time, but that's the story, isn't it? For the remainder of his time with us, Pencil Man couldn't do enough for his roommate. He'd set up his meals, prop him up in his wheelchair, and even assisted him to the bathroom. But he kept messing with him, too. You know, trying to pull him out of his deep funk."

"What'd he do?"

"He'd lift Dan's heavy head off his chest and say, 'Today I'm going to teach you how to smile like a Bible salesman.' Or when Dan got embarrassed after a farting episode, he'd pleasantly comment, 'Don't worry none, Dan. Just go ahead and toot your own horn, let the folks hereabouts know that you're still alive.' However, Nurse Hatchet and her ilk believed his actions were simply a ploy to get himself a favorable forensic review. But her party hadn't witnessed that transfixing scene down in the yard.

"A few nights later, I hear Diesel Dan making revving sounds like an 18-wheeler in their room—hadn't heard that in a while. So I knock on the door and find the pair sitting side by side, facing the window as if it were the windshield of a big rig, and they're driving down an imaginary highway. No kidding! There was Pencil Man gripping a pizza pan like a steering wheel, while passenger Dan had Pencil Man's dog-eared Motor Carrier Road Atlas laid over his lap. Heck, they had even positioned the night light so it shone on their faces like a lit-up dash."

"Crazy!"

"Yeah, but true. Now I'm the sort to join in the fun, so I stick out my thumb, and Diesel Dan emits a perfect imitation of air brakes. Then Pencil Man leans across him and shouts out the pretend cab window, 'Hop in, kid!' So I sit on the bed behind the pair, and the atmosphere they created was so real, I could visualize the pull-cord of the air horn, and a mike hanging from the CB."

"Sounds like you're still hallucinating, O'Hara."

"No, Ols, I'm not. That's just how real it was. Next thing, Pencil Man looks over his shoulder and asks me where I'm headed. So I say, 'Anywhere but here.' He lets out a chuckle, and says to Dan, 'I always pick up hitchhikers, less they're swinging an axe or baseball bat,'cause they help shorten the long road. Never had trouble, neither, and I've picked up hundreds of all sorts and varieties, hoping their uncertain road leads 'em to Lady Luck.'

"Waxing philosophical, the trucker continues, 'You hear all these stories about psycho hitchers, but I never met one. Strange enough folk, to be sure, but harmless, 99 out of 100, and I never encountered that last one. I gotta believe that all God's people carry goodness in their hearts. Moreover, I've often heard that Jesus tramps these highways in disguise, and I ain't ever gonna pass up the opportunity of meeting my main man. You with me on that one, Dan?'

"'Amen, to that,' Dan replies, still thrumming down the highway.

"I lean between the happy pair, 'Where are we, anyway?'

"Pencil Man points to the stained atlas in Dan's lap: 'I-15 North, headed for Butte, Montana. A wild mountainous stretch—got to use all 12 gears in my box. Time to shift, Danny boy.'

'Va-room!'

"Pencil Man shifts his pretend gears. 'Need more throttle.'

'Va-rroomm!'

"Pencil Man grins across at his wingman. 'Damn, Dan, you're freaking amazing!'

"Then Diesel Dan turns and smiles back at me, and I take it as his way of thanking me for finding his Tylenol stash a few nights earlier. So I just sit back, and enter their fantasy, as Pencil Man keeps up a steady spiel as he passes through their fictitious landscape.

"'Pretty country, ain't it? Just look at those majestic pines! But hold your Polaroid, Dan,'cause there's a stand of fir south of Portland that'll make them look like bonsai trees in a pot. Stick with me, good buddy,'cause your eyes are gonna pop like Toasties when you see where this glorious road takes us.'

"He brings me into the mix. 'Hey, hitchie, your mama give you a name?'

'Kevin, but you can call me Kev.'

'Okay, Kev. Tonight we're gonna bunk down in Helena and get ourselves some cowgirls. You in?'

'Sure thing.'

'You know that cowgirl's expression—save a horse, ride a cowboy?'

'Yippee-ki-yay!' yapped Diesel Dan.'"

I was pretty far gone in my drug-fueled rendition of the story, when Ollie interrupted me. "You know, Kev, you're crazier than your patients, truly the lunatic running the asylum."

"C'mon, Ols, I had to join in. I'm the donkey nurse, remember, so I've got to graze with the herd."

"Yeah, until one wild stallion finally kicked your ass."

I shrugged, and reached for my water before continuing. "I was on vacation for a week, and came back a few days before the cowboy's court hearing. Working evenings, staff told me that Dan and The Man had been at their traveling caper just about every night since. So I passed my pills, finished my charts, walked into their room, and stuck out my thumb.

"Once again, Pencil Man stops to pick me up, but this turns out to be a bad stretch of road. Yep, all the strut is gone from his voice, and he's flatter than the Texas Panhandle. He's telling Dan a tearful tale, a woeful country tune. Went something like this . . .

"'It was at the Silver Lady, north of Portland, where I first met Geraldine. Pretty name, but a prettier gal. Helluva pool player, too. Patrons called her Queen of the Rails, but that had a double meaning, since she also had a love affair with cocaine.

'But every time I walked into that roadhouse, she'd drop her cue, walk to the juke, and play an 'arm an arm' song, as she called it. Before I could crack a Coors, we'd be dancing. The first night she took me home, it was a dream, so long since I made love to a woman who gave something back. For a spell, she kept asking if I'd park my rig in her yard. Wish I had now, it might've saved us both from our addictions.

'After doing a few runs along the coast, I'm back at the Lady, but a friend of Geraldine's meets me at the door, sobbing like. She tells me how Geraldine left the joint a month back and failed to negotiate a hairpin on her way home, and plowed into one of those majestic firs I've been telling you about. That was nine years ago, Dan, and you might think I'd be over it. But time is like an accordion, ain't it? Stretches way out there, then squeezes right back in again. Sometimes I go hundreds of miles off-route just to say a prayer to that white cross nailed up to that Douglas fir.'

"Now, Ollie, it was Diesel Dan's turn to comfort. 'I figured you were running away from something, and I'm truly sorry for your loss. But I hope that's not the reason you've been driving the Interstate like a loon. You could get yourself killed, old pal, or kill somebody else, which to me would be way worse.'

"A long silence filled the cab, and I had the thought, being a therapist and all, that I should say something. But what could I say, Ols, that Dan hadn't already said?"

But Ollie offered no comment. "Ols, are you still with me?"

I turned toward him, figuring he nodded off during my long-winded tale. But I saw tears streaking down his face, and knew they weren't being shed for Pencil Man.

"Ollie, you okay?"

He cleared his raspy throat. "Yeah, I'm here."

But I knew I'd hit a nerve, a raw one. "Hey, we can finish this story another time."

"Naw, go ahead, I'm good."

But Ollie was far from good, and I realized that I had struck the wrong note with my potentially suicidal roommate, so I quickly lightened my tune. "His 20 days up, the court gave Pencil Man a green light. No jail time, no revoked license, just mandated monthly blood tests."

Ollie forced a reply, "He lucked out."

"Better believe it. Then in the morning group on the day of his discharge, Pencil Man divulged the secret of his instant bond with Diesel Dan.

"'Three weeks ago, when I was in a coma in your do-or-die unit, I had some kind of powerful dream. I'm driving my sky-blue rig and find myself lost at a fork in the road on a foggy night. I knew this was no ordinary fork 'cause one road led to my salvation and the other my damnation. But I hadn't a bull's notion of which path to follow. Just when I started to go left, this old gent jumps out of the gloom and waves me wildly to go right. That's when I awoke from my coma.

'Now, that dream would've passed me by like a summer shower, 'cept when I laid eyes on old Dan here that first day down in your yard. Boy Howdy! I say, this dude is the spitting image of that dang gent who frantically directed me in my comatose dream.

'That very same night in our room, Dan asked if I'd ever traveled to the Northwest Territories, and that he's got himself a collection of license plates stored away, and the only one missing—the one he's been longing for since a kid—is one shaped like a polar bear from way up there. And if I was ever to travel that way, would I be kind enough to keep an eye out for one.

'Now, I know my brain-box has been rattled some, but the way I figure, Dan guided me right in my dream, and I'm guessing he's guiding me right again. The only difference is I'm awake this time, but I'm still at that same dang fork. If I go back to hauling produce, I know I'll be back to snorting speed in no time—thus my damnation. So I've decided to take some time off and heed my dream guide's message. Yesiree! I'm gonna bobtail up to the Northwest Territories, somewhere

where I've never been, and find Dan that polar bear plate. His quest is my quest. I'll find his dang plate, and in the search, find my own sobriety on that long winding road to my salvation. Not sure how, but I know it's so.'"

"Where are the Northwest Territories?" Ollie was again fully engaged.

"Way up in Canada, just east of the Yukon. More than three thousand miles from here. Pencil Man had even marked out his route on the road atlas, and handed it to Dan with a promise to call him with a progress report every other night. With that, he tipped his black cowboy hat to the group saying, 'Y'all are saints of the fun variety,' and strode off the unit with a determined stride."

"Did he make it?"

"Hold your donkeys, and let me tell it proper. Two weeks go by, and Pencil Man kept to his word, calling Dan every other night from the Trans-Canada Highway: Ottawa, Winnipeg, Saskatoon. But then he falls off the radar, with nary a blip.

"Dan's a mess, of course, sitting by the phone every night with the open map in his lap. Surprisingly, Sammy the Snit stepped up to keep him company, sitting like a faithful dog at his feet, and saying it would bring a tear to a glass eye to see anyone so lonesome."

"So Sammy really did have a good side."

"He did, indeed, though you'd have to dig a bit to find it. We'd given up hope when forty days had gone by—just the length of Lent—when suddenly we heard this blaring air horn. We race to the kitchen windows and, holy bejaysus, there's Pencil Man's flashy sky-blue rig taking up three full spaces in the Administration Only parking lot. In minutes, he swaggers onto the floor, carrying a flat packet in his hands. He's road weary, yes, but looks happy and healthy. Clean as a whistle, too, he later told us.

"We gathered up every chair and circled 'round our cowboy trucker, with Diesel Dan sitting smack dab in the middle, as Pencil Man shared the tale of his odyssey.

"'After a week on the Trans-Canada, I veered northwest after Edmonton and braced myself for some serious trucking. It got really tough after I passed Fort Nelson and turned due north toward Fort Liard, just into the Northwest Territories. That 200-mile desolate stretch gives a new meaning to the word boondocks. Dang, I saw more bear, bison, and moose than I did people.'

"Pencil Man looked down at Dan. 'That's where I fell off your map, good buddy. Phones were few and far between, and got to admit I strayed a bit out in the wilderness, heading for the ends of the earth. Had some dark nights too, suffered a rash of temptations. Then I didn't want to call again till I'd completed our mission. So, sorry for that, old boy. But here I am, in the flesh, bearing a gift.'

"Our road warrior waved around his thin packet. 'Before I open this, I have to tell you how I found it. When I finally arrived at the frontier town, I found it populated by Inuits and Eskimos. First Nations People, they're now calling 'em. At a trading post, I approached a father and his sons, but this far north they had no more English than a store-bought parakeet. So I drew 'em a polar bear plate, and one of the kids nearly jumped out of his furry boots and pointed to Pink Mountain. I figured by his gibberish that an abandoned vehicle was up there with a plate still tacked to it.

'So I circled Pink Mountain, and I might be circling it still if I wasn't in the Land of the Midnight Sun. But I kept my faith in the Good Lord, and finally spotted an old rusty pick-up in the thick brush off the road. I jumped from my rig and went running toward it like a man possessed. And, Boy Howdy, I see this red-and-white polar bear plate still attached to its front bumper. In good shape, too.

'So there I am, whooping it up and doing a happy dance in the middle of nowhere. Anyone see me, they'd think I was straight out of a loony bin.'

"He winked down at Dan, 'They'd gotten that right.

'I was thrilled to find Dan's treasure, true enough, but it was far more than that. A strange feeling came over me, like a shiver from the Holy Ghost, that lifted that dang clawing monkey clear off my back. Somehow I knew I'd never go back to druggin', that I was clean for life. Don't know how, but I just know it's so.'

"Ollie, at that point Pencil Man took the wrapping off the packet and handed Diesel Dan his prize; a 1973 Northwest Territories license plate in the shape of a walking polar bear. 'Hope this is what you sent me up there for,' Pencil Man said with a grin, 'because I ain't ever going back again.'

"At first, Dan was so overcome that he couldn't even utter a thank you. Nope, he just stared down at the plate, tears streaming. Finally, through heavy sobs, he thanked Pencil Man, and lifted the polar bear plate over his head to tremendous applause.

"I gotta tell you, Ols, I've seen many wondrous things in my thirty years on the Jones Wing, but that stands out in my memory. Frozen in amber, it is. Two roommates saving each other through the miraculous intervention of a piece of tin. We all gathered round, staff and patients alike, to sing the praises of the duo, though each downplayed his role. It was truly inspirational."

I turned again to gauge Ollie's reaction, and found a smile creeping over his bruised and bearded face.

"Wow," said Ollie, "that's some way to kick a drug habit. Must have cost him a pretty penny in fuel, but you can't put a price on sobriety."

"That's for sure. But the best part is they remained good friends. Pencil Man hooked up with a regional carrier, and would often take Dan on short runs to St. Johnsbury, Vermont. He never went back to drugging either, as far as I know. Of course, Dan never recovered completely, but lived out a tolerable life till his natural end."

At that moment, in walked our med nurse, Stephanie. "Good grief, it's 2 a.m., and you're both still awake?"

"How can anyone sleep with a roommate who never shuts up," Ollie joked. "Any chance for a room change?"

"Only Room 500 at this time of night," Stephanie said, referring to the morgue, "and I don't think you want to go there."

After we'd gotten our meds, Ollie drawled out pensively, "Hey Kev, I know we're both looped, and I don't want to get all sloppy, but I have a thought. How about we go on our own imaginary journey, just like Dan and The Man. Let's make it a Greyhound, but not like the one Ratso and Joe Buck take in *Midnight Cowboy*, nobody dying in the other's arms. Just road-tripping to recovery. Being an Army brat, I've traveled the length and breadth of this country and know it as well as Pencil Man. What'd you say, you in?"

"Sure, why not. What's our destination?"

"Yuma, Arizona," he blurted without hesitation. "My happiest days were spent there."

"OK, Yuma it is."

"We'll be great travelers, like Lewis and Clark, or Livingston and Seagull."

I laughed: "Stanley and Livingston, I presume."

"How about Huck Finn and Tom Sawyer? Didn't they raft down the Mississippi together?"

"That was Huck and Big Jim, I think. Tom and Huck painted fences."

"Or you and your jack-ass walking around Ireland, like your brother Dermot told me."

"My donkey, Missie, was a jenny, and I was the jack-ass. But it's a long haul to Yuma. There'll be plenty of obstacles."

Ollie's spirits were on the rise. "Yeah, like stingy med nurses, crabby aides, and idle undertakers. But we'll need handles of our own, like Dan and The Man."

"I'll be Kevlar, one of my many nicknames before my protective shield wore out. How about you?"

Switching off his nightlight, Ollie said with a catch in his voice, "Fat Boy. After the Harley I purposely smashed up on Sunday."

WEDNESDAY:
DISORDERLY PASSIONS

"Hey, Kevlar, are you enjoying the ride?"

"Wha'? Hunh? Who?"

"Kevlar, that's you, and Fat Boy, that's me, and we're riding the bus to Yuma together. Remember?"

I lifted my aching head, to take in where I was and who was talking. "Say again?"

"Our bus ride to Yuma, you clown!"

I reached for water, and remembered my aching back, already regretting my middle of the night promise. "Are we there yet?"

"Are you kidding!" Ollie laughed. "We just passed Eire, nosing for Ashtabula. You know that Bob Dylan tune, 'I'll look for you in old Honolul-a, San Francisco, Ashtabula . . . '"

I looked over at my balladeering roomie. "My, you're lit up like a Christmas tree."

"That's because I finally convinced my new Indian doctor friend for a rare PRN. So right now I'm higher than a giraffe's ass. But I'm mad at you."

"For what?"

"We're supposed to be traveling buddies, like Diesel Dan and Pencil Man. So I go and talk our bus driver into detouring out of Buffalo to see Niagara Falls, and you never once looked out your window."

"We passed Niagara Falls?"

"C'mon, Kevlar, play the role here," he chastised me. "We've got four days and over two thousand miles on our bus trip to Yuma, by way of San Antone and El Paso, and I'm counting on you for companionship. So get with it."

I sighed and shut my eyes, wondering how I could get myself out of this latest predicament. Presently, our assigned nurses and aides bustled in to kick our day into gear—bed bath, medication, and all—and it wasn't long before I was back on our imaginary bus, more welcoming to Fat Boy and our buddy routine, ready to play my role.

Settling in side by side, he asked, "How'd you ever become a nurse, anyway? Were you a medic in 'Nam?"

With improved spirits, I got right into ancient history. "Nope, I was a crash-rescue firefighter, spending long hours on the flightline at Cam Ranh Bay. I did that for five months before our stationmaster realized that a scrawny kid wouldn't be much good at dragging in a brawny pilot from a burning aircraft. So for the last seven months of my tour, I worked the Alarm Room, dispatching fire trucks across two of the busiest runways in Southeast Asia."

"Many crashes?"

"Not many, thank goodness. But we once had a fully-loaded B-52 spitting up sparks down our foamed runway. If that baby had blown, I sure wouldn't be your traveling buddy. But to answer your question, it was during that year when I first thought about becoming a nurse, inspired by Dr. Tom

Dooley."

"What?" Fat Boy cackled. "Inspired to hang down your head and cry? Poor boy!"

"Not that Tom Dooley, you dolt. Dr. Dooley wrote a book that I read while there, *The Night They Burned the Mountain*. He was a great humanitarian, a U.S. Navy doctor with an Irish Catholic background, that I could relate to. He was assigned to help with refugees from North to South Vietnam after the partition in '54, eventually leaving the Navy to establish his own hospital in Laos. He died young, but his clinics continued to operate for years, and helped inspire the Peace Corp. I was so moved by his mission that I volunteered for our local MEDCAP team, going out with doctors and corpsmen to assist the sick and wounded in the villages outside our airfield."

"Wasn't that dangerous?"

"A little. But we never ventured too far, and we were always back on base by nightfall. Besides, we had a battalion of fearless ROK'S—Korean marines—protecting our perimeter, after the convalescent center of our sprawling base was attacked by sappers that August."

"What would you do for MEDCAP?"

"Drive the deuce-and-a-half, mainly, carrying supplies. That, and do little things like distract the kids when they were getting vaccinated. Quite a primitive start to my medical education. Man, I'll never forget the time I witnessed a young mother squatting on a milking stool to give birth in a catcher's position. I think about it every time I see our Maternity nurses setting up their elaborate sterile fields."

"Gives a new look to natural childbirth," mused Ollie.

"Got that right. Anyway, while at Cam Ranh, I wrote to the Dooley Foundation in San Francisco, asking how I could help. They wrote back immediately, saying they were in desperate need for nurses. So, bingo, a nurse is what I would be. After discharge from the service, I'd earn my nursing degree, and sign up to work at Dr. Dooley's first clinic in Muong Sing, Laos."

Fat Boy groaned: "Why would you ever want to go back to that hell hole?"

"I loved the kids for one thing, but I mostly felt guilty about my role there. I was only a firefighter, sure, but every time a Phantom Fighter took off loaded with napalm and TNT, I knew that maimed and dead bodies were the aftermath. They never ceased, those bombing runs, day and night, and gnawed at me something awful. During that stretch, I adopted Dr. Dooley's motto as my own, 'From the wretchedness of Asia, I learned what my job on this earth was to be.'"

"The call to vocation."

"Pretty much." I reached out gingerly for the water on my bed stand. "Then my commitment grew stronger."

"How so?"

"On the day I was promoted to buck-sergeant, the chief granted me a three-day furlough to Saigon. So I hopped a C-130 cargo prop to Tan Son Nhut, 200 clicks south, to visit Sam Samolis, a friend I'd made at Bergstrom Air Force Base in Texas. Now that was some transformation. How can you keep 'em down on the base after they've seen Saigon? I was so enchanted by the 'Paris of the Orient' that I managed to visit the capital six more times before my tour ended, and risked every stripe on my sleeve to do it."

"In what way?"

"Writing fake orders, for starters."

"Whoa, that'll work. Sounds dumb to me."

"Real dumb," I agreed. "But I was bored at Cam Ranh, an isolated spit of sand in the sea, enlivened only by moments of danger, enemy rockets or a fiery crash, with only my weekly runs with MEDCAP to look forward to. Having seen the loose security at both air terminals during my first legal furlough, and having a set schedule of three consecutive days off every three weeks, I got hold of official 12th Tactical Wing stationery, typed up my own orders, forged our base commander's signature and—hot-diggity—I was back in Saigon."

"Setting yourself up for a dishonorable discharge."

"Discharge nothing! I'd wind up hammering license plates at Fort Leavenworth. I mean, think about it; fake orders, forged signatures, and being AWOL from my assigned airbase in a war zone, which borders on desertion. Sam always warned me that I was looking at anywhere from five to 20 years, if caught."

"So why'd you chance it?"

"What can I tell you, Fat Boy? I was 20 and felt invincible. I was also charmed by a teagirl or two, for sure, but I came to find out that my buddy Sam was a father-figure to a dozen street urchins living in wooden crates along the waterfront. After a few visits, I knew most of the kids' names, and even picked up a bit of the language. Each succeeding visit, my conviction of joining MEDICO, the medical arm of the Dooley Foundation that supported both orphanages and clinics , grew stronger. I couldn't wait to become a nurse and begin my three-year stint in Laos."

Fat Boy tried to whistle but barely managed a puff. "Three years!"

"Yep. My self-imposed penance for participating in that dumb war. So once I returned stateside, I finished my short military stint at Edwards in California, and returned home to embark on my medical quest. My first night at the dinner table, I passed around pictures of the waterfront gang to my parents, telling them of my plans to return to Southeast Asia once I became a nurse."

"They must've freaked."

"If they did, they didn't show it. Though I suspect they started a nine-day novena that very night, praying for the return of their wayward son's senses.

"Then within a week, by happy coincidence, my brother Dermot, who was working as an orderly at St. Luke's Hospital at the time, came home with news of two sudden orderly openings at Pittsfield General. Two vacancies that occurred in the oddest of ways."

Fat Boy shifted his pillow, in search of an elusive comfort, and prodded, "I'm all ears, Kevlar."

"Evidently, two orderlies were called to an old patient's room to prop him up in bed. While there, one found a loose curtain weight on the windowsill, much like a ball bearing, and stuck it in his pocket. When leaving the room, the old timer, on the brink of death, let out a groan. The pair looked back and saw his mouth agape. So the orderly with the curtain weight took it from his pocket and pretended to dribble it like a basketball. His buddy picked up on the game and started to mimic Johnny Most, the voice of the Boston Celtics; 'Heinsohn to Havlicek, back to Heinsohn, over to Cousy, he fiddles, he diddles, he stops, he pops—.' The inspired shooter lets loose the projectile that finds the old man's gob and straight down his gullet. Swish and goodbye!"

"Damn, they wouldn't have made that shot again in a thousand tries."

"Unfortunately, they only had to make it once."

"What did they do?"

"Tried to cover it up, I guess, saying they'd found him that way. But the ensuing coroner's report sealed their fate."

"They do time?"

"Naw, not back then. Just a swift dismissal. Probably swept under the carpet, with the ongoing merger between the two hospitals at the time. Nor did the old chap have any family, so I suppose he was bound for Potter's Field, anyway."

"True story?"

"I believed so at the time. But once I landed the job, I asked a few of my fellow mates about it. Some of them debunked the story, attributing it to the mudslinging between the two hospitals, saying the pair were actually canned for stealing dozens of surgical Kelly clamps, and selling them as roach clips. You know, to hold the butt end of a joint."

"I know what a roach clip is. I've been around the block a time or two."

"Well, whatever transpired, I landed the perfect job to pursue my nursing career. But it was some ordeal, I tell you."

"In what way?"

"The job called for a two-week probation period, to see if hospital work was right for either worker or hospital. And believe me, if I wasn't so committed to my Asian quest, I would've thrown in the towel—a bunch of towels—that first day."

"That bad, huh?"

"Bloody awful! Fortunately, Dermot had clued me in on a number of distasteful orderly duties, but never in my life—."

I trailed off, drooping my arms over the sides of the bed, pretending to be too weak to continue.

"C'mon, man, off your chest," Fat Boy encouraged me.

With a deep sigh, I commenced the tale of that foul and repulsive first day. "Monday morning, 0700 sharp; chief orderly, Ed Crosby, a retired cop, is not in the best of health or the best of moods after the two recent firings. With barely a welcome aboard, he hands me a white uniform with matching bucks, and two lists with names and room numbers. One was headed 'Local Care,' the other 'Enemas.'"

"I know what an enema is, but what's local care?"

"Scrubbing the privates of every male patient who has an indwelling catheter. Tons of fun, hey? So around I go, dressed like the Hood ice cream man, entering rooms, drawing curtains, lifting men's johnny tops, and giving their toolboxes one royal polishing for a whopping $2.33 an hour. No wonder some jokers in the hospital referred to us orderlies as 'scrotum-scrubbers.'"

"Scrotum-scrubbers," Fat Boy chortled. "Maybe that should be your new handle?"

"Don't you dare," I warned my traveling mate. "After I finished my nine scrub-a-dubs, Ed led me to a sink where he demonstrated enema preparation, filling a quart-size enema bag full of a soapy solution of steaming water, and hanging it up on a squeaky-wheeled IV pole, with the instructions, 'Remember the old orderly adage: high, hot, and a helluva lot.'

"Placing a jumbo tube of KY jelly in my other hand, he led me into a crowded elevator bound for Five South. There I stood, leaning on my pole, clutching a tube of lubricant, and surrounded by a bevy of St. Luke's nursing students tittering behind their textbooks."

"I'd hate to have been your first victim."

"Fortunately, Dermot had given me sounder advice—tepid water, not hot, and moderate the flow if the patient showed any signs of cramps or discomfort. Actually, the first two went okay, but the third patient pegged me as a greenhorn and ordered me out of his room, shouting, 'Find yourself another asshole, asshole!'"

"Was this a hazing?"

"Hazing? No way, Fat Boy. It's what orderlies do. That, and other disagreeable tasks like shaving male patients from nipple to knee before surgery, or preparing the deceased for the morgue with shroud, toe tag, and three cotton balls up the poop chute."

My road buddy had to catch his breath from laughing. "Three . . . cotton balls . . . up the . . . poop chute!"

"Yep, otherwise known as Cotton Ball Derby."

"You're one sick pup, Kevlar, you know that."

"It's foxhole humor, Fat Boy. The way we hospital folk get through tough times."

Fat Boy wasn't buying it. "Yeah, right."

"During that long, miserable first week, I went from butt to butt and scrotum to scrotum, and hardly saw a face unless it needed to be shaved. But despite my best efforts, Ed pulled me aside that first Friday and said I wasn't cutting the mustard."

"What was his beef?"

"He called me out on a few local cares where I neglected to clean under the foreskins. And he didn't like the way I buddied up to the doctors, many of whom I knew from my caddying days at the Country Club. I did my damnedest that second week, but I could tell Ed remained less than keen on me. But that Thursday, with just one day left in my probation, two improbable events occurred that kept my Asian dreams alive."

"Go on, tell me, ye olde enema-giving scrotum-scrubber."

"I'm sitting with the other orderlies at morning coffee break. I remember them all, Joey Powers, John Quill, Scotty Ingram; good guys feeling bad for me, knowing the writing was already on the wall. The day was hectic from the start, and just as John bit into his jelly donut, he got paged to Five North.

"He throws down his pastry and says, 'Dammit, that's Mr. Reynolds in 527, wanting to use the bedpan again. He's already gone twice this morning, but nothing ever satisfies his need to go. He's convinced he's got a torpedo stuck up there.'

"I volunteered to go with John, in one last attempt to ingratiate the boss, or maybe just to escape his cold glare. Now, Mr. Reynolds was a blubbery behemoth, and John and I struggled to roll him onto his side in order to wedge the metal bedpan beneath him. Once he was on board, so to speak, we drew the curtain and waited outside. A couple of minutes later, Mr. Reynolds wailed his standard plea, 'Did I go, Joe?'

"We shouldered him off the pan, and John eyed its contents like a hopeful prospector panning for gold. 'I'm afraid not, Mr. Reynolds, but remember you've already gone this morning—twice, in fact.' Unappeased, he violently shook his bed rails. 'Twice, bedamned! I'm still waiting on the mother lode!'

"I'd later learn that such bowel obsession is a common sign of early dementia, but there was nothing more to be done, until we were called back at lunchtime for a repetition. This time, once the patient was rolled onto the pan, John was paged elsewhere, leaving me alone to await the wished-for evacuation. I was loitering outside the room when I spotted a leftover baked potato on top of the lunch cart. With Mr. Reynolds again hollering, 'Did I go, Joe?' I got one of my crack-brained ideas, and popped the potato into my pocket.

"Somehow managing to roll him off the bedpan, I slipped the potato into the pan with a deft sleight of hand. When he roared his query once again, I lifted the pan in triumph and rumbled around its weighty nugget over his head. 'By golly, Mr. Reynolds, did you ever!'"

"Did he buy it?"

"Buy it? He swooned with relief, exclaiming, 'Now, that's music to my ears! Just the nagging log I've been waiting on!' So I flushed away the evidence and returned to his bedside, expounding on its length and girth to his profound gratification. Just as I was leaving Mr. Reynolds with a smile of satisfaction spreading across his broad face, my name was paged over the loudspeaker: 'Kevin O'Hara, Two South. Kevin O'Hara, Two South, please.'"

"Never a dull moment in the life of an orderly, I guess."

"Plenty of them, but this was my lucky day, remember. So when I got to the floor, I reported to Miss Mae Cummings, the sweetest charge nurse of all. 'Kevin, could you go into Room 217 and get Mr. Abbott up for lunch, as his wife is here to feed him. The poor man has Parkinson's and is little more than skin and bones. He also hasn't spoken a word in months, so don't expect a thank you.'

"I entered the room and greeted the missus, who stepped out into the hall to let me work. When I pulled down the bed sheets, I saw that Mr. Abbott was as thin and stiff as an old rusty lawn chair. I lifted him, pivoted, and plopped him into his Geri-chair, with less than my most attentive care. As I was going to retrieve his wife, a dry rasp followed me out the door, 'Get back here you idiot, you've sat me on my balls!'"

Fat Boy cracked up, "No wonder you were going to get

canned the next day."

"Sure, but then the missus rushes in, ecstatic upon hearing her beloved's voice once again, but thankfully, not having heard what he actually said. As I repositioned him more comfortably, she smothered him with kisses. He pushed her away, feebly and irritably, 'Dottie, could you please hold off your affection until I have my lunch.' Despite the rebuff, Mrs. Abbott looked up at me as if I were a miracle worker."

"Oh, yeah, that natural healing touch of yours."

"Say what you will, Fat Boy, but word of Mr. Abbott's breakthrough got around the hospital, with my name attached to it. But the topper came the next day, Friday, my scheduled doomsday. A large fruit basket was delivered to Two South, with a card that read, 'To Kevin O'Hara, Ward Angel. With deepest gratitude, the Abbott family.'"

"Damn, you're one lucky ball washer!"

"Don't I know it! Once the basket was presented to me by Nurse Cummings, I removed the cellophane, picked out an apple, and offered the basket around to the nurses and aides, modestly saying, 'We're all ward angels.' Then I strolled down the corridor, basket in hand, taking a satisfying bite of the apple, and imagining the chorus of admiring whispers in my wake:

'Why, that's the son of James O'Hara, the longtime chauffeur at St. Luke's.'

'Just home from Vietnam. A hero, no doubt.'

'What a healer! Did you also hear what happened yesterday with Mr. Reynolds on Five North?'"

Fat Boy chirped up: "There goes Orderly O'Hara, known the world over for his enema expertise."

I scowled at my roommate playfully and continued. "In

the cafeteria, I presented the remainder of my fruit basket to Ed and the crew, 'Help yourself, guys. It's probably the last thank you gift I'll ever get.' I thought I might have scored a few points with Ed, but his glower told me otherwise. He plucked out a grapefruit and rolled it from hand to hand like a cannonball, and asked skeptically, 'So, O'Hara, how did you get Mr. Abbott to talk yesterday?'

"'I guess he finally had something to say,' I ventured. But Ed's hard glare showed me he wasn't buying it, so I finally blurted out the truth, 'I accidentally sat him on his family jewels, and he complained when I was leaving the room.'

'And Reynolds?'

'I slipped a baked potato into his bedpan that he mistook for a Lincoln log.'

"I bowed my head and meekly awaited the end of my hospital career, and all its accompanying sorrows. Instead, Ed let out a roar that turned every head in the cafeteria. 'A baked potato? Now, that's one helluva brilliant placebo!'

"Hearing Ed's proclamation, my fellow orderlies stood up and slapped me happily on the back, as Ed reached out a hand and granted, 'Kevin, I didn't think you had the heart or stomach for this job, but you've proved your mettle, and you've proved me wrong. Welcome aboard, son!'"

"Saved by a potato," Fat Boy pondered. "Just the thing for an Irishman."

"Yep, one baked potato that kept my MEDICO dreams alive."

*   *   *

Despite my initial reluctance, I had relaxed into my

road-buddy role-playing with Fat Boy. I always enjoy telling tales, and it took my attention away from bodily woes. Plus, I was pleased with how responsive Ollie was, as I took my mission from Dr. Carter to monitor his mood. He certainly retained his sense of humor, and can there be a better barometer to one's mental health?

So stuck on our imaginary bus, we talked through the day, though I'd occasionally catch a glimpse of him looking blankly down the hospital corridor, as if reliving the moment of his crash. I was happy to keep talking about my ups and downs, in hopes Ollie might eventually choose to share some of his own dark stories.

"Okay," Fat Boy perked up, after reeling in distant thoughts, "so Kevlar dodged another bullet, survives probation and becomes an orderly. What next?"

"Getting into nursing school. As a veteran currently working in a hospital, I figured I'd be a shoo-in for admission, but it didn't turn out to be so easy. The department chair at Berkshire Community College, a sympathetic elderly woman named Gwen Lawson, looked over my transcript and informed me that my high school grades were well below their standard."

"Were you dumb in high school?"

"Let's just say I was an underachiever. Missed some school days earlier on, then never caught up. Mrs. Lawson was helpful though, advising me to take prerequisite courses and try again the following year. I pleaded with her, and told her my dreams of working at Dr. Dooley's clinic. I even showed her the letter I'd received from his foundation, MEDICO."

"You didn't tell her about your three-year penance?"

"Naw, she'd probably think I was crazy. Even my parish priest, Father John Foley, thought my repentance bordered on the extreme. But taking her advice, I enrolled in three evening classes. I needed a B average or better to stay in the running. Psychology and Sociology came easy enough, but Speech was a killer."

"Speech? I find that hard to believe. You haven't shut up since I've met you."

"Yeah, I know, but I was intimidated by a few tough cops in that class, looking to get a pay boost by earning an associate's degree in Criminal Justice. Our last assignment was a show-and-tell to present tangible objects dearest to one's heart. That December evening, I pulled out all the stops, bringing in my three Dr. Dooley books, my MEDICO letter, and a stack of photos of the waterfront gang taken the day Sam and I treated them to the Saigon Zoo.

"Basically, I told them everything I've been telling you, but they weren't good listeners like Fat Boy. As I rambled on about the kids, especially Willie Joe and his endearing little sister, Phuong, everything I was saying started to sound hollow and absurd. Yep, right there at the podium, it dawned on me that the after-effects of war take on many shapes, what we now call PTSD. My friend Johnny came home from the war and spent his days bouncing a rubber ball against the brick wall of our old school. Tommy came home and spent his days fishing without a hook on the line. Kevy came home and dreamed of saving droves of orphans from the perils of the Orient.

"Next thing, my voice is quaking, and I can't get to my conclusion. Nope, I just stood there, silent and immobile, until I felt the warm arm of our professor, Dr. Kataoka, ushering me back to my seat. There I sat, trembling and fighting back tears, as the next speaker handed out flashy brochures of time-shares in Florida, the next big thing."

"Sounds bad, Kevlar."

I took a large gulp of ginger ale, wishing it were a frothy pint.

"When my grades arrived that January, I couldn't believe my eyes—all A's. So I eagerly enrolled in three more classes the following semester, and switched to night duty so I'd have more time to study. During that stretch, I spent many nights in the ER making friends with interns and residents, who knew of my MEDICO plans and taught me a lot of stuff that orderlies aren't supposed to know: how to suture wounds, lance boils, even help set simple fractures. When questioned by attending physicians, Dr. Kiti, our chief surgical resident from Thailand, would reply, 'Kevin is going to Laos in a few years, and he'll need these skills.'

"Meanwhile, the war raged on, and every night I'd crouch in front of our small black-and-white TV to watch Walter Cronkite. Whenever a clip of Saigon was shown, I'd put my nose to the screen, hoping to catch a glimpse of one or more of the waterfront gang. Crazy, huh, but one never knows. What my poor parents must have thought back then—their daft son intent on saving the world."

"There's far worse pursuits," Fat Boy sagely observed.

"Yep, but then everything unraveled. The war soon spilled into both Laos and Cambodia, which forced MEDICO to abandon their clinics. Took me a long time to get over it. As you may know, whenever a dream dies, it's devastating. But my family, parents and siblings alike, were a great comfort, though they probably thanked every saint in the heavens the whole time. And while my mission in Laos was no more, I still had my professional dreams to pursue."

"Well, Kevlar," said Ollie, clearing his throat of phlegm

and spitting into a kidney basin, "your story certainly made the miles fly by. We're halfway across Ohio already, but now I've gotta take a snooze. Look forward to hearing the rest of your journey to nursing further down the road."

With that, Ollie fell back into his cacophonous snoring, and I had to wonder how a man with just one working lung could blare so loud. Just as well, I suppose, because my story was about to take a sad turn, not a suitable thing for a suicidal man to hear.

After MEDICO'S closing, I found myself going through the motions in my coursework at BCC, and doubted whether to pursue nursing as a career. Why enter a largely female profession now that I'd be staying stateside? A male nurse wouldn't faze the orphans at Muong Sing, but I could already hear the ribbing I'd get from my hometown buddies, "A nurse, really? Gee, O'Hara, why not a cosmetologist?" At the time, male nurses were few and far between, and the phrase itself seemed oxymoronic.

This was an issue I discussed with my mother, who set me straight. She explained that Nursing was a ministry suitable for men and women alike. She cited St. Benedict, St. Gerard, and the Hospital Brothers of St. Anthony, and how hospitals were really an outgrowth of medieval religious orders. Even "Bedlam" itself, Bethlehem Hospital in London, was founded in response to a vision of the Virgin Mary. I'd read about Walt Whitman's nursing days during the Civil War and recalled my teenage impulse to become an Edmundite missionary, so the idea of nursing as a ministry had a natural appeal for me.

Mom didn't stop there, urging me, "Think of all the good you could do as a nurse, all the lives you could touch. You could join the Peace Corps and travel to any number of countries, even Asia." She went and retrieved a handbook, *Mental Nursing*, from her own nursing days during World War II in England. As I thumbed through the book, she shared stories of her days at St. Andrew's Hospital in Northampton, reputed at the time to be one of the most prestigious psychiatric facilities in Europe.

Mom's favorite patient was the Honorable Violet Gibson—daughter of the former Lord Chancellor of Ireland—who attempted to assassinate Benito Mussolini in Rome in 1926, and resided at St. Andrew's until her death in 1956. Her gunshot struck him in the nose, but Mussolini took the attack lightly and saved her from an angry mob, reputedly saying, "Calm yourselves. It is just a simple joke with a pistol shot." Rather than being convicted, Violet was committed to St. Andrew's.

"Miss Gibson rarely spoke to anyone," Mom shared, "but one morning, out of the blue, she asked if I'd help her sew little pouches into the shoulders of her black dress. Once done, she'd go filling these pouches with breadcrumbs and sit perfectly still in the rose garden, where redbreasts and sparrows would alight on her shoulders and begin to feed. She did this for years, mind you, and we'd often tell her that her cheeks had been caressed by the wings of a thousand birds. Our words never failed to make her smile."

She also told me about Saint Dymphna, the "Lily of Eire," who remains the patron saint of the mentally ill, and of those who care for them. With my mother's encouragement, a different vision of nursing began to take shape in my mind, less about hordes of orphans on distant shores, but more about troubled mental patients closer to home.

Mom inspired me, but night duty at the hospital unsettled me. They call it the skeleton shift for good reason. The silent halls seemed haunted by the spirits of the sick, past and present. I felt like another ghost, patrolling these lonely wards, my dreams retreating faster than I could advance. With Dr. Dooley's mission no longer my beacon, I was lost at sea, and oppressed by the responsibility of being the lone orderly in a house of 265 beds.

Say, for instance, I'm called to Five South to assist the nurses in persuading a confused old man back to his bed. He's standing naked by the elevator, holding his catheter bag in his hand like a briefcase, insisting he needs to attend an important board meeting. On the day shift, such a scene might elicit witty remarks from my mates. But at this ungodly hour, the plight of the senile gent is piercing beyond words.

Paged from floor to floor, I'd encounter one unfolding trauma after another: a Mayday in Coronary Care, an auto accident in the Emergency Room, a call from Nursery to remove a stillborn to Room 500, hearing the distraught wail of its mother as I cradled her warm bundle in my arms.

All this misery took its toll, and the call to vocation got fainter and fainter. But in the dead of winter, I was called to Four East, the Isolation Unit. It was unusual for me to be summoned there, since I'd never been fully trained in sterile techniques. I reported to Mrs. Anna Doyle, the charge nurse, who greeted me with an urgency that overturned my dark of night lethargy.

She filled me in on a burn victim named Julie Potter, a 30-year-old woman who was seared over 60 percent of her body when she lit a portable gas stove at home the night before. Nurse Doyle would need my assistance twice nightly for the duration, an assignment cleared by Mary Jane, our nursing supervisor. Mrs. Doyle gave me a quick but detailed lesson in asepsis and helped me into a gown, cap, mask, and gloves at the doorway of Room 404.

Nothing I'd ever experienced, not even as a firefighter in Vietnam, prepared me for the sight and stench of what confronted me upon entering Julie's room. I staggered and nearly retched. There the naked woman lay comatose, her flesh charred and livid, on an air mattress attached to a large circular stainless steel bed. Gel dressings covered her breasts, and a forest of IV poles surrounded her.

The room itself was suffocating, set to body temperature as Mrs. Doyle explained, since Julie had so little skin left, and therefore was susceptible to pneumonia. With sponges and sterile water, we began the laborious task of removing the antibacterial Silvadene cream applied earlier by the evening nurses. That done, we applied a new coat.

I was terrible at the job. My hesitant fingers, clad in rubber gloves, left thick clumps across her abdomen, while Mrs. Doyle spread the cream over Miss Potter's seared body like melted butter.

She noticed my tentative fingers. "Don't be concerned about hurting her. The poor girl won't feel any pain until her nerve endings begin to rejuvenate in a few days."

I looked down at the young woman's unmarked face, in repose despite my haphazard treatment. Unconscious of her own plight, she'd soon wake to a life so horribly changed, and I shuddered to think of her moment of realization.

During my rounds, I gathered from the residents that Julie Potter would be dead within two weeks, most likely from shock after her first debridement—removal of dead tissue—in the operating room. Even if she survived that, they agreed, there was a strong likelihood of kidney failure, pneumonia, or fatal infection.

I told Mrs. Doyle what I had heard, but she promptly dismissed their prognosis. "I've been a nurse long enough to know there's more to a patient's survival than what's written in the medical books. And, Kevin, if you and I set our minds on losing Julie in two weeks' time, we'll certainly succeed in doing so."

Thus Mrs. Doyle enlisted me in a joint mission, "you and I," so every night that I was on duty, at two and five in the morning, the team of Nurse Doyle and Orderly O'Hara would stand to either side of our patient, applying cream to her limbs and torso. After a week, Julie regained consciousness, and was sent to the O.R. for her first debridement. She returned oozing and in agony, and had been so heavily medicated during the procedure, that Mrs. Doyle had to ration out her pain meds— or hold them altogether—in fear of an overdose.

Those nights passed endlessly. Julie screamed at the lightest touch of our fingers, cursing us and her own sorry existence, no longer wishing to live with such pain. I had to take short but frequent breaks by the window, where I looked out at the fresh swirling snow, in such contrast to our stifling room. I glanced back at this horrific scene through the window's reflection, trying at the same time to banish these terrible hours from memory.

But one night slipped into another, and Julie survived.

Up to that time, as an orderly, I'd generally shuttle from floor to floor, rarely engaged in one patient's care for any length of time. But now, despite the abject misery of my mission, I began to feel privileged to witness firsthand the healing art of Nursing in the capable hands of Mrs. Doyle.

After Julie's second debridement, she fell ominously silent.

"Slipping into herself," Mrs. Doyle feared, stressing such withdrawal could be as life-threatening as any infection. So through her mask, Anna Doyle became a chatterbox, talking animatedly about her large family—fifteen children—sharing their everyday adventures and small triumphs. During those nights, I began to marvel at the way this mother of such a huge brood, this tireless middle-aged nurse of Polish descent, could do what she did night after night, buoyed by immeasurable faith, without let-up or complaint.

After a while Mrs. Doyle encouraged me to join in on the conversation. I felt awkward at first, though I'd already noticed Julie taking some interest in Mrs. Doyle's ramblings. So I piped up, and in time Mrs. Doyle prompted Julie to join in and speak her mind. And my, did she ever, cursing God and every living thing! But then she broke down and wept, the anger draining from her voice, and I could see Mrs. Doyle sigh in relief behind her mask. In short order, Julie rallied and became more engaged.

Why, if you had walked by Room 404 some late-night as January slipped into February, you'd have thought there was a party going on, with all our jokes and banter. Once I made Julie laugh so hard, she had to ask Mrs. Doyle for "breakthrough" pain meds. I pledged then and there I wouldn't crack another joke. But soon we'd be at it again, full throttle.

One other night, following a Silvadene treatment, Julie asked me about Vietnam, since Mrs. Doyle had mentioned to her that I was a veteran. I was slow to reply, wishing to put those days behind me. But Julie was insistent, so I surrendered a few inconsequential stories. But as someone well acquainted with grief, she wanted to go deeper into the horrors of the war.

I hesitated for Julie's sake, and for my own, but Mrs. Doyle coaxed me, wiping her own beaded brow with her sleeve. "Go on, it'll help get that weight off your chest. Won't it, Julie?"

Julie gave me a wink, and managed to quip in her feeble voice, "I'm not going anywhere until you do."

Bonded with these two women in the dark of a winter's night, sharing a legacy of pain and caring, I unloaded a black bag of random memories: the plight of orphans at Dong Ba Thin; the frail and frightened young Viet Cong prisoners chained for hours in the punishing sun; the river children of Saigon scraping eggshells and fruit rinds for sustenance; the club-footed girl named Nhung selling individual Chiclets from a rusty Sucrets tin; C141's taking off from Cam Ranh to Dover Air Force Base, loaded with a cargo of young soldiers in body bags. And, lastly, the chance of returning to Southeast Asia to right my wrong.

Once I started rummaging through the mental relics of that unhappy time, I could hardly stop, for there was no end. After my litany of sorrow, Julie piped up with the wisdom of painful experience, "It's time you left that foolish war behind. You're a young man, the world at your feet. If I were you— and believe me, I'd gladly trade places—I wouldn't be moping about like a beaten dog. You've got to get on with your life. Am I right, Anna?"

Mrs. Doyle brushed Julie's hair back from her comely face. "You're darn right."

Julie then spoke of her own predicament, which may have been Mrs. Doyle's intention all along. She shared stories of her happy college days in Ithaca, and how she enjoyed camping at the Finger Lakes. She also spoke of falling in love for a "brief spell" with a young man from the Catskills. And finally, how her life had been irrevocably changed by the simple striking of a match.

Those following nights I found myself getting stronger while Julie grew weaker, as if she were lending her lingering reserves to replenish my own. All the while, I could see that Mrs. Doyle was praying silently behind her mask, as if administering the rites of passage to the two of us.

When I reported to Four East in early March, Mrs. Doyle led me to the sunroom, out of earshot from Room 404. There she held my hands and revealed, "Julie will only be with us for another night or two. For all her strength and heroism, her kidneys are failing her."

I started to protest and insist upon the possibility of recovery, but Mrs. Doyle knew when to maintain hope and when to relinquish it. She said Julie had accepted her impending death, and suggested we not hold out false hope, "It's time for us to let go, too."

When we entered Julie's room, I noticed that her legs were severely bloated, and her catheter bag nearly empty. We provided comfort measures only; wet packs to her abdomen and a cool washcloth to her forehead.

Julie spoke in a whisper, thanking us both for our care and kindness. At one point, she looked me straight in the eye, "How you made me laugh, you scoundrel! That humor will serve you well as a nurse. Keep it up. You'll do that for me, won't you?"

"I will," I promised her, and meant it.

She slipped in and out of consciousness, and there were times when I thought she had passed on, but then her eyes would open for another brief postscript. With her remaining strength she shared that her tragedy had become a revelation, and despite her grave misfortune, she'd never felt closer to God. "Wasn't I stupid," she murmured, "to embrace God only at the end. What have I lost for not loving Him sooner?"

Julie died on a Wednesday. I'll always remember because Ed came in and stayed with me for the first hours of my shift. After he left, I couldn't bear to visit Mrs. Doyle at two or five, so I waited until my six-thirty rounds. Afraid to accept the truth of it all, I suppose. When I finally arrived on Four East, I looked into Room 404 and noticed that Julie's circular bed had been replaced by a standard one, and that the room was scented with clove disinfectant.

Rather than go directly to the nurses' station, I walked into the empty sunroom where I struggled to get a grip. Imagine, two arduous months of hoping and caring, all for naught. To rein in my grief, I thought of all I wanted to say to Mrs. Doyle; how she was a gift to her profession, how she had kept Julie alive, as well as preparing her for death. Lastly, how she had inspired me to pursue the ministry of Nursing without further doubt.

Drying my eyes, I left the sunroom and walked toward the nurses' station, where I found Mrs. Doyle jotting notes with her back toward me. I started to speak, but all I had hoped to say got caught in my throat. So mumbling only a hurried "Good morning," I collected her lab and diet slips and walked down the quiet corridor, leaving Anna Doyle to ponder what nurses must always ponder after a long stand with a doomed patient.

With that melancholy reflection, decades later, back on Neuro Stepdown as a patient myself, I fell asleep.

*   *   *

That evening, settled and dosed to a pleasant glow, Fat

Boy and Kevlar set off on the long, straight bus ride through Indiana to Chicago, seated side by side and passing the miles together as congenial companions. I entertained him with a well-rehearsed tale that I had often sung for my supper. It went something like this . . .

When spring arrived, Ed thoughtfully pulled me off the graveyard shift, so I could enjoy the lengthening days, and offered to put me back on nights once I got into nursing school.

It was wonderful to reunite with my old mates; Joey, John, Scotty, and a new recruit, George Champoux, who became a fast friend. George was a conscientious objector with a mystic bent, doing two year's alternative service at the hospital. He spoke Latin and joked of being a recent "escapee" from a Connecticut seminary. We called him Padre Pio for his mystical tendencies, or occasionally less flattering monikers like Padre Pie-O-My, since his New Age-y beliefs sometimes bordered on the woo-woo.

One morning I found George in Room 500, praying over a recently deceased patient. He confessed that he was watching for a green luminescent soul to rise from the body. He also had a penchant for astrology, and had drawn up a complex star chart for me, filled with arcane symbols. As he was reading it to me, he uttered a long "Hmm!" and jotted down a date on a scrap of paper, then handed it to me: "June 16, 1973."

"What's this?" I asked.

His vibrant blue eyes danced. "That, my friend, is your wedding day."

Not likely, since that was just over a year away, and I had no romantic prospects whatsoever. That was soon to change, though. The following week in the cafeteria, I espied a surprising candidate among a group of medical technology students from the Philippines, and with uncharacteristic assurance, made my own prediction.

"See that lovely Filipina with the yellow ribbon in her hair? I'm going to marry her," I boasted to my mates.

They were quick to provide a reality check, each saying something to cool my jets.

"You're shopping at Macy's, O'Hara, when you belong at Zayre's. It's nice to raise the bar, but hell, you can't jump over the moon."

"Let me tell you about dating a Filipina, which a buddy of mine did. You ask one out, and three others will tag along as chaperones. You'll wind up paying for all four, and forget which one you were actually dating."

"Just so you know, her name is Belita Suarez," informed George. "She's from the southern island of Mindanao, and I hear she's something like a princess over there."

Well, I was no Prince Charming, that I knew, but looking over at this beautiful, spirited girl having fun with her friends, I was resolved to embrace my newfound passion and move in the direction of my dreams.

Early mornings I'd see Belita drawing blood, and try to ingratiate myself by always pulling a stunt when she caught me going about my mundane orderly chores. For instance, I'd make her laugh by draping a towel over my forearm and carrying an empty bedpan on the flat of my palm, like a waiter in some classy joint. But then I'd see her enjoying lunch with the surgical residents, and my heart would sink.

Maybe my fellow orderlies were right, she was out of my league. I was near the bottom of the hospital hierarchy, dressed in a stained white smock. Interns and residents wore fashionable gray scrubs; they were getting ahead in the world, learning valuable skills, while I was still preparing for my medical education to begin.

But on my 23rd birthday, April 20th, I rallied to the occasion, figuring I had nothing to lose by asking Belita for a date. I wrote a note in my finest penmanship: "Belita, would you like to go to a movie some evening?" I drew two boxes labeled "YES" and "NO," adding, "Check one, please. If you say NO, don't feel too bad. Today's my birthday, so I have a cake waiting at home. Fondly, Kevin the Orderly."

I dropped the note beside her food tray and retreated to my table. Minutes later, she returned the note with her own box drawn and checked—"MAYBE"—and whispered, "I'll have to ask my sister after my Hematology exam. By the way, Happy Birthday!"

I was discouraged when our date didn't pan out right away, for family reasons I never was privy to, but I took consolation from another positive turn in my life. One May morning, after getting three more A's on that semester's report card, I ran into Mrs. Lawson, chair of the BCC Nursing department, in the hospital lobby.

"Congratulations on your marks, Kevin!" I gave her a double take. "Oh, yes, I've been keeping an eye on you, and I fully intend to matriculate you into our program for the upcoming fall semester."

With a thumping heart, I dashed home and grabbed my dictionary to look up the word "matriculate."

With such good news in hand, I quickly emptied the coffers once earmarked for my return to Southeast Asia, and celebrated by buying a new car: a VW Karmann Ghia. Now, with sporty wheels beneath me, I rallied my courage for another assault on Castle Belita.

The Angelus was ringing from nearby Holy Family Church when I parked my blue Ghia in front of the hospital's Bishop-Clapp building, a century-old brick residence now housing medical students. Feeling both lucky and blessed, I boldly asked the receptionist if she'd ring up Belita Suarez for me.

The gatekeeper eyed me doubtfully, "Is she expecting you?"

I fibbed, "Oh, yes, but I'm a little early."

I nervously paced the lobby as the receptionist called up to the third floor.

She turned to me, "Belita will be down in a minute."

I took a seat on a deep leather couch in front of the fireplace, but jumped to attention as the lovely señorita descended the handsome oak staircase.

"Hi, Kevin. What's up?"

"I just bought a new car, and I wonder if you'd like to take a short spin with me?"

"I'd have to ask my sister, but she's working till eleven at St. Luke's."

"I'll have you back in twenty minutes, promise. Just enough time to buy you an ice cream cone."

She peeked out the lobby window at my shiny sports car. "It's so cute. What kind of car is it?"

"It's a Karmann Ghia, a Volkswagen chassis topped off with an Italian-style body."

"Twenty minutes, promise?" She looked at me with some apprehension.

"I promise."

I waited at the car as she went upstairs to get ready. But when this raven-haired beauty came skipping down the red sandstone steps toward me, I couldn't help but blurt out something stupid.

"Listen, Belita, I know this might sound weird, but you've got to hear me out, okay?"

She retreated a step. "Okaay?"

"If we're sitting together in this car when the odometer turns ten thousand miles, that'll mean we're married."

Belita backpedaled a second step. "How many miles on it now?"

"157."

"Well," she giggled, "that should give us plenty of time to get to know each other."

So began the orderly's courtship with the princess of Mindanao, generating gossip at both hospitals. My parents were won over by her kindness and charm, and soon I won the favor of Belita's older sister, Cheryl, who gave us the green light to pursue our courtship. Free as any lovebirds, we romanced our way through New England in our little blue sports car, from Rockport to Newport, as well as spinning around to local attractions.

In particular, I remember a Bobby Goldsboro concert—the things one will do for love—at Wahconah Park, right across the street from the hospital, where I became jittery on the long queue.

Belita noticed my uneasiness. "Kevin, what's wrong?"

I wiped my sweaty brow, and confessed, "This is the first time I've ever actually paid to get into this old ballyard. I've always jumped over the right-field wall."

Belita looked at me quizzically, but luckily did not begin to wonder what sort of local riffraff she had fallen in with.

After completing three more summer courses at BCC, and counting on the principle that absence makes the heart grow fonder, I left Belita in August to take a long-anticipated trip to Ireland with my brother, Dermot. That became another defining turn in my life, foreshadowing many journeys in the decades to come. For Belita, I brought back a lovely Aran knit sweater, then went back to the hospital for part-time night duty and entered nursing school on the GI Bill.

Sixty nursing students filled BCC's Melville Hall on Orientation Day, including twelve males, the highest number of men ever accepted in any state nursing program.

"Welcome and congratulations," Mrs. Lawson kicked off the proceedings. "We're a proud institution with high standards, so it's an achievement for you to be sitting here. But do not think you can rest on your laurels. You'll have to work diligently to stay here. We have a record to maintain—for the past ten years, our graduates have scored a 100 percent passing rate on the Nursing Boards, far exceeding many three-year diploma and four-year baccalaureate programs. So, some of you will be weeded out in the process, as we expect ten separations each year. Concentrate on your work, and do your very best. We intend to give you a preparation for a nursing career second to none, but it depends on you to put forth your best effort."

Our assembly shifted uneasily, glancing from side to side, realizing that one in three wouldn't make the grade. Mrs. Lawson continued to show her sterner side, reciting a long list of dos-and-don'ts, and concluding. "Have I made myself clear?"

Our class responded in chorus, "Yes, Mrs. Lawson!"

The nursing chair then introduced the seven starched and stoical women sitting to either side of her, along with their areas of expertise. I wasn't sure how "magnificent" these seven were, but they sure looked as tough as any bunch of gunslingers. In fact, they flashed me right back to my days in Boot Camp. One was as hard-jawed as any drill sergeant. She radiated such command, that right then, and forever after, I thought of her as The Colonel. I'd learn that she had flunked more students than all the others combined.

I sat upright in my chair like an eager recruit, waiting for just one of these professors to crack something like a smile. I'd find out the armed services analogy was not far off, that most nursing schools were fashioned after the military model, stressing rigid discipline throughout the years of training. This standard evolved from the first nursing school established by Florence Nightingale, following her service in the Crimean War.

After we picked up our uniforms, the guys milled around the quadrangle: an eclectic mix of Vietnam vets, conscientious objectors, shop guys laid off from "The GE," and a lone cowhand. The group put me in mind of the Twelve Apostles, plucked from diverse jobs to follow a higher calling, though the similarity probably ended right there.

"You can thank me for getting us all in," boasted an alpha-type named Jeff. "For three years I've been writing to the Board of Regents claiming discrimination, and they finally caved in. But we have a big bull's eye on our backs, because Chief Lawson and her nasty squaws don't want any braves in their tribe."

"Well, we should support one another," was the diffident suggestion of Arthur Ruff, the soft-spoken son of missionary parents who'd grown up in Burma. Arthur was painfully shy, but we'd been in Speech class together, and he credited me with bringing him out of his shell. We'd since become fast friends.

Despite all our efforts, individual and communal, Mrs. Lawson's prediction proved spot-on. Ten students either failed or dropped out that first semester: seven women and three men, including Jeff.

When classes resumed in late January, I missed many of the departed, especially Kathy and Sarah; two energetic, good-hearted women who, by my reckoning, would've made fine nurses. I'd heard rumors about "nurses eating their young," but now I had witnessed it firsthand.

In the meantime, my courtship of the Filipina princess was making headway, and on my 24th birthday, Belita and I were engaged to be married one year hence, after my graduation and before Belita's student visa expired on July 1, 1974. Rather than an engagement ring, I bought her a Baldwin spinet piano, since she loved to play and I figured it was something she couldn't throw back at me. But shortly after our announcement, I found Belita crying on the front steps of Bishop-Clapp, a letter in hand.

Her visa was cut short by a year, following the institution of martial law by President Marcos in the Philippines. It was barely two months till she would have to leave. I brushed away her tears and held her close, but secretly couldn't have been more delighted with the news. I knew just what to do, how to stand up to adversity and right a wrong.

"No problem," I nuzzled up to her reassuringly. "We'll just move our wedding up a year, if that's okay with you?"

Her tear-stained face looked up at me. "You certain?"

I took her back into my arms. "Never been more certain. Heck, we can call it our bonus year together."

Next morning, I called our parish priest to set a date for

the wedding ceremony. Wishing to cut it as close to the deadline as we could, I asked for Saturday, June 30th. Sadly, Father John Roach was booked that day, but offered the 23rd.

"That'll be great, Father, thank you," I replied. However, he called back the following day to say there'd been a mix-up, but the 16th was still available.

"We'll take it, Father. Thank you!" After I hung up the phone, it dawned on me. June 16, 1973, was the day my orderly friend George had predicted I'd get married, and I still had written evidence to prove it.

Soon after, as Belita and I were going over the rushed details of our wedding, I received a phone call from Helen Downey, a Coronary Care nurse at the hospital. Her father, Louie Lamone, was the photographer for the famous artist, Norman Rockwell. He was taking a series of portraits of various ethnic types for the artist to incorporate into a celebration of America's melting pot for its upcoming Bicentennial, and Helen had thought of Belita as a model.

Thrilled to bits, Belita and I drove to Stockbridge the next Saturday, and entered the cluttered studio behind Mr. Rockwell's home. A portrait of John F. Kennedy sat on an easel, and a recent oil painting of Arnold Palmer was drying on a wall. Mr. Rockwell soon came through the door, famous pipe and all, while Belita's picture was being taken by Helen's father.

"Are you here to be photographed?" he asked me.

"Oh, no, Mr. Rockwell. But my fiancée is right now." I pointed to Belita across the room. "She's from the Philippines, and we're going to be married next Saturday."

"What's your name?"

"Kevin O'Hara."

He pulled the pipe from his mouth, to grin at me and shout to Mr. Lamone, "Louie, better take a picture of this Irishman. Can't do a portrait of America without our friends from the Emerald Isle."

Three years later, we finally got to see the finished illustration, "Spirit of America," a double-wide horizontal image filled with diverse portraits in profile, all looking up to the right against the backdrop of a waving American flag. Mr. Rockwell and his wife, Molly, are depicted at the far left, but in the right panel Belita stands out in the foreground, with the artist's signature stenciled against her long black tresses. Just above and behind, he's done equal justice to the long-haired mug of yours truly. To say the least, this is among our most treasured wedding pictures.

We also have many prized images of the wedding day itself, a sunny Saturday with three hundred in attendance, including my nursing class and many friends from the hospital. Since Belita's parents couldn't make the ceremony due to martial law, her uncle, Dr. Jose Timbol, a gifted surgeon practicing in Toronto, gave Belita away. The reception was held on the spacious lawn of my Aunt Nancy's in Lenox, and the music was provided by my orderly pal, Joey Powers, and his Potter Mountain Road Band. Our tireless caterer was none other than my dear boss, Ed Crosby. Whoever would've thought?

Belita and I left the party at six, having made reservations for dinner at the Top of the Hub in Boston. The next morning, we were to fly to San Francisco for our honeymoon. Zooming down the turnpike in my little blue roadster, I suddenly pulled off at a rest stop, hopped out of the car and ran to open Belita's door, to usher her around to the driver's side. "You've got to see this!"

"What? What's going on?"

"Trust me. Just sit here."

"I don't get it. Do you want me to drive?"

"No, just check the odometer. What's our mileage?"

"Oh my gosh, Kevin, it's 10,000 miles! You must have set it?"

"Never touched it, honestly."

"How did you know this would happen?"

"Lucky, I guess."

"Lucky?"

"Yes, I've always been lucky," I enveloped my new bride in my arms. "Lucky to have a loving family. Lucky to have a bunch of great friends. Lucky to have my faith, my health, and working toward my new profession. And, most of all, lucky to have spotted a yellow bow in the cafeteria line attached to the loveliest raven-headed girl in the world."

We kissed a long minute to the bugling horns of passing motorists.

After our first summer of bliss together, I buckled down for my last grueling year at BCC. I squeaked through my lengthy Medical-Surgical rotation, thanks to our warm and wonderful instructor, Pat Fasce, well known as "the mortar between the bricks."

Next, a short rotation at Northampton State Hospital gave me my first taste of psych nursing. The main Gothic Revival building, dating from 1856, looked like the setting for a horror film, a real-life "Snake Pit." Even the surrounding apple trees seemed to gnarl their boughs and sour their fruit in response to the neglect, abuse, and misunderstanding to which mental patients were subjected.

Inside the peeling green walls of the infirmaries, some

patients shuffled about aimlessly, while others muttered to themselves, or occasionally let out a scream or squawk. One male patient worked his fingers beneath a locked window screen, and scraped up pigeon droppings from the outer sill and ate them, an eating disorder known as "pica." My closest classmate, Elaine Allen, spoke for us all when she asked plaintively, "Is this the best we can do for the insane?"

I was surprised to recognize a male patient my age, barely identifiable as an old buddy from Little League days. I called out to Fred, but he glanced at me uncomprehendingly, and lumbered back to his fellow inmates, on their endless trek to nowhere. I couldn't believe that Fred, 24, looked like an old man—missing teeth, sallow skin, balding hair—a mere shadow of the star shortstop I had known twelve years earlier.

The ward nurse verified Fred's identity and explained that he'd suffered his first schizophrenic break during his freshman year in college. He'd been confined to "Old Main" for the past five years. His wizened appearance was my first actual glimpse of how devastating this disease could be.

Back on the BCC campus, I was getting more A's than B's going into my final semester, so it was a shock to receive a dreaded "D" slip from The Colonel at mid-term. I figured it was a mistake and made an appointment to see her. But there was no mistaking her tone or her intention.

"You may have earned good grades, Mr. O'Hara, but after reviewing your Nursing Care Plans, I find that you haven't a clue about Nursing Process. Without clear knowledge of nursing objectives based on scientific principles, why we do what we do, you simply don't qualify as a nurse."

Stunned by her criticism, deep down I knew she was right. For the life of me, I couldn't grasp the concept of the Nursing

Process—assessment, diagnosis, planning, implementation, evaluation —as it struck me as too abstract and theoretical.

Finding myself on the ropes, I countered, "But nursing isn't just a science. Isn't it also a ministry from the heart, an expression of sympathy and compassion?"

The Colonel would have none of it, slapping an open hand on her desk for emphasis. "Tell me, Mr. O'Hara, when has the heart alone, however well-intentioned, cured anyone of disease?"

I knew this was an argument I could never win, so I flinched and submitted. "What can I do in order to pass?"

"You'll be with me for your final rotation in Isolation, is that correct?"

"Yes, ma'am." I had dreaded those last two weeks the entire semester.

"On your last clinical day, you'll hand me a Nursing Care Plan that shows me unequivocally that you have a grasp of the Nursing Process. And we'll see where we go from there." With that, she waved me out of her office.

During my make-or-break Isolation rotation in May, I was assigned to Mr. Daly, a confused old man with septicemia. He was in Room 404, the same room in which I had cared for Julie Potter two years earlier. With able and extensive assistance from classmates Arthur and Elaine, I put together a Nursing Care Plan on Mr. Daly second to none. Arthur also coached me on the reasoning behind my objectives, in case The Colonel grilled me on each.

On the morning of my last clinical day, The Colonel stopped by to collect my Nursing Care Plan. Snapping it out of my hands, she said she'd be back at 2 p.m., with her final decision. Before leaving, she watched in irritation as I donned my isolation garb at the door of Room 404. Her hard glare made me so nervous I clumsily tied my mask strings into my long hair.

"Time you lowered those ears, don't you think?" she snorted before marching away.

At two bells, I made certain everything was shipshape for The Colonel's last decisive round. I propped Mr. Daly comfortably on his pillow, emptied his catheter bag, and placed a fresh pitcher of ice water within his reach. Since it was time to take vitals, I inserted a thermometer into his mouth and wrapped the cuff around his arm to take his blood pressure.

Just as I removed the stethoscope from my ears, I caught sight of The Colonel standing in the doorway. She was scanning the room, searching for the slightest infraction to cast me from the ranks. Anything to round out our graduating class to an even forty. Standing off to one side, I followed her gaffe-seeking gaze with due confidence, certain I'd done a dandy job with Mr. Daly.

Then I spotted it and went green at the gills. I had committed the ultimate cock-up—I had popped a red-tipped rectal thermometer into Mr. Daly's gob rather than an oral blue-tip!

I slumped against the wall and watched in horror as the tell-tale thermometer flashed its cherry beacon around the room. Wracked by guilty apprehension, I thought of blowing the whistle on myself, rather than letting The Colonel discover my glaring violation, which, I was certain, would lead to instant dismissal.

But, just as I cleared my throat to do so, The Colonel motioned me toward her, saying, "Kevin, your Nursing Care Plan is quality work, worthy of our profession. And I do believe Nursing can be a ministry, provided it's based on sound nursing principles. Don't you agree?"

I stood directly in front of her, doing my utmost to obstruct her view. "V-very much," I answered with a full and racing heart.

"Well, then," she smiled, "we'll see you on Graduation Day."

The Colonel about-faced and marched down the long corridor, as I turned and plucked the rectal thermometer from Mr. Daly's mouth. I then dropped to my knees and whispered a thank you to the guardian spirit of Julie Potter, who seemed to abide in this room and to lead me at last into my destined profession.

We were pulling into the Chicago bus station, as I turned to my road buddy and said, "Well, Fat Boy, you wanted to know how I became a nurse. Now you know more than you probably wanted to. What do you make of that?"

Clearly, Ollie had fallen asleep some miles back as I rambled on. But we certainly had covered some ground over one long day—my disorderly progression into a lifelong nursing career.

THURSDAY: PATIENT CARE

I woke with a jolt from another fantastical dream.

"Kevlar! Top o' the morning to you!"

I looked over at Ollie surfing channels on his small TV. "You've been sleeping through the Land of Lincoln, and just missed the impressive skyline of Springfield, not to mention a buddy of yours named Charlie."

Head still swirling, I slowly gathered my senses. "Charlie? Oh, Charlie Mendes. Did he say anything?"

"Said he'd be back later. Seems like a nice guy."

Noticing my breakfast tray, I reached for a bite of cold toast. "Charlie's a great guy. He's run the activities program on Jones Three since it opened twenty-two years ago. Hey, Fat Boy, do me a favor and tell me what my catheter bag looks like?"

He glanced down at the receptacle hanging beside my bed. "Still red, I'm afraid."

"Same red as yesterday, or more pinkish?"

"Same red, unless you want me to lie."

I let out a groan, "Not getting out of here today." Still

trying to orient myself, I glanced at the wall clock and saw it was just before eight in the morning. "How about you, Fat Boy? How you doing?"

"Counting the minutes till my next Dilaudid, what else? I'm just glad Nancy Nurse isn't working today. She's always questioning my pain level. 'Hey, look,' I want to say to her, 'I've got a pump draining fluid out of my left lung, a crushed leg held together by an Erector Set, and a mysterious abdominal bleed. So you tell me!'"

He winced as he tried to look my way, "As a nurse, were you so stingy with the meds?"

"On the contrary. Nurse Hatchet often called me Pez Nurse."

"You mean, like the candy?"

"Yep. She even presented me with an actual Pez dispenser, crowned by a nurse's capped head: the only redheaded nurse I could ever call my own."

Fat Boy's merriment brought on a coughing spasm. "Damn, Kevlar, I've told you not to make me laugh."

"Sorry to be so amusing. Sometimes I just can't help myself. But to answer your question, I was never stingy with prescribed pills unless the patient was clearly med-seeking. In fact, I rarely told anyone to punch a pillow, hug a stuffed animal, or hit the showers. Drugs generally proved to be the most reliable intervention, aside from normal human contact."

I grappled my pillow free of the bed rail, and buried my head in it, suddenly very tired again.

"Hey, what are you doing? Floating away on me already?"

"Sorry, gotta go, my eyelids feel like curtain weights."

"So I guess I'll ask our bus driver to pull over until you wake up."

"Whatever, Fat Boy. Just wake me if Charlie stops by again."

"Sure thing," came a distant voice, as I slipped into a dream that unspooled in my head like a classic movie, with Charlie playing the starring role . . .

"Courtyard to Jones Three."

I pulled the walkie-talkie from my pocket, "Go ahead, Charlie."

"Kev, we're coming up. Can you meet us at the back door?"

"You bet."

I waited at the top of our landing, listening to the shuffling feet and muttering voices ascending the courtyard from three flights below. Patients arrived at the door, huffing and puffing, smokers and non-smokers alike. Charlie, a young man of Portuguese descent, stood at the rear after securing the courtyard gates below.

"Everyone up?"

I counted on my fingers, "Yep, all seven of 'em."

Charlie bonked me with the plastic cigarette bin. "Nine, you lunkhead. Always gotta be a wise guy, don't you? Now make yourself useful and help me round up the crew for morning group."

I walked into the kitchen and cupped my hands like a megaphone. "Nine o'clock, everyone. Charlie's Group!"

Charlie turned on his way to open up the conference room, "Come on, Kev, get it right. It's not my group, it's Community Meeting."

I re-cupped my hands: "Community Meeting, everybody!"

Being both medication and milieu nurse, I did my best to attend this first official assembly of the day, as I found it a valuable barometer of the goings-on of the floor. After my second announcement, I rounded up a few stragglers, much like a sheepdog rounding up an errant flock.

At nine sharp, Charlie took a deep breath in preparation for the certain surprises that lay ahead, and grabbed the group's attention, "Good morning, everyone! Glad to see all of you here on this beautiful morning."

A medley of grunts, groans, and giddy good cheer filled the spacious room of straight-back chairs arranged in a circle, on which patients had draped themselves in erratic postures, an ill-sorted lifeboat of survivors from the shipwreck of life. "Good morning, Charlie."

Sunlight streamed through the room's high, metal-screened windows that offered a stunning view of nearby Bishop-Clapp, the hospital's handsome Redstone Victorian building, built in 1877, to train and board nursing students. A flock of pigeons, nesting in the eaves of that storied infirmary, wheeled through the summery sky in flecks of black, white, and gray; their wing-claps audible in the clear morning air, seemingly catching the attention of no one but myself.

Nine of fifteen patients were in attendance, a good turn-out considering the acuity—or mental clarity—of our current clients. I sat between Blanche and Penelope, two of my perennial favorites. Blanche, an elderly woman confined to a wheel-chair, suffered from emphysema and chronic anxiety, the two conditions a common tandem. I had made a hit with her on Day One after she became embarrassed when fellow patients noticed her medication—three red capsules—doing somersaults in her tremulous hand. "Oh, look," I announced to the curious onlookers, "Mexican jumping beans!" Since that first wisecrack, Blanche had found me good company.

Penelope, or Penny, a roly-poly single woman in her 40s, had a comical, cherubic face that would make a perfect bobblehead doll. However, she'd often go into tantrums and pout for long periods of time, thus creating her infamous "bubby face." She wore open sandals due to a stubborn fungal toe infection, a condition so severe that I spent ten minutes each morning applying an array of ointments to her feet.

"How are my piggies doing?" she'd asked me that morning.

"They're improving, slow but sure."

"Will I ever be able to stand on my tippy-toes again?"

"For sure. But I wouldn't think of auditioning for Swan Lake anytime soon."

Her angelic countenance switched into her inglorious bubby face.

"I'm just saying," I quickly backtracked, "Believe me, your little piggies will soon be going to market. But right now, I'm afraid they'll have to stay at home."

After everyone in attendance had introduced themselves, Charlie kicked the ball into play. "Today is Wednesday, June 25th, and you may know that the Red Sox lost again last night, but still remain seven games back in the AL East."

Charlie looked around to see nine goose eggs staring blankly in return.

"Okay, no baseball fans," he shrugged with a laugh. "Moving right along, Dr. David Raskin is our psychiatrist today, and Ceil Roosa is our charge nurse. For those of us present, JoAnne Provost will be working with Blanche, Allison and Penelope. Rob Mickle is working with Robin, Uncle Rupert, Larry, and Gustav. And Kevin here, our illustrious Pez Nurse, will be working with Percy and Jake."

I acknowledged my two charges with a friendly but

cautious nod.

Percy, a well-dressed gray-haired gentleman, was a retired Ivy League professor, the most brilliant man to ever grace our unit. He had kept his bipolar illness in check for decades, thanks to Lithium and his wife's loving care. But following her untimely death, he dropped his Lithium for bourbon, which not only inflamed his illness, but, for some reason, spawned caustic behavior toward all women. Indeed, Percy boasted of being the floor's "resident bipolar misogynist."

Percy had been more labile of late, his moods switching from euphoria to depression on a dime. When level-minded, he was most amiable, living up to his name, Percival, the noblest of the Knights of the Round Table. During one tranquil stretch, I asked him what one book I should read before I die. Without hesitation, he replied, "*The Eve of St. Agnes*, by John Keats."

Jake, still actively detoxing, was an irritable poly-substance abuser. His idea of a Friday night buzz consisted of a 12-pack of beer, an eight-ball of coke, and a few 'Vico-mints' to take the edge off. A known troublemaker, he was deemed a "pod-king," the unofficial term on our unit reserved for Alpha-like males most likely to act out physically.

Ceil often assigned me to such volatile patients. Being the self-designated donkey nurse, I had gained the perilous reputation of having a knack for "defusing hotheads."

After announcing the day's assignments, Charlie reported on the current weather, patient chores, and community issues. A typical daily complaint was aired hotly by females, imploring males to clean up their "dribbles" after using the co-ed bathrooms.

"Okay," trumpeted Charlie, "let's jump right in to

everyone's favorite topic, 'This Day in History.'"

Jake interrupted, "We're not going to get quizzed on this later, are we?"

"No, this is just fun, informative stuff," Charlie assured him.

Jake leaned in threateningly toward Charlie, "You sure?"

Charlie nodded decisively, "Positive."

"Well," Jake spewed, "some jerko in the ED asked me a slew of questions, and that's probably why I'm here and not at McGee Detox where I belong. Out of the blue, he asked me to name the last five presidents! How the hell do I know? I don't even vote."

Professor Percy shook his head in disbelief, "My God, young man, you boast of such ignorance. You mean you don't know the names of our famous leaders of the free world, during your own lifetime?"

Jake fired back, "No! Do you, asshole?"

"Not only those five, but the 39 who preceded them," answered the professor. "I could probably name their First Ladies, too, except for the 15th, James Buchanan, who despite his reputation as the worst of the lot, was smart enough to never marry."

"Whoopee shit! Go to the head of the class."

The professor calmly retorted, "I think it's safe to say I'm already at the head of this particular class. That's indisputable."

"Yeah, well, Mister Professor," chided Jake, "did you hear about the constipated mathematician?"

"No, I don't believe I have."

"Well, good news. He was able to work it out with a pencil!"

The professor sat unfazed, though titters circled the room, especially from the women who'd been objects of the professor's scorn in the past.

Charlie quelled the group's amusement with a simple lift of his hand, "All right, everyone, calm down, please."

Abruptly, Uncle Rupert, our bearish but genial older chronic, lifted his moistened index finger to the sky and proclaimed, "There's one thing neither President nor First Lady has ever seen, and that's squirrel poop."

Jake rocketed off his seat, "Squirrel poop! What the hell has that got to do with anything? This place is absolute bullshit. I gotta get to McGee."

Charlie gave Jake a warning glance, "Watch your language, Jake, or I'll have to ask you to leave the group."

Allison, a pale and ghostly woman in her 30's, badgered chronically by inner voices, roused from her torpor, "Yeah, don't you see there are ladies present."

Percy shifted his ire from one target to another. "Ladies present, Allison? *That* is a debatable proposition."

Verbal jabs filled the room, but this time Charlie remained silent, unruffled by the ruckus. He allowed patients to vent, but remained vigilant for any overstepping of bounds. He behaved much like a seasoned TV daytime host amongst unruly guests. Having worked with Charlie for so many years, I knew his every nuance. He was brilliant in allowing patients to express themselves, offering leniency, yet he could put his foot down when comments became willful or vindictive. His confident posture in the presence of enraged pod-kings like Jake was also commendable, though it helped to have earned a third-degree black belt in Aikido.

At last, after everyone had their say and settled down, Charlie continued, "Okay, okay, let's finally get around to This Day in History. Here's a good one. On this day in 1178, five

Canterbury monks reported to their abbot that they had seen an explosion on the moon."

"Probably drinking too much moonshine," laughed Robin, a 20-year old with a marginal IQ, whose doughy face was blotched with rosacea. She was admitted this time around after losing her best friend of ten years, a goldfish named Crispy.

Astoundingly, Robin had bought Crispy for a dime at the Fin and Feather, half her lifetime ago. It grew to be 10 inches long—"an inch for a penny for every year"—she'd fondly say, and had kept it in its original bowl by her bathroom window. She explained how Crispy would swim wildly around its bowl every time she entered the bathroom. In time, Robin changed the small bowl for a larger one, thinking Crispy would appreciate the added space. But Crispy began to refuse his evening flake, and soon listed belly-up white, until she returned him to his original glass dome, whereupon his sinking spirits lifted.

Sadly, just that past week, Robin found her longtime companion dead on the bathroom floor, having evidently jumped clear from its bowl. Despite her tragic loss, she continued to share her favorite joke, "How do you tune a fish?"

"How?" we'd ask her, though we all knew the punch line.

She'd squeal out the answer as if for the first time, "It all depends on the scales, you stupids!"

As Charlie continued to share historical facts, I reflected on the numerous admissions that had been precipitated by the loss of a beloved pet over the years—cats and dogs, mostly. Actually, a young schizophrenic recently had been admitted after her social worker discovered she had baked her parakeet in a microwave. When asked why, the poor woman sullenly replied, "I was afraid it would fly away."

Another client had babysat two cockatoos for a friend on vacation. Feeling sorry for the white-feathered pair cooped up in their birdcage the long day, he released them to fly around the house. Regrettably, one flew out an open window.

"Why didn't you just go and buy another one?" someone asked. "Cockatoos all look alike."

"I thought of that," said our distraught patient, "but it'd taken the owner nine months to teach it to say, 'Praise the Lord!' How could I accomplish that in two days?"

A loud, unmuffled belch from Uncle Rupert brought my attention back to the group.

"In 1630," went on Charlie, "the fork was introduced to American dining by Governor Winthrop."

Robin, exhibiting an unusual display of good humor, chimed in again, "Boy, those pilgrims must've been really sick of using their fingers!"

"I guess so," said Charlie, "Or maybe spoons. Or even knives. You might have heard the verse that goes, *'I eat my peas with honey/I've done it all my life/It makes my peas taste funny/But it keeps them on my knife.'*"

"Oh, that's funny, Charlie," laughed an appreciative Allison, bringing a taint of color to her pasty cheeks.

Charlie smiled and continued, "In 1798, the U.S. passed the Alien and Sedition Act to give President Adams the authority to deport dangerous aliens."

Charlie and I winced at the very mention of the "Alien" word, knowing the group's direction would shortly be headed for the Milky Way. We looked over at Larry, a barrel-chested carpenter in his 40s, docile and disinterested prior to the utterance, admitted a week earlier after ranting to a female bank teller how he'd been taken aboard a UFO to have a certain bodily fluid drained. He catapulted off his chair, eyes beam-ing, "Sorry to inform all you evangelicals," he gushed, "but Bible stories are actually alien stories. Angels and fiery chari-ots are simply ancient astronauts and their spacecraft. Not to knock the Old Testament, but the Ark of the Covenant was a communication device set up by star-beings to literally 'Call Home.'"

Larry's copy of *Chariots of the Gods*, perpetually perched on his lap, was dog-eared, thickly annotated, and overstuffed with newspaper clippings on UFO sightings dating back years.

"How do you think acupuncture came around?" he ram-bled. "Chinese people are smart, real smart, but do you really think they were smart enough to know about conduits and meridians—our bodily energy channels—in 2,000 B.C.? And why do you think our government covered up the epochal events at Roswell, New Mexico in 1947? Because a UFO crash-landed there, with aliens aboard!"

Larry babbled on, fact after factoid. Nevertheless, not one person in the room would dismiss his statements as simple drivel.

"Believe me," Larry expounded, "our collected wisdom stems solely from the gifts of 'grays.' Why, even Socrates . . . "

Startled by Larry's outburst, the group's attention remained focused throughout his impassioned rant. When he finally paused from sheer exhaustion, the others chimed in with their own mysterious and otherworldly encounters.

"The TV sends me private messages all the time," shared Allison. "I wonder if that could be the grays talking?"

"I see pedestrian ghosts," Gus stirred from his profound lethargy. "Do you suppose the aliens come down and walk around Pittsfield sometimes?"

"I hear teeny, tiny voices," blurted Penny. "Could that be them?"

Jake spat out, "I see pink elephants all the time, but they ain't no damn aliens."

Said Percy, "Nonsense. All arrant nonsense."

After Larry had laid out his theories, Charlie thanked him for both his input and expertise on infinite matters, without giving his beliefs either credence or censure. "Okay, moving right along. On this date in 1876, Colonel Custer and the 7th Cavalry were wiped out by Sioux and Cheyenne braves at the Battle of Little Bighorn."

Percy shook his head in sad contemplation, "He should've listened to his Crow scouts. But, no, Custer was too arrogant, even though he'd graduated last in his class at West Point. Imagine his foolishness: 300 soldiers going up against a band of 3,000 braves defending their rightful homeland. One of the few survivors was one of Custer's officers' horses, ironically named Comanche. Everyone ought to read Evan Connell's classic, *Son of the Morning Star*."

"Yap! Yap! Yap!" spat Jake. "Can somebody put a muzzle on this guy?"

Undaunted, Charlie carried on. "Hmm, here's an odd one. On this day in 1977, Roy Sullivan, a ranger at Shenandoah National Park in Virginia, was struck by lightning for—get this—the seventh time."

"By jiminy!" exclaimed Uncle Rupert, as though hit by lightning himself. "He must've been going 'round waving Governor Winthrop's forks in the air."

Penelope chimed in, "Hit by a fork of lightning!"

"And Custer got the big fork, too," giggled Allison. "'Stick a fork in 'em!' squawked Crazy Horse, 'He's finished!'"

"You can joke all you like, but it's a true story," asserted the professor. "I remember reading about it at the time. Even made the Guinness Book of World Records. He's known as the 'human lightning rod.' Four or five times, it set his hair on fire. People started avoiding him when thunder rolled, and his wife got struck once while hanging out the wash next to him. Pity the old bitch survived. Sullivan wound up dead in bed with her, shot himself, or so they say. Appears that Thor was targeting him all along."

Jake, sneering, asked, "Who the hell's Thor?"

The professor buried his face in his hands and pretended to weep like a child. Slowly, he parted his fingers and peered across at Jake. "You mean to tell me that you've never heard of the Norse god who wields his famous hammer to bang out thunder and lightning?"

Jake pleaded to Charlie, "Can I please punch this guy's lights out?"

Charlie put his foot down this time, in fear they might go fisticuffs: "There will be no physical contact of any kind. Verbal disagreement is permissible, but within bounds."

Percy continued to provoke, making gestures as if firing lightning bolts at our pod-king.

"Cool it, Percy! I mean it. Do you want to end up in the Quiet Room again?"

"Quiet can be a delicious respite from this madhouse," said Percy.

Percy had been confined so often to the Quiet Room that he actually kept his spare pillow in there. In fact, Charlie and I had directed him to the QR only days before. It started innocently enough, with Percy, in the kitchen, proudly showing off his 'five-gallon' pin—a handsome gold pin shaped like a blood drop—recently awarded to him by the American Red Cross.

"Wow!" Robin had gasped, "You gave five gallons of blood! Instead of one doughnut, you should've gotten the whole box!"

Percy couldn't let such a ripe opportunity slip by, especially when it entailed a vulnerable young female.

"I've donated five gallons of blood in my lifetime, you half-wit, not in one sitting. The loss of a quart of blood would put anyone in shock! How old are you, anyway?"

Robin recoiled, "Twenty."

"Twenty!" Percy exclaimed, "I have a nephew, 20, taking pre-med at Fordham University. Do you think he'd ever utter something so profoundly ignorant to his lecturers?"

Hearing the professor's uproar, Charlie and I had rushed out to the kitchen to intervene. "Okay, Percy, cool it. Robin gets the message."

Percy, still frothing at the bit, continued to spit insults at Robin as though from a Gatling gun. "My God, such stupidity! What, pray tell, was your favorite subject in school, Pick-up Sticks? I weigh 160 pounds and carry approximately ten pints of blood. Why, five gallons would make up 30 percent of my total body weight," he swiftly calculated. "Damn, I'd be a walking bloodmobile!"

Meanwhile, back in Community Meeting, unflappable Charlie soldiered on, though his morning group was fraying at the edges. Since kick-off, three patients had left the room, two had scuttled in, and Jake was finally ejected following a burst of profanity that would've scorched the ears off a deaf nun.

"Now to today's birthdays," announced Charlie. "None of us here as far as I know. Well, here's one: George Orwell, born in 1903, the British author of the classic novels *Animal*

Farm and *1984*."

Our professor emeritus took special interest in the topic, "I've always thought that *1984* had one of the best opening lines in all of English literature, 'It was a bright cold day in April, and the clocks were striking 13.'"

Befuddled, Penelope looked directly at the professor, though her cream-covered toes had retreated into little fleshy balls, "That doesn't make any sense. Clocks only go up to twelve."

"Listen, my dear, dunderhead Penelope. That sentence immediately sets the tone and theme of the book, the mystery, and the menace. It combines the normal with the abnormal, creating a sense of disturbing dislocation. We know immediately that 'the time is out of joint.'"

Minding attentively to the professor's discourse, Allison abruptly left the room, only to return with a poster board on which she had pasted a collage of luxury watch advertisements.

"Speaking of time," she waved the poster in front of Percy, "every watch ad I cut out from magazines in yesterday's art group—Fortis, TeNo, Wittnauer, Bulgari, Rolex—all point to ten after ten. Why is that, Mr. Know-It-All?"

Percy, apparently bored, glanced at the poster, "Ten after ten is how most watches are advertised. It simply gives the timepiece an elegant look."

He snatched the poster from her grasp and pointed out a Rolex ad. "See how the two hands frame the watch's signature trademark and, at the same time, remain clear of its date window? Even the actual time ten after ten is perfect; not too early, not too late, time in the morning, time at night. You don't need to work on Madison Avenue to see its appeal."

Dumbstruck, Allison gazed admiringly at the professor,

"I've lived on this planet for 37 years, and I've never noticed that most wristwatch ads point to 10:10."

Rudely, the professor tossed the poster back at her, "It may seem like a lot to those who know little, but to me, it's just common sense. Something you women sorely lack."

Blanche spoke up, as if coming out of a trance.

"The clock of life is wound but once
No one has the power
To know just when that clock will stop,
At late or early hour."

"Why, Blanche, thank you for that lovely contribution," said Charlie. "Anyone else have something to add?"

Robin piped up, her rosacea in full bloom. "I once worked at a clock factory but got fired. Guess why?"

"Why?" we all asked.

She burst into laughter, "For making lots of faces, you stupids!"

Of course, no morning group was complete without Nurse Lite throwing a few bacon strips onto the sizzling pan.

"I had an odd realization about the relativity of time back in March."

"Tell us, oh bearded one," said Percy, with a profound and lengthy, audible yawn.

"I was at my niece's basketball game, and there was a time-out just before the end of the third quarter. And in that pause, it came to me that was exactly the point I'd reached in my own life."

"Okay."

"So, I said, 'Holy Cow. That's me. That's my age!'"

"How so, pray tell?"

"I'm going on 60. Get it?"

"Not yet, but I'm trying, honestly."

"Say I live to be 80, right? Every quarter is 20 years. Age 20, first quarter, age 40, second quarter, age 60 . . . "

Percy's eyebrows disappeared into his hairline, "Now it's coming 'round."

"See, I'm just about to start my last quarter. Time is running out on me."

"Cheer up," giggled Penny, "maybe your game will go into overtime."

"Yeah," said Allison. "Lots of people live to be a hundred. That's a whole 'nother quarter!"

"Maybe we'll all get lucky and you'll just foul out," grumbled Percy.

"First you're a cube, then you're a square, then you're dead," blurted Uncle Rupert.

Charlie looked at me with dry amusement, "Wow. Thanks again, Kevin, for provoking *so* much. And speaking of time, it's time to wrap up. Anyone leaving us today?"

Gustav, our poor toothless chronic, raised his hand half-mast.

Jake, who'd been hovering outside the door, poked his head in, "How the hell can he be leaving, and me still stuck here? He's nuttier than a Payday!"

Charlie paid no mind to the exiled group member, and brandished the book of quotations with which he always closed the meeting. "So Gus, before you go, pick a number from one to 100."

Gus pondered his choice a long moment.

The professor griped, "Pick a number already, this isn't a quadratic equation."

"Sixty-nine!" shouted Jake from the doorway.

"Thirteen," chimed Allison.

"Ten, I guess," Gustav offered flatly.

Charlie thumbed to the page, "Okay, our quote for the day comes from the Irish playwright, George Bernard Shaw, 'A happy family is but an earlier Heaven.'"

"Earlier Heaven," muttered Allison, "My family was but an earlier Hell."

Charlie closed the book, thus signaling the conclusion of another community meeting.

"Next up, Sensory Room at 10:15," he called to patients as they scurried out the door.

Penelope pushed Blanche's wheelchair up the corridor, "Oh, goodie, the Sensory Room is my favorite group of the day."

The professor followed at her heels, "Why is that?"

"Because we can help Robin feed the fish in the aquarium, listen to ocean wave music, and lie on green beanbags the size of baby elephants. It's so peaceful I just let my mind go duh."

"Duh," repeated the professor, "I surmise that 'duh' is your mind's natural state."

Penelope stopped dead in her tracks and stamped her feet in annoyance, making her little piggies squeal. She then delivered a verbal snub as close to cursing as one is ever likely to hear from a bobble-headed doll sporting a bubby face.

"Oh, Percy, go poke your nose in the Poconos!"

* * *

Riding through the day on waves of pain, and troughs of opiate relief, I bobbed to the surface once again, and reached for the call button. By the time I was floating peacefully again,

Charlie came back to visit, and we had a good laugh over my vivid cinematic dream, and other memories of our two decades together on Jones Three.

When Charlie went on his way, I turned to see Ollie in conversation with our nurse, rattling pills in his med cup, "What's this red one here?"

"That's Colace, a stool softener. We give it to patients on opiates, such as yourself."

He turned to me, "Should I take it?"

"I would, unless you want to start passing billiard balls."

Ollie nodded to the nurse with a smile and took his meds with a sip of water. Duty done, and nurse departed, he thought a moment and then asked, "Hey, Kevlar, you've been a nurse for what, thirty-some years? How many pills do you figure you've dished out in your career?"

"More and more over the years, that's for sure. But I figured it out roughly not too long ago, pills-per-patient-per-day, and I came up with over a quarter million."

Fat Boy gawked at me in disbelief, "A quarter-million pills? No way!"

"It's the truth," I answered. "Before I switched to my weekend schedule, I'd been the designated med nurse for nearly 20 years. Now, figure our average patient is on five pills a day. Add a few PRN's, and we're talking 60 pills a day among an average daily census of 12 patients. During that stretch, I was working about 230 days a year. Sixty times 230 is what, 13,800. Multiply that by 20 years and, presto, we're looking at a whopping 276,000 pills."

"Wow, what are you, some kind of a math whiz?"

"I play darts, Ollie, and our breed is known for two things; good arithmetic skills and drinking better beer. By the way, we recently had one unfortunate woman taking 33 pills a day."

"Thirty-three pills! She probably didn't even need to eat. Just think of the cost alone."

"Yep, talk about big numbers. There are blockbuster anti-psychotics and anti-depressants that gross five billion dollars a year, in an overall market of something like sixty billion. Pill-pushing is what psychiatry has become."

"But do they really do any good? I once knew a woman on wacky pills who grew a beard, and another guy who grew breasts."

"My traveling friend, there's a new line of medication with fewer side effects called neurolyptics, far better than the old standbys like Thorazine and Haldol, introduced way back in the '50s."

"The notorious chemical jackets?"

"You got it. But those two antipsychotics helped empty out our state's institutions. Without them, patients would still be living unimaginable lives."

"They still in use?"

"Yep. In fact, Haldol is still a first-line of treatment in some cases. But you have to keep an eye out for bad reactions. The most dangerous side effect is NMS—neuroleptic malignant syndrome—which can be fatal. We've had a few close calls over the years, but the ICU folk literally brought our patients back from the brink. Good as new, too.

"But the most frightful-looking side effect of Haldol is oculogyric crisis. That's when a patient's eyes rise high in their sockets. Add a writhing jaw, twisting torso, contorted limbs, and poof, the patient looks like Regan in the movie, *The Exorcist*. Fortunately, there's a ready antidote, Cogentin, that quickly reverses the symptoms. Recovery is so swift that you feel like you've performed a successful exorcism."

"Too bad about those side effects."

"Yes, but drugs are more humane than the barbaric treatments tried over the years."

"Like what?"

"Fat Boy, treatment of the mentally-ill has been a real horror show for centuries, with one prescribed physical abuse after another, and none of them doing any good. Bleeding, purging, blistering, confinement in hideous contraptions. Even while other forms of medical knowledge advanced to become actual cures, treatment of the unstable person seemed more like torture; so-called hydrotherapy, hypothermia, insulin-induced comas, lobotomies."

"Ah, the old ice pick through the eye socket."

"True enough, though eventually they dressed it up as neurosurgery."

"Lobotomies didn't really work, did they?"

"Depends on the result you were looking for. It certainly made patients less violent and more manageable. There were thousands of such operations back before my time, but I saw the results at the beginning of my career, when we got patients who'd been released in droves from Northampton State Hospital, wearing the telltale scars on their forehead, like they'd been kicked in the head by a shod horse. Fortunately, the discovery of Thorazine put an end to that brutal treatment, as well as shutting down those houses of horror.

"Let me give you an example of how strong Thorazine is. We had a chessmaster on the ward, and two hours after his morning dose—at the height of the pill's potency—I could beat him in four moves, 'fool's mate' they call it."

"That's wrong, O'Hara, real wrong."

"It was his idea. But, boy, would he whomp my ass any other time of the day."

"What about shock treatment, like in that Jack Nicholson movie. They still use it?"

"Yes, but that's been tidied up too. Now it's called ECT, for Electro-Convulsive Therapy. Has a nicer ring, don't you think?"

Ollie screwed up his face, "Not really. Is it effective?"

"Like everything else, sometimes yes, sometimes no. I've seen it work on some kinds of intractable depression, but I've seen it fail a lot, too. Today it's quite different from that movie version, or in my early days on Jones Two. No more flopping around like a fish out of water. Voltage is also better controlled, and patients are given muscle relaxants beforehand."

"How does it work?"

"Truth be told, nobody knows. Just a jolt to the system, like jump-starting a car, or rattling a pan of marbles so they settle differently."

"Wow, Kevlar, that's some 21st-century scientific explanation. I can just see some hotshot shrink telling his depressed patient, 'No worries, sir, we're just going to rattle 'round your marbles with a few jolts of electricity.' And what are the side effects of that?"

"Slight headache afterward and temporary amnesia. I'd often tell a patient a joke before their treatment, and tell them the same joke after, and they'd laugh as if hearing it for the first time. Two laughs for the price of one. But if I showed them where I put their cigarettes, they'd never forget after their treatment. Interesting, huh?"

"Addiction never forgets. I'm afraid I know a thing or two about that. Tell me one more thing—what about Freudian psycho analysis, shrinks still pushing that line of nonsense?"

"That approach has certainly fallen out of favor since its heyday. Not a lot of one-to-one talk therapy going on these days. Insurance companies don't want to pay for it, for one thing. And many pill-oriented psychiatrists today don't hold as much reverence for Dr. Fraud, as he's now sometimes called."

At that point, a nurse came in to interrupt our conversation and check on our well-being. Once settled again, Ollie continued inquisitively, "So, of those tens of thousands of pills you've dispensed, how many mistakes have you made?"

"Three or four."

"C'mon, three or four! That you know of, right?"

"Oh, believe me, you'd know, sooner or later. Thankfully, my errors never sent anyone to ICU or Room 500, though I had a few close calls."

Ollie struggled to adjust his pillow. "Go on, out with it. Spill the beans."

"Okay, if you insist, but these stories don't put me in a flattering light. Gotta go way back to my first memorable mistake, not so much a med error, as getting careless after the fact. We had a young female patient, Dolly, with a dubious diagnosis of schizophrenia, but a for-real eating disorder. Pretty girl, but ravaged by anorexia, and looked like someone near the end of a prolonged hunger strike. She'd been in and out of hospitals throughout her teen years, when she became institutionalized, and learned to become a master manipulator. She was also known to be wild at times, so her scrawny butt cheeks were pockmarked and leathery from receiving countless injections to sedate her.

"The funny thing is, she could be a real charmer. Years later, I'm delighted to say, she made a startling recovery."

"That's good to hear. But how did she survive on your floor?"

"It wasn't easy, because she was so strong-willed that we failed miserably to regulate her diet. When her weight dropped below 80 pounds, we had standing orders to start an IV, as well as to force-feed her. This entailed having a doctor insert a nasogastric tube through her nose to her stomach. Of course, she'd fight us tooth and nail—who'd imagine that a skeleton could be so strong?—that we had to put her in wrist and ankle restraints so she couldn't pull out her IV and feeding tube. Believe me, it was an agonizing experience for all involved."

"Sounds terrible. So how did you mess up her meds?"

"At the time, her weight was hovering around 80 pounds, and her labs came back showing poor kidney function due to dehydration. So she was given yet another ultimatum—eat willingly today or be force-fed tomorrow.

"Working a double-shift that day, I took Dolly as an assignment, and had dreamt up a few off-the-wall interventions that might entice her to eat. The thing was, once she started to munch on anything, however small—a grape or a Hershey's Kiss—she'd keep it up, and her intake would remain steady for a while. First thing that morning, I invited her to play a game of pool."

"Wait a minute," interrupted Ollie. "You had a pool table on your nut ward."

"Yep."

"With real billiard balls and cue sticks?"

"For years, Fat Boy, and without incident, until the Department of Mental Health spotted it during an annual inspection, and out the door it went. Anyhow, when Dolly agreed to play, instead of stripes and solids, I racked up apples and oranges. She got a kick out of my prank and our eccentric little game, but I still couldn't get her to eat, even after she sniffed the tangy effervescence of a peeled orange.

"Later that morning, while passing pills, I handed her a medicine cup full of M&M's. She laughed again, but still no dice. In the afternoon, I delivered a Mail o' Gram to her room marked Special Delivery. Again she chuckled as a graham cracker fell out of the envelope, but still she didn't bite.

"Next thing I knew, I was called into the psychiatrists' office. He'd gotten wind of my antics and read me the riot act, calling my interventions unprofessional and counterproductive. I meekly replied that no other treatment had worked, and at least I was showing her that we cared. But he just gave me a steely glare, as if to say how I dare question his superior judgment.

"I was pretty green at the job, so you can imagine how I felt. But I didn't give up, and at nine o'clock that evening, after I'd given Dolly her potent prescribed sedative, Placidyl, I made one final plea for her to eat in order to avoid the inevitable showdown in the morning.

"Much to my surprise, she relented with a smile and asked for a large bowl of Rice Krispies. I immediately dashed down to the kitchen, grabbed a fruit bowl, and filled it with milk and cereal to the brim. When I returned to her room, I raised the head of her bed, and placed the large bowl on the bedstand in front of her. There I watched happily as she gobbled up spoonful after spoonful.

"I soon left her at it, not wishing to disturb, and went about distributing my nighttime meds to the other patients. As you can imagine, my head was in the clouds, thinking of how our esteemed psychiatrist would be eating crow next morning."

"A hero, after all!"

"I thought so, too. But then, ten minutes later, I was at the end of the hall when my heart did a backflip. It suddenly struck me that I had left a heavily medicated Dolly tottering over a deep bowl of cereal. I bolted to her room where, holy bejaysus, I found her face flat in the bowl, submerged up to her ears in milk."

"Dead?"

"Can't say she was in the land of the living."

"Damn!" gasped Ollie, "What did you do?"

"Do? I pulled her head out of the bowl, fingered the cereal out of her mouth, and started mouth-to-mouth resuscitation. Just when I thought I'd lost her, Dolly coughed, sputtered, and let out a sweet, sugary burp. Then she opened her doe-like eyes, nuzzled her head up against my chest, and fell asleep."

"You must've been shitting bricks."

"Fat Boy, I could've built a 20-room schoolhouse. Tell you one thing, it was a long time before I ate Rice Krispies again."

Ollie chortled, "Gives a whole new meaning to Snap, Crackle and Pop. Did she eat enough to avoid her forced feeding the next day?"

"More than enough! Next morning, when our psychiatrist made his rounds, he watched cheerfully from the kitchen doorway as Dolly polished off a stack of pancakes."

"Did she remember anything about nearly croaking to death?"

"Nope."

"No signs of brain damage?"

"Naw. I pulled her out in time."

"You report it?"

"And muddy my pristine waters with the doctor? No way!

He actually praised me at Grand Rounds. However, I did think of writing an article under a pseudonym for RN Magazine, so other nurses might learn from my blunder. The working title: *'Near Drowning on Lake Placidyl.'*"

"You're whacked, O'Hara. Seriously whacked."

"Maybe so. But I was giddy with relief. I certainly dodged a bullet that time, early in my career, too. If Dolly had died, I would've lost my job, my nursing license, and been rightfully sued for negligence by her family for leaving her narc-filled head nodding over a deep bowl of milk. Worst of all, I would've carried Dolly's tragic death to my grave."

I opened a pack of Fig Newtons left over from my lunch tray.

"Hey, how about the others?"

I tossed him the packet.

He tossed them back. "Not those, you idiot, your other mistakes."

I took a deep, painful breath and resumed my confession, "Okay, fast forward ten years ago to Jones Three. A guy named Frank, a bonafide hothead, came to the nurses' station and asked for his meds. So I said, 'Got 'em right here, Frank.' He swallows the five capsules, hands me back the empty med cup, and walks away. A second later, I dropped to my chair as if sucker-punched by Manny Pacquiao. 'Holy Moly,' I gasped, 'those weren't Frank's pills, they were Justin's.'"

"How did you mess that up? Too much Guinness the night before?"

"I haven't a clue. Maybe a misfired synapse, or just a statistical inevitability?"

"Could they have killed him?"

"No, but he wouldn't be tying his own shoes for a while.

So I'm a mess, right, and go chasing after him, bracing myself for one royal egg-beating. 'Frank,' I say, 'I'm terribly sorry, but I just gave you the wrong pills.' Instead of getting angry, he calmly replied, 'Yeah, they didn't look like my usual ones.'

"So I answer, 'Frank, I'm afraid you'll have to drink some ipecac to vomit them up.' And he says, 'Naw, I'll just toss 'em up the old-fashioned way, with my fingers here.'

"With two digits raised, he walked into the bathroom, upchucked, and pointed at the toilet, saying, 'Is that what you're crapping your pants about?'

"I peered into the bowl and saw a flotilla of colorful capsules bobbing on the surface, all five accounted for. I tell you, Ols, those little vessels of evaded doom looked as beautiful to me as sailboats in a Monet seascape."

"No wonder you're nicknamed Kevlar. Did he blow the whistle on you?"

"Not when I was the guy supplying community smokes."

"Did you blow the whistle on yourself?"

"Why? It ended up clean. No harm, no foul."

Ollie stared at me disapprovingly.

"C'mon, Fat Boy, we're talking a few mistakes in over two hundred thousand pills here."

"Why didn't you check Frank's wristband, like the nurses do on this floor?"

"I do, most of the time, but I just shot this one from the hip. By right, if I followed hospital protocol, I should've sat Frank down with his Medication Kardex in hand, identified every pill, and gone over the benefits and side effects of each before he took them. But that's not feasible on our ward, because I'd be passing out my morning pills 'til late afternoon."

"Nurses seem to do it here, no problem."

"Yeah, but they usually find their docile patients tucked away in their beds. But on Jones, it's more like herding cats."

"How so?"

"For starters, most of our patients hate taking their pills and scatter to the four winds at my approach. They hide beneath beds, crawl under sinks, or hit the showers. Others play possum in bed, pretending deep sleep. Then we have patients who cheek their meds."

"Cheek?"

"Tuck the pills beneath their tongues, or stick 'em to the roof of their mouth, or under their dentures, to spit 'em out later. Oral Houdini's, we call them. Others flat-out fib, and say the doctor just changed their order. Others swallow their pills and hightail it to the bathroom, from where you'd hear a gag-reflex and accompanying flush of the toilet. Still others look you straight in the eye and say, 'These aren't my pills!' Or, 'I only take brand name, not these cheap generics.' Or maybe, 'These aren't the same color as the pills I take at home.'

"Others bellyache and say, 'Hey, what are these, horse pills? You gotta crush 'em up in chocolate ice cream. No, make that strawberry.' Or, 'I can't take my pills until I have something to eat, and right now I'm not hungry.' A few would simply look at me and say, 'I ain't taking no goddamn pills from a bearded nurse!'"

I continued, "Then we have patients on Rogers Orders, court-ordered to take their neuroleptics; pills like Zyprexa or Risperdal. If they refuse, we have no choice but to give them an injection of Haldol, which often sets up a showdown that could rival the *Gunfight at the OK Corral.*"

"How does that play out?"

"First, we call Security for reinforcements, and draw up the injection in the Med Room. Meanwhile, staff put on gowns, latex gloves and protective masks in case the patient spits or bites, or is positive for Hep B or HIV. When the Blue Coats arrive we approach the patient, who is usually confined to the Quiet Room by this time. We must look like a phalanx of gladiators to them, armed with leather restraints, body net, and a silver syringe glistening at the ready. Best case scenario, they jump off the bed and say, 'All right, already. I'll take my stupid pills.' But the physical violence—anticipated, threatened, or actual—is the worst part of the job."

I swept my hand down the length of my bedridden body, and Ollie nodded in acknowledgment. He then worked his straw through the lid of a styrofoam cup, making it screech, and said, "Maybe your injury is a blessing in disguise; get you out of there for good. Sounds like you're a little burnt out."

"Burnt to a crisp, to tell the truth. But listen, Fat Boy, I haven't told you the half of it. On the other side of the ledger we've got our med-seekers, eager to swallow any pill, whatever color or shape, with whatever effect. We had one woman so notorious that we referred to her as Anita Pill. She could identify any medicine from aspirin to Zoloft, and any pharmaceutical company from Abbot to Zeneca. She would've made one helluva drug rep if she weren't so ill.

"And get this: a few patients get so attached to their meds they dress up in coordinated colors, and I don't know whether it's conscious or subliminal. I remember one woman who always wore a nightgown the exact pink-and-red colors of her nightly Sinequan, and another in a lime-and-green outfit that perfectly matched her life-saving Librium."

"Hah, I've always said you eventually become the drugs you take. How about your third mistake?"

"Actually, that was a scary doubleheader. A real doozy. It was five years ago, and if I wasn't guilty of negligence, I sure demonstrated the danger of relying on assumptions. If one or both patients had died and the case had gone to trial, the 12-member jury would've gladly taken up hammers to help build the gallows."

"That bad, huh?"

"Not a leg to stand on, your Honor."

"I'm not a judge, just a captive audience. So out with it, Kevlar. As Dr. Carter keeps telling me, sharing the truth will set you free."

"Okay. This was a bad mistake, a real wake-up call, but in a way, it's kind of funny too."

"Scary and funny. Just like a good horror movie. Let me have it."

"It was a typical Saturday morning in December, and I was back on the floor, fresh from five days off, my usual happy-go-lucky self. That same week, I had learned from an insider that I'd been short-listed for Nurse of the Year award. After morning report, I began to dish out my pills, starting with the smokers, so as not to delay their morning hurry-up to the courtyard. Next, those who'd been up since the crack of dawn. I let the sleepyheads snooze, and once the majority of folk were down in the yard, I'd get around to the most tedious or complicated of meds.

"We had two elderly women admitted during the week— Mrs. McCarthy and Mrs. Rosen—both suffering from dementia, and each prescribed with a hodgepodge of a dozen morning pills. I prepared their meds and then walked over to the table they were sharing. First I turned to the rosy-cheeked old lady whose forebears must've hailed from the Lakes of

Killarney. 'Good morning, Mrs. McCarthy. I have your morning pills.'

"The poor creature was so confused she couldn't even put the med cup to her mouth. So I placed her pills on a saucer and assisted her with each, one at a time, a ten-minute ordeal. That done, I turned to Mrs. Rosen, straight out of the roadshow cast of *Fiddler on the Roof*. She had trouble swallowing, so I crushed her pills—the ones allowed—with mortar and pestle, and fed them to her in applesauce. No problem.

"Come midmorning, Mrs. Rosen was scheduled for a nitroglycerine patch. I was tied up on the phone, so I handed the patch to Ross Cookis, a fellow nurse, and asked if he'd apply it to her for me. Then I looked up and saw him putting it on the old Irish woman, Mrs. McCarthy. So I shouted out, 'Hey, Ross, I said Mrs. Rosen!' He turned to me and replied, 'Kev, this *is* Mrs. Rosen.'

"Fat Boy, I shiver every time I think about it. I remember dropping the phone and seeing my nursing career going up in flames, not to mention my two patients. To my dread, I soon learned that Annie O'Connor had married Isaac Rosen, and Sarah Weinstein had hooked up with Patrick McCarthy. Imagine the odds, two mixed marriages from an era when that was seriously frowned upon, and they both wind up on our floor at the same time. And neither lucid enough to know either their own names or pills!"

"Old story, Kevlar, don't judge by appearances. Again, why didn't you just check their wristbands?"

"They weren't wearing any."

"Why not?"

"Many demented elders chew on them or try to pull them off, and since the bands are made of plastic, they often cut into their paper-thin skin. I took their identities for granted, because of the way they looked. And this wasn't like Frank the hothead, when I recognized my error right away. No, this was two hours later, and my only option was to rush them both to the ED to get their stomachs pumped, and even that would've been for naught."

"Since you're apparently still a registered nurse, how did you squirm out of this one?"

"Before I raised the alarm, I ran to the Med Room and laid out their Med Kardexes side by side. Of their dozen pills, five were identical, and four were interchangeable, like Prilosec and Prevacid for gastric distress. Add two innocuous vitamins, a low-dose benzo, and, presto, I was off the hook!"

"Off the hook? It couldn't have been that easy."

"True, I couldn't believe my luck. Their numerous pills were basically a harmless swap, like Coke for Pepsi. I breathed a sigh of relief, but before I could throw up my arms in triumph, I double-checked the list and found one giant discrepancy: they were both taking Lopressor for hypertension, but one was on 75 milligrams, the other 7.5."

"I gather that's bad news."

"Oh yeah, cataclysmic."

"What did you do?"

"I have a friend in Pharmacy, John Betters, who, over the years, was always good about answering my dumb questions without making me feel too dumb. So I called to tell him the situation—one old lady getting ten times her prescribed dose of Lopressor—and asked him what to do. After a moment of silence, Johnny muttered, 'Pray.' 'No, really,' I pleaded. And he replied, 'Kev, there's only one thing you can do, call the MET team, stat!'

"So I put him on hold, called the Medical Emergency Team, and then got him back on the phone to brief me on what to expect. He told me Mrs. Rosen's overdose would peak in an hour and make her blood pressure plummet. He suggested that I keep her active and push fluids as tolerated until the MET team arrived.

"Meanwhile, from the nurses' station, I could see Mrs. Rosen, my wild Irish rose, pushing her walker through the ward, little suspecting her ticking time bomb was about to go off. I hung up the phone and asked Ross to take her BP, and he shouted back, 'Seventy over fifty, with a heart rate of 48. And that's being generous!'

"I raced to give Mrs. Rosen a glass of water, but it just dribbled down her chin. She had become so weak that Ross and I had to carry her to her room, her toes dragging along the floor like a drowned victim being pulled to shore. No sooner had we got her into bed than the MET team rushed in—three highly-skilled nurses, a med resident, and my nursing supervisor, Sue Earle—to whom I sputtered my grievous mistake."

"Mistake? More like 24 mistakes?"

I shrugged, "Why confuse the issue? Only one pill made a difference and had to be dealt with immediately."

Ollie looked at me wryly. "Uh-huh, how stupid of me."

"C'mon, you can't make me feel any worse than I did at the time. I stood in the corner like a dunce as the MET team started an IV and ran an EKG. It looked like the start of a full-blown Mayday. Thankfully, it wasn't long before these seasoned professionals had the situation under control.

"But then things took another bad turn. No sooner had the MET Team left the unit after stabilizing Mrs. Rosen, than Reception called to say her family was here to visit. Now, at that moment, Annie O'Connor Rosen looked more suitable for Calling Hours than Visiting Hours, so I asked my fellow nurse, Jo Jo Provost, to apply a little color to her pallid cheeks, while I dashed down to meet the family and stall their advance."

"How did that go?"

"Not too good. The family was an incorrigible bunch of bashers from the Jersey shore, captained by the eldest daughter, Ronnie, who immediately struck me as a tough nut to crack, or maybe a nutcracker herself. She snapped her chewing gum with blue-collar authority, and intimidated me enough to abandon my usual policy of 'Tell the truth and shame the devil.' So I started fibbing to beat the band, in my high-pitched and Irish-accented voice designed to be as ingratiating as Darby O'Gill's.

"Just outside their mother's door, I did my best to warn the family that Mrs. Rosen was indisposed at the moment, and they ought to come back in a couple of hours when she had recovered.

"'Recovered from what?' asked Ronnie, as she pushed past me into her mother's room, followed by the rest of her tribe. 'Hey, what gives with the IV?' she snarled at me, and 'Why is my mother so zonked out?' Her whiny little daughter chimed in, 'Mommy, I don't like it when Grandma's tongue hangs out of her mouth like that.'

"Ronnie next glared at my badge, wondering if I was the keeper of the joint, or a mutineer who'd led an uprising, with the real charge nurse bound and gagged in the Quiet Room."

Ollie snorted, "Can't say I blame her."

I gave him the cold eye. "Anyway, I tried to explain that we had to adjust Mrs. Rosen's medication and assist with her dehydration, and she simply needed to rest while it took effect.

I suggested they go have dinner or catch a movie and come back at seven, when Mom would be purring like her old loveable self again. At first, Ronnie would have none of it, but I continued to wheedle in my most weasel-y manner, and eventually I was able to shoo them out of the room and off the floor."

"Kevlar, you're one smooth operator."

"More sickening than smooth in this case, but at least it worked. In truth, I've been known to live and die by the tongue. Of course, that wasn't the end of it. I went back to check on Mrs. Rosen, and found one of the ward's blabbermouths loitering by her door, asking if he could have her dinner tray since she'd be in no condition to eat. After I told him I'd consider his request, he said, 'Hey, Kev, why don't you just toe-tag her and be done with it? I know you made a big mistake this morning because I saw your jaw drop when you shouted out to Ross. But don't feel too bad because she wasn't long for this world, anyway. She just happened to bump into you on the way out.'

"In the meantime, Ross was taking Mrs. McCarthy's BP, and reported with alarm that it was 210 over 112, along with heart palpitations. What an idiot I was! So preoccupied with Mrs. Rosen's overdose, I had forgotten all about Sarah Weinstein McCarthy's underdose. Again, I had to deal with our annoyed on-call doc and get a stat dose of Lopressor, which soon put her back on an even keel. So, that night, I had to write up two incident reports that you seem so concerned about."

"Still, you got off easy, with your usual Irish luck. But wait a minute, what about the Rosen family? You had to face them sooner or later."

"That's the miracle of the whole story. Before they returned, our activities guy, Bingo Bill, had announced Bingo to the community. And, somehow, at the sound of that word, Mrs. Rosen's blue eyes flickered back to life, and her blood pressure rose steadily. By the time gum-snapping Ronnie and her crew came back, they found their matriarch sitting at the table, shouting Bingo at every number called. Saints be praised."

"And sinners saved."

"Well, the following day, Sunday, when I hit the floor with a truckload of guilt and trepidation, I was overjoyed when I saw the elderly pair jabbering away senselessly at the kitchen table, no worse for wear. I tell you, Ols, you can be sure I never mixed them up again. And in the process I learned a lesson that I'll never forget: check, don't assume. When it comes to caregiving, it's better to be careful than sorry."

"Do you think your mistakes kept you from winning the nurse award that year?"

"Probably. But Ceil Roosa, our fabulous weekday charge nurse, won it, and deservedly so. But it had been within my grasp, Fat Boy. I was on top of my game the entire year, except for my Irish-Jewish gaffe. Now time is running out on me, and I'm afraid my chances are little to none."

"Cheer up, Kevlar. Maybe you'll still win it. After all, if you didn't get in front of that crazy Nathan, he could've seriously clocked his step-mom, and she and her husband could've sued the hospital big time. By my reckoning, you saved the hospital a bundle."

"Thanks, that's very kind."

"But you know, after hearing all your stories, I'm just glad about one thing."

"What's that, Fat Boy?"

"That you're not the nurse passing my goddamn pills!"

*   *   *

That night, after I'd gotten my usual visits from family and friends, and Ollie his usual none, we received our pain killers and basked in the cheery afterglow, road buddies rolling down that mythical highway once again.

"Kevlar, check out the Gateway Arch. Impressive, lit up at night like that, ain't it?"

"Yeah, beautiful. So this is St. Louis. Is that the Missouri River?"

"Nah, that's the Mississippi, Father of Waters. The Missouri flows into it just north of here. We'll be switching buses here in old St. Louie and heading down the river to Memphis and New Orleans, where we'll be playing hide and seek with the Big Muddy along the way. Wait till you see it after the Ohio River runs into it at Cairo, that's one helluva mighty stream."

"Wow, Fat Boy, you sure know your rivers. You seem pretty passionate about them too. Is that your Norse heritage?"

"Don't know, but I got it from my dad. He was born on the Big Muddy just north of here, Davenport, and loved to fish. He truly had a love affair with America's waterways. It was the best part of what I learned from him. Mom used to tell me I never truly knew him, because he was only a shell of himself when he returned home from Vietnam. Drinking was his main curse, but whatever shape he was in, sober or hung over, he always took me fishing on Saturdays."

"Was your mother also from Davenport?"

"Sure, high school sweethearts, what else? That's the way it was in the Midwest back in the day, I guess. Mom even dropped out of her senior year of high school, just to marry him. Before he was deployed, she insisted they try for a child and, sure enough, I was four months old when Dad returned home from 'Nam. He tried civilian life for awhile, but that was a disaster, so he re-upped. Lucky for him. If the Army hadn't taken him back and exerted some stern discipline, he would've died a lot sooner than he did."

"That's tough, losing a parent so young."

"I was in my 20s at the time, but, yeah, it was hard. I never really felt that close to him, except when I was standing beside him on a grassy bank, side by side, fly-fishing. That's why the sight of a river, any river, big or small, calls up this nostalgia in me."

After this surprising outburst of personal testimony, Ollie fell silent for so long I thought he had fallen to sleep. But then he mumbled something, and I had to ask him to repeat it.

"I guess we'll be in Yuma in two days, three if our bus connections are bad." He groaned loudly as he shifted his position, so much so that I felt his pain. "By then, you'll be discharged, and I won't have Kevlar to keep me company. Nope, I'll be stuck here in this room, unless something worse happens to me. You know, I have this ugly feeling that something is going to go wrong any time now. Sort of a premonition."

"C'mon Fat Boy, I don't think your premonition is true. I've seen you improving a little every day, and that will continue with whatever roommate you wind up with. Don't be so sure I'll be getting out soon, either. I've got another scan coming up, and as long as my urine is red, I'm stuck here, too."

"Yeah, but look at you. You can get to the bathroom, with

assistance at least, and do your business solo. I'm weeks away from that. That's what I hate most, calling for the bedpan."

"I wouldn't fret too much about that. As someone who's emptied hundreds of bedpans, I can assure you it's routine for nurses, no big deal."

"Hundreds of bedpans!" The thought diverted him from his foreboding. "I wouldn't mention that on your next resume, if you decide to move on. But now that we're adding up numbers again, how many patients do you think you've worked with in your career?"

"Spencer and I recently talked about that, and we figured between four to five thousand."

"Wow! You must've seen a real cross-section of the community, though heavy on the lower end of the scale, I imagine."

"You'd be surprised. We get all kinds. I like to say we've had everyone from taxi drivers to taxidermists, but maybe the sing-song says it best, 'Rich man, poor man, beggar man, thief, doctor, lawyer, Indian chief.'"

"I doubt you ever had an Indian chief for a patient."

"Well, no. But I remember one who was certain he was descended from an Indian chief."

"I bet there's another story there. Do tell, kemosabe."

"Sure. This young man was referred to us from McGee Detox with a diagnosis of idiosyncratic intoxication, which is a condition where the person has an extremely low tolerance to alcohol. Just a thimbleful would shoot him, and others afflicted like him, into moonshine orbit."

"Sounds like fun."

"Not really. It can lead to hallucinations, delusions, and aggressive behavior. We had one young woman with the same diagnosis who'd taken a sip of champagne at her sister's wedding, and before her rampage was over, she'd kicked a hole through the drummer's bass drum and punched out the lead singer.

"So this polite young man arrived on our floor, and given his fixed obsession, soon earned the nickname of Micmac, for the Canadian tribe, and that's what I'll call him. Micmac had been adopted at birth by a French-Canadian couple—there's a sizable community of them here in the Berkshires—and they told him as he was growing up that his birth parents came from two Northeastern tribes, the Micmacs and the Pequots."

"Do you think his drinking problem stemmed from his Native American background?"

"We thought there could be a link. But let me start from the beginning. When he reached his teens, Micmac became totally immersed in his presumed heritage. He searched for arrowheads in the forests, hunted deer and turkey with a bow, and built a wigwam for a high-school project. He even constructed a birch bark canoe and paddled down the Housatonic River into Pequot country."

"Damn, a real Last of the Mohicans. Did he look like an Indian?"

"Naw. He looked more like a friend of mine from County Galway. And, unlike most Native Americans, he shaved daily. But he certainly carried himself as proudly as any brave.

"When he turned 21, he decided to celebrate at an annual powwow, held in those days on the summit of nearby Mount Greylock, the highest peak in Massachusetts. He was decked out in buckskin, moccasins, and his favorite beaded necklace. He swore that a turkey, his spirit symbol, appeared to him that first night in a dream. Unfortunately, this proved prophetic, since his favorite firewater became Wild Turkey."

"What happened after he drank?"

"Who knew, an absolute crap shoot. And since he'd go completely blotto after he drank, he wasn't much of an historian. But I do recall a few escapades attached to his chart."

Fat Boy reached out for his water, grimacing with pain, "Let's hear 'em."

"One January night, after taking a nip of firewater, Micmac got it into his head that he had to touch the flashing red light on top of a radio antenna to save the Northeast Indian Federation. This was winter, remember, and those poles are sky-high and thin as needles.

"The cops got there shortly after he began his climb, but all they could do was watch from below. According to the report, it took Micmac forty minutes to ascend, and four hours to descend, because the winds picked up, the antenna swayed, and his hands froze. In his cell that night, he raved on about touching the red eye of the demon, thus saving his two tribes.

"To this day, when I pass that antenna, I can't believe somebody actually climbed it. Drunk, no less, and on a bitter winter's night. You know, it's a fine line between a madman and a shaman, and not so easy to tell which is which, though Mic's tendency to self-destruct might offer a hint.

"Two other incidents confirm that he seemed to want to get his ass kicked. One time he walked into a bar in Amherst and started ranting that Lord Jeffery Amherst, the British commander during the French & Indian Wars, was the 'granddaddy of biological warfare,' for spreading smallpox to Indian tribes with infected blankets. True enough, as far as that goes, but not the wisest thing to spout off about in that particular watering hole."

"Ouch."

"Same thing again, in a moment of triumph, when Micmac was coming home from Boston after winning a blue ribbon in a statewide turkey-calling competition. He strutted into a bar proud as a peacock, but after a whiff of Wild Turkey and a whisper from his demon bird, he hopped up on the bar and started parading back and forth like a randy Tom, bearded and red-faced, gobbling and fanning his tail feathers in a bid to attract some bar hens. The hens remained unimpressed on their perch, but a gaggle of in-house Toms dressed down this invasive turkey, but good."

"Lucky he wasn't stuffed, cooked, and served on a platter."

"Got that right. Sadly, MicMac was in and out of our facilities for many years. One time when he was out and attending an AA meeting, his sponsor suggested that he take a DNA test to validate his Indian heritage. If he turned out positive as a bonafide Pequot, he could collect a share of the money minted from the Connecticut casinos."

"Not bad advice."

"In theory, perhaps. Poor Mic saved his pennies to have his tongue swabbed and waited six weeks for the results. In no surprise to me, they came back 90 percent Irish, without a drop of Native American blood. No longer the proud descendant of native tribes, he took to calling himself a drunken Irish bastard. He wound up back on Jones Three after going on a mighty binge that led him to slit his wrist at home. Luckily, he was found by a neighbor before bleeding out.

"Back on our floor, he lamented, in group, the loss of his Indian heritage, and tried to figure out how his adopted parents, now both deceased, had gotten it so wrong. After sharing his cheerless tale, Sammy the Snit cruelly shouted, 'Hey, Micmac, sounds like you got Paddy-whacked.'"

"Mic should have scalped him, Indian or not!"

"Fortunately, as Mic dried out, he calmed down and seemed to be adjusting to his altered identity. The day before his discharge, I got permission to take him back to his apartment on pass, to clean up the scene that hadn't been touched since his suicide attempt. While he put away groceries, I removed the basin of blood that had jelled in his living room."

"Basin of blood?"

"Yep. Mic didn't want to ruin his landlord's carpet."

Ollie scratched his head. "That was mighty thoughtful of him."

"Meanwhile, I looked around his apartment, which could have passed for a gift shop along Route 2's Mohawk Trail. The walls and furniture were decorated with Indian memorabilia, everything from velvet portraits of White Cloud and Sitting Bull, to dinner plates of Geronimo and Chief Joseph. He had dream catchers hanging in every window, and a large feathered headdress draped over a lampshade. It seemed like a hard place to find yourself a new identity."

"Did he make it?"

"Not really, sad to say. He just kept relapsing, three days sober and three weeks mad. Cirrhosis finally got him in the end, and he died up in Medicine at age 37. Looking back, he was one of many patients who had wrung my heart like a sponge. Micmac was a great guy without a bad bone in his body. I mean, think about it: most of us know our parents, and most of us can have a drink without going mad. But one sip of alcohol for Mic was a passport to grief. Strange how his body yearned for its particular poison."

At that point, Krystal from Dietary came into our room with a tray of evening snacks. She knew about our fictitious road trip, and asked, "Where you boys headed tonight?"

Ollie reached for an ice-cream sandwich from her tray, "Traveling downriver to Memphis." He gave her a wink and a pat to his pillow, "Want to come along? We can stop at Graceland, if you like."

Always chipper, she departed with a bird-like laugh, "No thank you. You two weirdoes are meant for each other, and I'm not part of your fantasy."

Ollie bit into his ice cream with relish, like a man who was regaining his taste for life. He had seemingly forgotten his grave foreboding. "You know, I've hung out with plenty of hard drinkers, but none quite like Micmac. I worked with a bunch of guys at a tire center in Tucson, the sort who could throw back a case of beer at night and come in next morning to do an honest day's work."

"You worked at a tire center?"

"Yeah, great career choice, right? I really needed to have all my spark plugs firing to balance and rotate tires. All I took away from there was a pair of busted eardrums."

"I don't know, he-man work must have done you some good. Look at you, you're biffed. Your biceps are bigger than my thighs."

He flexed his left arm. "Oh, yeah, these guns got me into tire town, but I never had the brains to get out. I wasted seven years of my prime there. Seven years. Hell, that was ages ago, and I still got grease under my nails." He looked at his fingertips and suddenly brightened.

"You're big into nicknames, right? We once had a pair of twins working with us that we used to call 'Pins and Needles.'"

"Pins and Needles?"

Fat Boy let out a painful laugh, "Yep, because they were

both pricks!"

After his Pleur-evac settled down, he piped up again. "Hey, I've got a tire story right up your alley."

"Do tell, Fat Boy. We've got nothing but time on this long, lonely highway through the night."

"Okay then, here goes. There's this guy driving down a desolate dusty road, and one of his wheels blows off and goes rolling through the sagebrush. The guy gets out of his car, retrieves the tire, but can't find any of the lug nuts. In a panic, he looks around and sees he's right across from a funny farm, some state institution plunked down in the middle of nowhere. So he peeks in and sees a patient peeking out, and asks, 'Hey, bud, how far to the nearest garage?' The inmate says, 'Twenty miles.'

"Hearing this, the motorist throws up his hands, grabs his head in despair, and moans, 'Oh my god, what am I going to do?' So the inmate shouts out, 'Hey, pal, get a grip! You got a jack and a lug wrench and a spare tire in your trunk, don't you? So simply remove a lug nut from each of your three mounted tires, and use 'em to put on your spare. Then drive nice and slow, and you'll reach that garage, no problem.'

"The driver is dumbstruck by the inmate's practical knowledge, and says, 'Hey, bud, you're pretty smart. What are you doing locked up in Chuckletown?' And the inmate shouts back, 'Oh, I'm crazy all right, real crazy, but being crazy doesn't make me dumb!'"

I laughed appreciatively, "That's a good one. Spot on, too. Mental illness is not stupidity. I've known plenty of patients who were brighter than a 200-watt bulb, but just had a glitch in their wiring. Your story reminds me of one patient who made a fool of an uppity intern during a recent intake interview.

The patient was well known to me and simply needed a short admission to have his meds tweaked, but the intern was irritated by my shortcuts, and insisted on doing a standard mental status exam; day, date, year, that type of thing. He came to the question about naming the last five presidents, which I consider pretty comical, because this was a while back, and so many people, sane or insane, can't remember Gerald Ford."

"Oh, I can. He pardoned Nixon, played football without a helmet, fell down stairs, bad golfer."

"Very good, Fat Boy. You pass with flying colors. Well, this patient kept getting more and more agitated at the whipper-snapper intern, till the veins in his temple were about to burst. But the intern carried on and asked, 'How many nickels are there in a quarter?' With an exasperated glance in my direction, the patient answered, 'One.' The intern jotted it down on a pad, and double-checked, 'One nickel in a quarter? Is that your final answer?' The patient then jumps off the gurney and gets right into the intern's face, and sneers, 'Yeah, jerko, and two goddamn dimes!'"

Ollie braced his chest as he let out a roar, "That must've sent him back on his heels."

"Yep, and a good lesson learned, to boot."

Fat Boy and I finished our snacks in a jolly mood, and once settled in for the night, he turned to me, "So, Kevlar, of all those thousands of patients, is there one that you regret?"

"Like a blown case?"

"Yeah, sort of, if you don't mind me asking."

I shifted uneasily in my bed, and lamented, "Actually, I blew a case a few years ago that still haunts me."

Alarmed by my somber tone, Fat Boy backpedaled. "Hey, let's drop it. I was only trying to make conversation."

"Naw, it's okay. I've learned over the years that sharing a tough story can be very helpful."

"All right, then, but only if you want to."

I raised the head of my bed as high as my broken back would allow. "It all began one summer night way back in the '70s, when I was an orderly working the graveyard shift. I was sitting in the ER with the nurses when, nearing dawn, the police scanner reported a house fire across town. A young medical resident from Ohio, Dr. Robert Taylor, turned to me and said 'Let's go!'

"As you know, I'd been a firefighter in the Air Force, both crash-rescue and structural, so the idea didn't seem all that crazy to me. Once I got the green light from Mary Jane, my night supervisor, I followed him out the door, and hopped into the back of a responding ambulance.

"We quickly arrived at a large triplex engulfed in flames—a three-alarm blaze—the house was surrounded by fire trucks and swarming with firefighters. A distraught mother was being held back by a number of neighbors and police. She was screaming hysterically, 'My baby's inside! Toby, my baby!' "

"Shouting, 'I'm a doctor, let me through,' Dr. Taylor surged past the firemen who were emerging from the burning structure empty-handed, and I followed him up a smoldering staircase to the second floor. We searched every nook and cranny in the smoke-filled house, until we found a young boy—only a baby to his mother—in the deepest recess of a closet, cradling a lifeless Yorkshire terrier in his arms. Dr. Taylor and I took turns giving him mouth-to-mouth, begging him to give us a single breath, but it wasn't his to give. Finally, we felt the strong hands of the fire lieutenant pulling us away, 'He's gone, docs. You've got to let him go.'

"As Dr. Taylor and I left the scene with burning eyes and rasping throats, we watched the fire chief approach the young boy's mother, and heard the mother's repeated wail rend the night, 'Toby, my bay-beeee!'

"Fast forward to three years ago, when a middle-aged female named Tanya was admitted to our floor with chronic suicidal ideation. I'd often see her around town, always walking alone, as if climbing a steep hill—head stooped and bent forward—seemingly weighed down by immeasurable guilt. She was never assigned to me, per se, but I did spend time with her doing ceramics in our Activities Room. I tried to use that as an opening to get her to talk, but I made no inroads in her deep-seated depression.

"So I felt an enormous pang of regret when I heard she succeeded in killing herself shortly after her discharge. A week later, when her case came up at Grand Rounds, her assigned therapist observed that Tanya had never recovered from the fire.

"'What fire?' I asked. 'Didn't you read her chart?' came the sharp reply. 'Not carefully enough,' I said to myself.

"Sure enough, back in the '70s, when Tanya was still living with her parents, she came home late one night, and sitting on the couch, she dropped a lit cigarette. When she couldn't find it, she assumed it was out and went to bed. Some hours later, the house went up in flames, and her younger brother, Toby, died in the blaze, and the rest of her life was filled with guilt and remorse.

"Fat Boy, if only I had made the unlikely connection between Toby and Tanya, I might have been able to address her darkest memories in a helpful way. Not sure how, but having been on the scene, and the first to find her brother, I may have been able to help her delve into the horror and come out the other side. Ever since my blunder came to light, I've taken a large particle of Tanya's demise onto myself, and I'm deeply sorry I wasn't able to save either her or Toby."

"Kevlar, I think you're being way too hard on yourself. You missed an opportunity, sure, but that doesn't mean it would've changed Tanya's fate. As my mom used to say, 'Time you crossed that bridge and got over it.'"

"Thanks, Ollie. I'd like to think that, too. But I've learned that a few comforting words at the right time can work wonders. And those words were at the tip of my tongue, if only I had read her chart thoroughly and discovered the connection. As many lives as a nurse or any medical professional may save, it's the ones you lose that stay with you."

"I'm sorry to have brought up such a dark memory," apologized Ollie.

"Not to worry, Fat Boy."

"I bet you still have an overall winning record over the years. So, tell me, who was your most rewarding case?"

"Oh, that would've been my Dad, hands down," I beamed, "though I didn't have much to do with his startling recovery."

"What? Your father was a patient on Jones? You never told me that."

"Fat Boy, I've only known you for four days."

"But wasn't that a problem, mixing job and family like that?"

"Not to me, but a few staff grumbled that it was inappropriate and unprofessional. It was really just a chain of circumstances. My Dad was first admitted to Jones Two, but was sent up to Jones Three after he jumped out a window."

"What?! You pulling my bad leg again?"

"Not at all. That's just how it happened. Kind of dramatic at the time, but more comical looking back on it."

"You seem pretty cool about it."

"Fat Boy, this was sixteen years ago. Sort of lost its initial drama. Besides, everything worked out fine, thank God, and my Dad's been in his grave for nine years now. It's just another incident enshrined in our family lore. Another story to add to our fond recollections of our dear old man."

Ollie grabbled with his pillow: "I'd like to hear this one."

"Okay, then, from the beginning. One wintry afternoon my mother rang me at home, sobbing. 'Kevin, your father has taken to the bed.'"

"Taken to the bed?"

"It's an Irish colloquialism, meaning one has given up on life. No surprise, because he'd been slipping for months. He was a natural-born caretaker who hated the thought of growing old. My father had been a man of great vitality, a little dynamo with a sharp wit, and our family always knew he wouldn't go gently into the good night. But his 'taken to the bed' at age 75, took us all by surprise.

"Things only got worse a month later when my Dad's younger sister, Nellie, died suddenly in Mineola, New York. I went into his room to break the news, and he took her death so hard that he actually keened."

"Keened?"

"It's this unearthly Celtic wailing. You should know, because it spooked your Viking ancestors when they invaded Ireland in the 9th century. It's the Irish version of the Bible's 'weeping and lamentation,' an expression of grief, but also of protest. It didn't prove cathartic for my Dad, and he just fell into a deeper depression, till we had no choice but to seek help.

And that's how he wound up on Jones Two."

"That must have been tough."

"Yeah, if he had to be hospitalized, though, I'd rather see him there than anywhere else. But, you know what? As soon as he was admitted, his depression lifted. He'd always been stimulated by meeting new people; 'a fresh set of ears,' he'd say, giving him a new lease on life. His admission was also a homecoming of sorts, since he had worked in the hospitals' Maintenance Department for years after the closing of St. Luke's Hospital, where he chauffeured the Sisters of Providence around in a Fleetwood Cadillac.

"For a few days, staff wondered why our family had checked him in at all. I'd visit in the evenings and find him leading a couple of biddies in the rosary, or regaling a captive and captivated audience with his rollicking Irish tales. He also got to highlight his favorite quips and sayings, like shiny new gems of wit."

"Give me an example."

"Oh, there were so many, a constant flow. Offhand, I remember, 'I'm too old of a cat to be fooled by kittens,' frequently addressed to his children. He used to dismiss a certain sort of person as 'neither useful nor ornamental.' Of various complaints, he'd say, 'It's not the cross you bear, but the splinters in it.' Or my favorite bit of wisdom, 'Whenever seven people are gathered in anyone's name, there's bound to be one jackass.'"

"Tell it, Dad! Ain't that the truth."

"Anyway, the lift of a new audience didn't last long. By the fourth day, he had fallen back into a deep hole, refusing to eat or participate in any group. He wouldn't even go to the courtyard to smoke his favorite briar pipe. Even at that, he retained some of his old humor. I heard about one group where they were doing some sort of survivors-on-a-deserted-island exercise, and he just walked out while the therapist was assigning roles. When asked where he was going, my dad pulled his unlit pipe from his gob, and replied, 'Forgive me, but I've decided to take my chances and swim home.'"

"I like this guy. No time for ripe bullshit. So how and when did he jump out the window? Aren't the windows barred?"

"We have wire-mesh screens, not bars. Patients who've tried to run through them bounce off like a trampoline. But this was Jones Two, which wasn't a locked unit at the time. All they had was a door buzzer back then. And since Dad already knew the hospital inside out, it was easy for him to skip out while the others were headed to dinner. He hobbled down the stairs to the Rehab unit on the first floor, slipped quietly past the nurses' station, and headed to the north end of the building.

"In the meantime, my colleague and good buddy, Colin Harrington, had noticed his absence and given pursuit down the stairwell. Chasing after, he caught a glimpse of Dad disappearing into the last room on the right, and arrived at the door just in time to see Dad jump out the window. It was a week before Christmas, and a heavy snow had just fallen. A good thing, because it helped cushion my Dad's fall. Only ten feet, but no small matter at his age."

"Was he badly hurt?"

"Just a few scrapes and a broken nose. By the time my mom and I got to the hospital, Dad was back in his Jones bed, sporting a snout the size of a goose egg. It was all a big kerfuffle at the time. The hospital had to go through a 'root cause analysis,' a procedure where administrators and managers get together to determine what went wrong, and how to prevent it in the future.

"As the only eyewitness, Colin was called upon to offer evidence whether Dad's intent was suicidal, or merely to escape. He testified to the belief that the jump was not suicidal, because the patient seemed future-oriented. How so? he was asked, and Colin replied that in entering the room, he had seen the patient straddling the open windowsill—one leg in, one leg out—and lighting his pipe. Therefore, it was Colin's opinion that if Mr. O'Hara was intent on dying, he wouldn't have bothered to light up."

"That's so funny!" Ollie erupted, his Pleur-evac kicking into high gear.

"Oh, sure, have a good laugh on my poor old man. Actually, it was the pipe that broke his nose. Anyhow, the incident got him transferred to Jones Three, for our father-and-son reunion. He was despondent at first, and took to the bed again, calling out my name plaintively when I was on duty, but not available for him. That was hard, but otherwise I could be sure he was getting the best of care. I had total faith in Dr. David Raskin, our psychiatrist, and the rest of my colleagues went out of their way to help my father. And sure enough, he did improve, and soon he was following me around the floor, and taking an interest in my duties, especially when I was passing pills."

Ollie snickered, "From what you've told me earlier, he'd probably do a better job passing them."

I folded my arms over my chest and looked across at my roomie, "Are we in Yuma yet?"

Fat Boy backtracked, "Glad your dad finally recovered. How long did he stay in your nuthouse?"

"Not even two weeks."

"What cured him? Meds?"

"Well, I don't know about cures in this business, but what turned him around was a person, someone who gave him something to care about again."

"And who was that miracle worker?"

"Larry Bird."

"The basketball player? You're gonna have to tell me more about that."

"On Christmas Day, we got to bring Dad home on a pass, for some of Mom's home cooking, and some time in the bosom of his beloved family. After the meal, my brother Kieran put the Celtics game on the TV. Dad used to love high school basketball, but never warmed up to the NBA. But these were the Larry Bird Celtics. What a terrific team they had that year, with Robert Parish, Kevin McHale, Danny Ainge, and Dennis Johnson.

"Kieran then had a great idea to mute the TV and put on the radio, to hear Johnny Most's hyperactive and hyperpartisan call of the game, in his guttural brogue. That turned the trick, and a passionate fan was born. Dad never lost interest in life again. I'm not saying he never had a bad day, but he never again took to his bed. And it was definitely Larry Bird & Company who pulled him out of his doldrums. After he was discharged from the hospital, his five sons celebrated by taking him to Boston Garden for a Celtics win over the Bad Boys from Detroit."

"How long did he live after that?"

"To the end of the Larry Bird era. He was 82 when he passed, so we were blessed with his presence for an extra seven years. I can still hear his voice in my head, always referring to my mom as his 'bride,' and always taking pride in his brood of eight children, three daughters and five sons. He liked to boast that not one of us ever brought a policeman to his door. On the other hand, he regretted that none of his five boys had a religious vocation. When asked, he would shake his head gloomily and say, 'A priest? I'm afraid I haven't a decent altar boy among them.'"

"Your dad sounds like a card, Kevlar."

"Aces, Fat Boy. We were lucky to have him, and I was lucky to care for him as a patient as well as having him as a parent, so that's why he retired as my Number One case. If he had worn a jersey, it'd be hanging off the rafters of Jones Three today like old number 33 at Boston Garden."

Smiling at the memory of the old man, I had one more story to tell: "I was just thinking about his wake, a sad occasion for sure, but illuminated by the legacy of his tireless spirit. My brothers had all come up from Boston, and each had planned to bring a little keepsake to place in the casket, but forgetting to inform me. So when the funeral director was about to close the casket, they each stepped up in turn. Mickey slipped a Kapp and Petersen pipe into his coat pocket, Jimmy added a pouch of Cherry Blend tobacco, Dermot placed a bottle of Guinness by his side, and Kieran, a biography of Larry Bird. Then they all turned to me, and the affable director, John Bresnahan, asked if there was anything I would like to bury with our father.

"Stuck for a moment, I finally offered, 'I've got a few gallons of old lead paint in my basement. Any chance to run home and get 'em?'

"We all had a good laugh, and I daresay Dad would've appreciated my humor. And with that final wisecrack, the lid was closed on our dear old man."

"I guess the apple really doesn't fall far from the tree, Kevlar."

"I guess not."

After a bit of rumination, Ollie finally settled in for the night, saying, "We'll be following Old Man River through the night. Have to change buses in Memphis early in the morning, so we better rest up while we can."

I struggled to flip over my pillow: "Sounds like a plan to me. Sleep well, good buddy, and I'll catch you downriver."

FRIDAY: THE WARD AND THE WORLD

The next morning, we were pulling out of Memphis on the road to New Orleans, disappointed to miss the music scene, but hoping to get off the bus in the Big Easy, when a candy striper came prancing into our room, and handed me a bundle of mail from her wicker basket.

Ollie looked over at me. "Man, you sure you're not the mayor?"

"What can I say, Fat Boy? I've been kicking around these parts a long time, so I know many people around here." Conscious of the disparity in our connections, I tried to make light of the stack of Get Well cards that I waved in my hand. "So whatever happened to those HIPAA Privacy Laws, huh?"

Thumbing through, one return address, on a lilac-colored envelope, leapt out at me. "Hey, here's one from Holly. How'd she find out I was wracked up?"

"Who's Holly? An old flame of yours?"

"No, but she's certainly Top Ten on my favorite patient list, a real sweetheart."

"You seem to have a lot of favorites."

"True enough, but Holly is special. A pretty young woman, always upbeat, with a flutey little voice, and a splash of vibrant freckles. Surprisingly she's genuinely good-hearted, despite a tough upbringing. I always think of her as a human pilot fish."

"How so? What's a pilot fish?"

"Oh, you know, Mr. Fisherman, one of those fish that swim alongside sharks. She was like that with other patients, always hovering near, ready to be of service. Ever hear of Herman Melville?"

"The author?"

"Yep. He wrote his classic, *Moby-Dick*, at his farmhouse, named Arrowhead, right here in Pittsfield. He even wrote a poem about pilot fish, how they *'find an asylum in the jaws of the Fates.'* That's Holly to me. She'll attach herself to anybody, saint or sinner, and even the toughest predator accepts her, and warms to her presence in the end."

"Sounds like a saint. So what's her problem?"

"I can't really tell you, HIPAA and all. Let's just say longstanding abuse by her mother once her dad died, to the extent of being locked away in their cellar for weeks on end. Her good qualities just never had the chance to flourish. She's thirty now, and doing pretty well, but she still ends up on our ward every so often. Nurse Hatchet is always telling her to work on her own problems, but Holly says she only feels good when she's helping others. On weekends, when Spencer and I are at the helm, we let her feed the elderly, run Bingo, things like that."

"Maybe you should hire her."

"We've hired many ex-patients over the years, but Holly's absolutely hopeless when it comes to patient confidentiality. She loves to blurt out the juiciest details of fellow patients to any visitor who strolls through our doors. Not in a mean, spiteful way, it's just her insatiable need to share."

After reading Holly's card, I reread the last paragraph aloud to Ollie. *"'I'll never forget our visit to Russell's antique shop with Hapless Happy that Christmas Eve. Remember, Kevin, how great he played his mom's piano? I cried that whole day in March when he died. I bet you did, too. But we did our part, didn't we, our little Christmas miracle!*

x's and o's, Holly.'"

"She sounds sweet," said Fat Boy, "But I didn't think you worked Christmas with your seniority."

"All staff nurses rotate the holidays, but I've always enjoyed working on Christmas, especially after my sons were grown."

"You won't be working it this year." He nodded toward my still-pink catheter bag. "But isn't it depressing to work on the fruitcake ward at Christmas?"

"On the contrary. We do our best to make the holiday festive. There's a psychiatrist on Jones Two, Phil Pryjma, a great guy and an artist to boot, who decorates his ward like the North Pole. NAMI—that's the National Alliance for the Mentally Ill—supplies gift baskets for every patient. And local school kids send colorful holiday cards. I remember one that read, 'I hope Santa isn't scared of crazy people like you!'"

"That one definitely got by the teacher."

"No harm done in that case, but it stuck in my mind as a common reaction to mental patients, out of the all-too-honest mouth of a child. Anyway, on Christmas mornings, a troupe of carolers come to our floor, and one of our nurses always brings in a large gingerbread house. Dietary also serves up a noonday feast with all the trimmings. That makes me think of something poor Hapless Happy once said, about what a far cry our holiday banquet was compared to the dry 'chicken on the bone,' they used to get at Northampton State Hospital."

"Kevlar, tell me about Hapless Happy. We've got 300 miles of Mississippi to travel before we stroll through the French Quarter."

"You asked for it, Fat Boy, so I'll give it to you from the start. Happy was descended on his mother's side from a distinguished New England family called Hapgood. At an early age he got the nickname Happy, and the name stuck, even as it became progressively more ironic. His mother died when he was a teen, and he started to exhibit a few mild symptoms of psychoses during high school. His stepfather didn't want to deal with him, and since there was old family money involved, he railroaded the kid into Northampton State, and then absconded. Happy spent twenty years wasting away there, until the Big House finally shut its doors and dispersed its inmates. If he wasn't clinically depressed when he went in, he sure was when he got out.

"When he returned to Pittsfield, no family member remained, and his only legacy was an heirloom baby grand piano, a white elephant in storage. But to Happy, it was an intimate contact with his beloved mother. She had taught him to play the instrument, and he moved it to an independent living apartment he got through Section Eight Housing, where it took up the entire living room. Playing the piano helped ground him and kept him something like sane. He became proficient over the years.

"But circumstances forced him to move to a smaller apartment, where he could no longer keep the piano. He had little choice but to consign it to an antique shop in town, where the considerate owner allowed him to come in and play it until it was sold. Happy's run of bad luck continued when he developed cancer of the esophagus, and that's how he wound up on our floor that Christmas."

"Was he a smoker?"

"No, the cancer developed from an old wound he got at Northampton. Evidently, he jammed a stick down his throat, or so I understand."

At that point, a pair of orderlies came in to wheel Ollie down to Radiology for a repeat CT Scan, still searching for his elusive abdominal bleed. Alone in the room, I had time to compose the story of Holly's and Happy's holiday in my own mind before regaling Fat Boy with it upon his return. With Holly's lilac-scented card triggering my nostrils, and painkillers coursing through my veins, I drifted back to that memorable holiday years ago . . .

Holly had been admitted a week before Christmas, a few days after Happy. Most clients wanted to be home for the holidays, but Holly begged us to stay. She was living with her mother and was afraid of being confined to the cellar again. Most staff advocated for her, but Nurse Hatchet wouldn't hear of it. "She's baseline, and should be discharged, *stat*. I heard from her social worker that the cellar she's always crying about is a fully-finished basement, more like protective custody than punishment."

My main adversary pointed her nose in my direction, "We all know that Holly's a champion manipulator, and a blue ribbon staff-splitter."

Dr. Joel Vogt, our goodhearted, attending psychiatrist, listened attentively to all factions of the argument, and kindly as Kris Kringle, opened her chart and took pen in hand. "Let's raise Holly's nighttime Seroquel to 75 mg., and set her discharge for Tuesday, the 27th. She can take it as an early

Christmas present."

When I told Holly the news, she literally jumped for joy, but little did I know the true intent behind her jubilation.

Christmas Eve fell on a Saturday that year, and a light, feathery snow accompanied my brisk morning walk to the hospital to work my 7-to-7 shift. According to my custom, I listened to the church bells blessing the old town before rushing through the corridors where I exchanged cheerful greetings with all I passed.

When I entered Jones Three, I was immediately accosted by Holly, decked out in her signature red-and-white stripe *Cat in the Hat* pajamas. But her usual feline smile was turned upside down, and her eyes were red-rimmed, as if she'd been crying through the night.

"Bad news, Kevin, bad, bad news! Happy learned yesterday that his mother's piano has finally been sold, and the buyer is picking it up this afternoon. He's a total wreck, and I'm worried sick about him."

She tugged at my coat sleeve desperately. "Could you take us to the antique shop today, so Happy can play his piano for one last time? Please, Kevin, please. You've got to. It'll make his Christmas. Oh please, Kevin, please!"

I gently freed myself from her feline claws. "Do you think Happy can manage it?"

"You could get a taxi voucher, couldn't you?"

"I could, but I'm afraid it'll take all your charm to get him motivated. He's been flatter than a pancake since his admission."

"You just leave that to me!" Holly skipped off on the run, a tireless advocate to all but herself.

That afternoon, with the ward somnolent following a

holiday lunch, a wan and wasted Happy approached the nurses' station, nudged firmly by Holly, who worked her fingers into his back like a snub-nosed revolver. Like a scarecrow in a rain-soaked field, his skin was as colorless as straw, and his winter coat hung heavily over his gaunt shoulders.

In a weak, hollow voice, he croaked, "I'm here to sign out."

"Happy, are you sure you feel up for this?"

Holly pulled a beanie smartly over his ears. "Of course Happy feels up for this. And I just called my friend Russell at the shop, and he said we'd best hurry because the buyer is due before three. Tell him, Happy."

I tried to look Happy in the eye, but his eyes remained downcast. He did, however, nod once and mutter, "Yeah, I wanna go."

Bundled up, the three of us took the short taxi ride to the antique shop. At the jingling of the front door bell, the amiable owner, Russell, came forward to welcome us. "Good to see you, Happy. It's been a while since you've stopped in to play. Sorry, too, about the piano finally selling. So go to it. See, I've even polished it for you—I mean, for the new owner—so try not to mess it up, okay?"

The Hapgood baby grand, a lovely Knabe with Victorian-era decoration and a walnut sheen, shone like a jewel amidst the clutter of brass fixtures and knock-off Shaker furniture. Happy sat down gingerly on the swivel stool, and stretched his cold fingers above the ivories. At his hesitation, Holly jumped in.

"Look at you, you're a mess." She pulled a handkerchief from her pocket and wiped his dripping nose. "You'd never see Mr. Cliburn hit the stage with a runny nose. And your fingers, they're frozen! Why don't you wear gloves, for Pete's sake?"

"I always lose 'em."

She blew her warm breath into his cold hands. "How can you play anything with these icicles?"

Trying the keys again, Happy's fingers soon began to limber up. He practiced some scales at first, before launching into a Chopin etude, which I recognized from my son Eamonn's long years of piano study. From there he was off, playing passage after passage from memory. Happy's transformation was remarkable, his spirit rose from the piano as if from a coffin.

When his playing attracted a circle of last-minute shoppers, Happy, surprisingly, did not close in on himself. Now in his element, he opened up to the group. He took requests, and ran through a medley of holiday favorites. Holly soon got the group singing along, leading the revels in a joyous, if ragged, rendition of *"Jingle Bells."*

As the impromptu concert wound down, and the audience moved on to their own Christmas Eve plans, one appreciative listener laid a five-dollar bill on the piano. "I don't see a tip jar, but that performance certainly deserves one. Bravo, maestro! Bravo!"

Holly smothered the pianist's capped head with kisses. "Your mom would be so proud! Just think, not only did you play your family piano so beautifully, but you got paid, too! That makes Happy a professional musician, doesn't it?" She turned to the voice of authority.

My voice squeaked back, "Certainly does. Happy might even have to join the musician's union."

That brought on a sight unseen before, a smile to Happy's face. He ran his fingers over the piano's casing as reverently as if it were his mother's casket. Slowly and quietly, he pulled the lid over the keyboard, stood up from the stool, reached out to touch the scrollwork music stand one last time, then turned and shook Russell's hand, thanking him for the final chance to play.

The occasion seemed too grand for us to go right back to Jones, so I proposed stopping for hot chocolate. Holly was delighted with the idea, and turned to shout out as she helped Happy button his coat. "Oh, goody! I'm going to have tons of whipped cream on my cocoa. What says you, Happy?"

Our hands were soon warming around mugs of hot chocolate at The Highland Restaurant, a fixture in downtown Pittsfield since 1936. A number of friends stopped by our booth with greetings of the season, though they no doubt were aware I was on duty with such novel companions: one bleary-eyed man well beyond his years, as gray and haggard as an old Union veteran of the Civil War; the other a sweet ragamuffin leaping up to greet everyone, like a spring-loaded Jill-in-the-Box.

I noticed Happy hadn't touched his drink. "Is anything wrong?"

Holly instructed the nurse. "Hot drinks irritate his dumb throat. It just needs to cool down. Isn't that so, Happy?" She leaned over and blew into his cocoa, surfacing with a dab of whipped cream on her freckled nose.

When the waitress arrived with our check, I reached for it, but Happy quickly handed her his newly-acquired fiver, "Please, I've never treated anyone in my life, so let me do it this one time." When she returned with the change, he held up his hands, and said, "No, that's for you. Merry Christmas."

"Ooh, look at you, Mr. Big Tipper." Holly reached out and laid her hand on his.

Happy looked down at the hand that tenderly covered his

own. "Easy come, easy go, I guess."

By the time we reached the hospital, Happy's moment of euphoria, or equilibrium at least, was waning rapidly. It had simply been a brief spark off a damp match. As we walked onto the floor, Holly gave him a poke, "Jeez, c'mon, cheer up, for Pete's sake, it's Christmas. We've got Bingo tonight for big prizes; I even hear they have fleeced gloves, and I intend to win you a pair."

Happy just walked dejectedly to his bed and burrowed in, and didn't even emerge for supper. Holly was oddly undisturbed by her friend's nosedive, and quickly changed into her Dr. Seuss pajamas, as if to hasten the holiday. When the house phone rang exactly at six o'clock, she dashed for it as nimbly as one of Santa's reindeer.

"Happy, it's for you! It sounds important, so please come quickly."

Barefoot and groaning, Hapless Happy emerged from his room and shambled toward the phone. He took it from his helpful companion, listened for a minute, and mumbled, "Thank you, Russ," before hanging up.

Holly jumped in front of him. "Cat got your tongue?"

"It was Russell. The buyer has decided not to buy my mother's piano, after all. So he says I can come back and play it whenever I like." He paused: "At least as long as I'm able."

Holly threw her arms skyward, and then wrapped them around Happy's brittle frame, the red and white stripes of her pajamas making the pair look like a tottering candy cane. "Holy Crackers!" she shouted to one and all. "Happy's piano has been spared!"

Her exuberance brought the other patients shuffling to the joyous scene, congratulating Happy on the good news. Amid the hullabaloo, Holly asked the shyly smiling pianist, "Now, Happy, what says you to that?"

Happy cleared his festered throat, "All I can think about is the Bible verse that says 'Rejoice with me, for I have found what was lost.'"

"Yes, the lost sheep. Luke 15:6," a chronic named Big Wayne piped up, with one of his always surprising bursts of lucidity.

"I'd given up on my mom's piano," choked Happy, "just like I'd given up on myself. But what was lost is found again. I know I'm a goner, but while I'm still able, once I leave here, I'm going to take every chance I get to play it."

Happy's pledge amazed staff and patients alike, not just for his heartfelt declaration, but because it was more words than he'd strung together since his admission. Nor was he finished, as he addressed his attending sprite directly.

"Holly, I want to thank you for dragging me to Russell's today. You've given me the best Christmas since my childhood days."

Holly, of course, was a bubbling mess, wiping her nose shamelessly on her red and white sleeves. Finally, in a heaving voice, she replied, "Oh, Happy, you're so welcome. I'm so, so happy that you're happy."

Composing herself with another swipe of her sleeve, she turned all business again. "Now we've got to get you something to eat before Bingo. C'mon, Happy, I saved your supper in the microwave."

Through the evening, I marveled at Happy's transfiguration, a small Christmas miracle. Not only did he eat a fair portion of his meal, but he helped clear the tables for Bingo—a first—with his little, lithe companion right by his side. So miraculous was his transformation, that it began to smell a little fishy to me. Pilot-fishy, to be exact.

I waylaid Holly outside the far bathroom. "It was you all along, wasn't it, this supposed piano buyer?"

She pirouetted coquettishly in front of me, and flashed her dazzling smile. "Yes, but it worked, didn't it? Even Russell thought it was a good idea when I explained it to him over the phone. Otherwise, Happy would've spent the whole day in bed, and his last Christmas on earth would've been very sad, and every Christmas should be more than precious. But, please, you won't ever tell him, will you?"

"You have my word. It worked out well, fair enough, but why would you put your old friend through all that misery. Think of how he must have felt last night when you fibbed about his piano being sold."

Holly stood high on her toes, her voice trembling with conviction, "You know how good it feels when you wake up from a nightmare and realize it wasn't true? Or when someone tells you a horrible story, and then says, 'Just kidding,' at the end? That's what I did for Happy. See, it took the jolt of thinking he lost his mom's piano for him to realize how much it meant to him. Or he never would have played it again."

Suddenly, she broke down and sobbed, and I thought she must be thinking back on her own Christmases, far from storybook endings. I stood before her, sorry for having questioned her angelic intervention. What is truth, next to hope?

"Holly," I choked, "I'm not always sure what you're thinking, but I do know you've got a heart the size of Montana."

"Why not Australia, it's bigger." She stamped her stockinged feet, but managed a smile through her tears. "Now I need a big hug, thanks to you." She spread her arms like angel's wings. "C'mon, nurses can hug patients on Christmas Eve, can't they?"

I gave her one long, heartfelt squeeze. "Merry Christmas, Holly."

She wiped her eyes and looked at me a long moment before she darted off to play Bingo in the kitchen. There, she grabbed five cards and a fistful of red markers, and sat down beside her rejuvenated buddy.

"Tonight, I'm going to win Happy a pair of gloves," she announced to the gang, "and this time my favorite piano player in the whole wide world is never ever going to lose them! What says you to that, Happy?"

"I says you're right on key," he winked, taking his own card and sidling up to the best friend he'd ever known.

*   *   *

When Ollie returned from his CT Scan, I had the story fully rehearsed for him, and it whiled away the time till lunch. After that, my roommate and I fell into a lull.

"Man, not much to see rolling through the Magnolia State unless we get off at Oxford and visit the Ole Miss campus," Fat Boy complained. "I'd love to visit Tupelo, just east of here, because I have a strange connection to that place. No chance of that, either. At least we'll get into New Orleans by 2000 hours, and maybe catch some live jazz at Snug Harbor."

"Snug Harbor?"

"Yep, up on Frenchman Street, the classiest joint in New Orleans. With any luck, we might even catch Ellis Marsalis on piano. Or any one of his four talented sons."

"Gee, Fat Boy, I didn't know you were such a jazz

aficionado."

"I love my rock 'n' roll, don't get me wrong, but my dad was a big jazz fan. I still have some of his old LP's at home; Dave Brubeck, Wes Montgomery, Paul Desmond, you name 'em."

Fat Boy stopped to glance again at the wall clock: 1:10 p.m. "Oh, great," he moaned, "another 50 aching minutes before I get my next shot, and I'm already cranky with the pain. C'mon Kevlar, distract me. Tell me what you'd be doing if you were working right now?"

"I'd be out in the courtyard playing basketball with Charlie and the gang."

"In the snow?"

"We play year-round. Helps keep you warm while you're out there."

"Patients must enjoy their time off the nut ward."

"You haven't a clue. It's the perfect in-between, half-way space for many, to be outside and inside the walls at the same time. You have to remember that many come to us because they can't cope with the outside world, but in the courtyard they can feel safe and yet not penned in. In nice weather we stay out for an hour and more."

"But isn't basketball a rough game? I can see it getting out of hand."

"Naw, we just play shoot-around games, like head-to-head free throws, Around the World, Horse. But instead of Horse, Sammy the Snit likes to play Pig, especially with pretty young women, so he can snicker when they say, 'I'm out. I'm a pig.'"

Fat Boy tried to imitate a snorting porker, but failed miserably.

"Patients look forward to the courtyard as the best time of

the day. A little freer, a little looser, even a bit closer to nature."

"Oh, yeah, I imagine a little wedge of asphalt between brick buildings, surrounded by a high, chain-link fence. More like a federal prison than a national park."

"You'd be surprised, Ollie. Our courtyard has a summer flower garden, and patients enjoy feeding our resident squirrels and hedge sparrows. One sparrow has a white head that makes him look like a miniature bald eagle. Said one female, 'Isn't it nice how none of the other sparrows pick on him. Pity we humans don't have the same tolerance for those different than ourselves.'"

"Out of the mouths of loonies."

"We once had a yellow parakeet join our squadron of sparrows. Must have flown the coop and out an open window. After a while, it was pretty torn and ragged, evidently not designed to flit through brambles at high speed. He didn't last long. I figure the first hard frost did him in."

"At least he didn't end up in a microwave like that other one."

"How do you know about that?"

"Duh! Because you told me. Man, are you ever way out there."

"Oh, shut your cakehole. We also have hummingbirds that visit our morning glories, and plenty of butterflies. One morning, a patient named Marty told us how he and his friends left their office one day for lunch. On the way, they encountered a panhandler who made the odd request for 88 cents. Marty's companions brushed right by him, but Marty emptied out his pockets of loose change, and was astonished to see he'd given him three quarters, one dime, and three pennies. Exactly 88 cents! Just as Marty finished telling us his improbable story, a

Monarch butterfly landed on his giving hand, as if to validate the tale. Crazy, huh?"

"Kevlar, I think I've told you before, everything you tell me is crazy."

I threw an empty tissue box at him. "Can I get off at the next stop?"

"The marshlands of Mississippi? You're welcome to 'em."

"We also hold summer barbecues in the yard, and every Christmas we build a life-size snowman, top hat, carrot-nose, and all. Once it's complete, Sammy, if he's with us, always sticks two fat snowballs on its chest and says, 'Da-dah, Mrs. Snowwoman.'"

Ollie laughed. "You hold groups down there?"

"Just informal ones. Mickey Goodrich, a talented musician and staff member on Jones Two, often brings his guitar down for a sing-a-long, and sometimes brings a special guest. Over the years, we've had the likes of Arlo Guthrie and Meg Hutchinson play for us. Tell me, what do you suppose our patients' favorite sing-along song is?"

"Hmm, that's easy: '*Crazy*' by Aerosmith."

"Nooo, guess again."

"Paul Simon's '*Still Crazy After All These Years*?'"

"Very funny, but you're way off. It's '*California Dreaming*' by the Mamas and the Papas, followed by John Denver's '*Take me Home, Country Roads.*'"

"You sound like you enjoy yard duty."

"Have to say, I wish I were there instead of here. It's the perfect meadow for this donkey nurse to graze. I'd often tell Nurse Hatchet and her ilk that they'd learn more about their patients in the yard than any formal session held upstairs."

"Is that true?"

"For certain. Our courtyard is comfortable, too. We've got a half-dozen Adirondack-style chairs, two picnic tables, and an actual bus stop shipped in from Buffalo, that makes for good shelter. Even our high metal fence is lined with thick shrubs and pines."

I chuckled.

"What?"

"Not long ago, a young discharged patient posted a sign on the outside of our fence. It read, 'Please Do Not Feed the Patients!' "

"Ha, that's a good one."

"Certainly everyone is more relaxed down there, whether they're a smoker or not. Smoking is the big draw for more than half our patients. And it's not just the nicotine, but the communal aspect. Even the most withdrawn patient seems to brighten with a cig in their hand. Don't smoke myself, but it's a pet peeve of mine that the authorities want to take away the self-medication that works best for so many. It's not harmless, but then neither are the drugs we give them. Many patients often open up in the yard, and lots of stories get told in a cloud of cigarette smoke. I don't want to be around when they take that privilege away from us."

"Maybe you should try a new career, be a salesman for Phillip Morris or R.J. Reynolds."

"I wouldn't go that far. I'm just telling you what I observe. One thing I've also noticed is the special relationship ex-cons seem to have with the courtyard, and the stretch of sky above. Some follow the phases of the moon, and others keep track of the flight paths of aircraft flying out of nearby Albany. I remember another ex-jailbird from Walpole pointing up to a mass of tiny white dots high in the blue sky, and exclaiming it was the largest flock of snow geese he'd seen all year. All year! It was the first flock I'd seen in my twenty years in the yard, and he had to point them out to me. Canada geese, sure, but the white ones way up there, I'd never noticed."

"James John Autobahn, you ain't."

I laughed, "John James Audubon, you clown."

"Anyone ever escape?"

"Yes, regrettably. A few years back, a troubled young man escaped through a gap in the fence, and committed a murder a few days later in a neighboring state."

"Ouch! Was it on your watch?"

"No, thank goodness. But it certainly muddied our reputation in the community for a while, let alone the deep sadness it brought to the victim's family."

At that point, our nurse came in with our afternoon injections. While Ollie was being tended to, my mind drifted down to the courtyard, where I could imagine Charlie and Bingo Bill clowning around with our current crew. Spencer, who visited daily, had given me recent updates on the latest ward news. Clyde and Ling-Ling were quickly "cast off" like stowaways on Monday after their three-day happy cruise on the Good Ship O'Hara. The following day, my assailant Nathan—along with fervent Jets fan, Roy—were both escorted by police to serve out 90-day sentences at Bridgewater State Hospital.

Once Ollie and I were settling back down in relative comfort, he turned to me, "You got any more stories about your cute little pilot fish, Holly? She sounds like a real catch."

"Funny you should ask, Fat Boy, because I do have another story that actually takes place in the courtyard."

With Fat Boy's encouragement, I launched into my tale, but in my drugged state, I couldn't be sure what I was saying. I believe it went something like this . . .

It was a lovely September morning down in the yard when Holly asked if she could run her favorite group, Sharing Stories. She was dressed in her signature horizontal stripes, but this time in an alternating yellow and gold jersey over black tights, making her look like a giant bumble bee.

Giving her the go-ahead, along with a fair warning to behave herself and not overstep her bounds, she sat on top of the picnic table, folded her legs beneath her and clapped her wings. Drawn to her bubbling buzz, the seven others in attendance happily swarmed around her, as if their queen bee.

"Okay, you loveable Grape Nuts, it's Sharing Stories time. Who wants to go first?"

There were no takers.

Holly reloaded, "Okay, who wants to go second?"

Penelope, our bobble-headed chronic with the stay-at-home piggies, hesitantly kicked the group into play. "I once opened a bottle of Coca-Cola and found a quarter tucked inside its bottle cap."

Holly rolled her eyes in disbelief, "Holy Cheerios! You gotta be joking!"

Penelope's cherubic face soured, thus going bubby. "Honest, I'm not! But I don't tell many people, because no one ever believes me."

Holly clutched her left breast with both hands as if cupping a fluttering bird. "Penny, I absolutely believe you! I mean, truly, who in their right mind would ever dream up such a far-fetched story unless it actually happened?"

Holly was most encouraging to her participants but, when opportunity arose, she could also become the undisputed queen of sarcasm. "Okay, then, who's going to be brave enough to follow Penny's captivating tale."

Bernice, who believed her deceased father communicated with her through the voice of Daffy Duck, flitted her hand high in the air. "When I buy Peanut M&M's, I make a small hole in the yellow bag so they pop out one at a time. Makes 'em last longer."

Holly scrunched up her freckled face, "Gee, I can't wait to see where this story's going."

"One day, the first seven M&M's that popped out were all colored blue. Yes, seven blue ones in a row! Can you believe it? The odds of that happening must be a billion to one!"

Holly dropped flat on her back, as if bowled over by the unlikely occurrence. When she righted herself, she exclaimed, "Why, Bernice, if that'd been me, I would've run out and bought 777 scratch tickets! Now, who's next up at the plate?"

Reggie, a troubled young man who'd experimented too often with LSD during his college days, raised his hand half-mast. "Sometimes I hear voices telling me to follow a radiant blue highway."

"Sounds like some dandy day-tripping to me," Holly giggled. "Tell us, have you traveled this blue highway that beckons you?"

"Twice, but I'm not going back again."

"Why not?"

Reggie abruptly bent down to fiddle with his shoelaces. Holly, in turn, drummed her fingers impatiently on the picnic table. "Hey, Reg, you gonna tell us, or leave us floating like a bowl of Rice Krispies?"

Reggie rose slowly from his task. "The blue highway leads to a marble temple where a buttery haze streams through gleaming white pillars . . . "

He stalled again.

"Go on, be brave."

"The people there are all dressed in white tunics, like senators in ancient Rome. And in the midst of the forum sits God."

"God?"

"Just like you'd picture Him. He's got long, white hair and a longer beard. But He's way skinnier, like an anorexic Santa."

"So why in Heaven's name don't you want to go back?"

"Because God hates me."

"Now, Reg, we all know that your compass doesn't point true North, but that's no reason for God to hate you. Besides, God is Love! And you're as loveable as the next person. How could you think that, anyway?"

A noticeable quaver accompanied Reggie's forced reply, "When all the others ask God a question, He answers them back in a deep, solemn voice, like a church pipe organ. But on my first visit, after I asked God a question, He answered me back in gangsta rap."

"Gangsta rap! You mean like Ice-T and Ice Cube, and all those chill brothers?"

"You got it. So I told my sister, Arlene, and she thought it had to do with the music I'd been listening to, and suggested I switch to country & western. So for a whole month, I suffered through Dolly Parton, Merle Haggard, and Travis Twitt."

"Tritt is the name. So did that work?"

"Nope. When I traveled back down the blue highway, God spoke to me this time with a southern twang, just like that goofy TV Marine, Gomer Pyle, 'Well, Gollee!' So I'm never going back, since I know He's just going to mock me again with whatever kind of music I listen to."

Amid muffled snickers, Penny spoke up. "Why don't you

try listening to *Sister Act*, where Whoopi Goldberg plays a nun who sings to God. Holy songs like '*My Guy*,' and '*I Will Follow Him.*' It's gotta be one of God's favorite movies."

"You think?"

"Either that, or a heavy dose of Gregorian chant," counseled the wiser Holly.

Leaving Reggie to contemplate his musical options, Holly turned around to fearlessly face a hulking mass of humanity. "How about you, Wayne. Any stories?"

Big Wayne was a frequent flyer on our floor, whose trademark duds honored his idol, Johnny Cash: a threadbare, black suit with scuffed cowboy boots. He fancied himself our reigning karaoke king, though his voice would shame a donkey. Subject to religious as well as musical delusions, he'd walk around with our battered house guitar held by the neck and slung over his shoulder like a cross.

"I walk the line, but I ain't going nowhere near your ring of fire. So that's that, I got no story."

"What do you mean, you got no story? A little birdie tells me that you're here this time because you think you're a bear?"

"I am a bear."

"Uh-huh. And I'm Queen of the Nile!"

Without any show of annoyance, Big Wayne reverently set down his guitar and took a knee in front of Holly. "I'm a bear because my teeth aren't like yours. Look, I've got sharp *insiders*." With that, he stretched out his lips like a thick rubber band.

Holly squinted bravely into the giant's cavernous maw. "Bear or no bear, I see that flossing isn't high on your priority list."

"Bears don't floss."

"Apparently. What do you do after you eat a tuna fish grinder, chew on birch bark or something?"

Holly clamped his jaw shut and looked him straight in the eye, something one should never do to a real bear. "Okay, Wayne, so you're a bear. Now, are you Yogi Bear, Smokey Bear, Papa Bear, Paddington Bear, Tubby Bear, Bipolar Bear, or my favorite, Sugar Bear?"

"I'm Kodiak Bear."

"Oh, yes, how stupid of me. A big boy."

"Here, I'll show you."

Big Wayne lumbered to the center of the yard, dropped to all fours, rose up on his hind legs, thumped his fists against his expanded chest, and let out a ferocious roar that surely rattled the cages in Hades.

His ear-splitting eruption sent patients scattering, sparrows soaring and squirrels scurrying, as our walkie-talkies squelched and squawked to life.

"Jones Three to Courtyard, what the hell is going on down there?"

Charlie got on the radio, "Sorry, Ceil. Wayne's just letting off a little steam, that's all."

After Big Wayne's trumpeting blast, he turned as docile as a circus bear and took up his guitar-cross once again. Holly gathered in her dispersed hive and resumed shakily. "N-now, who's gonna go next? But, please, let's be easy on the eardrums."

She scanned the congregation and singled out another young man, a workman with obvious mental deficits who was remanded by the courts on a charge of sexual assault.

"OK, Tommy, your turn."

He rifled back a ready reply, "My lawyer told me to keep

my big trap shut."

"C'mon, Tommy. You know my motto, 'What's said in the yard, stays in the yard.'"

"Nope, from here on in, I'm all zippered to the chin."

Tommy had good reason to be cautious, though the donkey was already let out of the barn, so to speak. There'd been a legal hearing held in our conference room—judges, attorneys, bailiff, and all—where the story was told. He'd been painting a large, Victorian house and frequenting a nearby sandwich shop for lunch, where he started to hanker after the counter girl, Sally, and finally got the nerve to ask her out. She obliged, but on their first and last date, she discovered he was all hands and wouldn't take no for an answer. What happened next was in dispute.

Sally claimed sexual interference, but Tommy claimed she was just trying to get back at him since he never asked her out again. The he-said-she-said could have gone either way, until the prosecutor pointed a knowing finger at Tommy and accused him of accosting Sally. Hearing this, Tommy leapt to his feet, and cried out, "That's a lie, Your Honor. Sally didn't *cost* me nothing!"

With that, the gavel came down on him, and he learned the hard lesson of shutting his kisser. Holly moved on to her next likely target, Bert, a rustic sort in his mid-thirties.

"I don't have any good stories, but I can tell you how I got here."

I interrupted him, "You sure, Bertie?"

"Sure, I'm sure. It's the law that's stupid, not me."

He turned to the assembly. "I live with my mother on a small farm, and I'm here because I got busted for four measly pot plants in my vegetable garden that the state police helicopter spotted on their flyover two weeks ago. I've been growing these plants for years, and harvesting them as Christmas gifts. You've all heard of Toys for Tots, right? Well, I do Buds for Buddies. Plus I roll one fat doobie for myself that I call my Yuletide Log. That's it. I don't sell it or nothing.

"I've never had any run-ins with the law, so I freaked out when three state police cars came screaming up our dirt driveway. I can't explain why I started acting like some besieged criminal holed up in a Hollywood movie climax, but I barricaded myself in my bedroom by sliding a heavy pine chest and a big oak dresser against the door.

"Soon a police sergeant was banging on it, ordering me to open up. My mom was with him, all weepy-like, begging me to cooperate. I still don't know what got into me, but I shouted back, 'No way, Sarge! In fact, I'm going to swallow one Tylenol tablet every two minutes until your cruisers leave our property.'"

"Oh Bertie, you didn't." Holly leaned forward with genuine concern.

"I did, crazy as it sounds. The sarge didn't believe I had pills at first, so I shook my full bottle so he could hear 'em loud and clear—*chug-a-chug chug, chug-a-chug chug.* I swallowed my first one and hollered, 'There goes Number One!' After two minutes of them still pounding on my door, I shouted, 'There goes Number Two!'

"Then I looked out my window, and saw two more cruisers screaming up the driveway. I now had half of Troop B barracks in our yard for four freaking pot plants, maybe worth two hundred bucks—if I sold it. A couple of 'em, dressed in ridiculous Hazmat suits, yanked my plants out of the ground. It was a total farce, so I went yelling out the window, 'Hey, guys, you afraid of catching Ebola?'

"Back in my barricade, I continued to shout out each pill as I took it, first like an auctioneer, 'Number Six going once, going twice. Number Six sold to the lady in the blue hat.' Then I became a Bingo caller, like those in a church hall, 'B-7, Lucky 7! B-8, Garden gate!' B-9, Up your Behind!'

"After that, things got totally out of control. My mother was still going batty as the troopers tried to pry open the door. Next, a hook and ladder came blaring up our drive, followed by a whining white ambulance. As the situation got crazier and crazier, so did I, and I started to gobble up the remaining pills like they were chocolate Goobers at the movies.

"Then I got sick to my stomach. Real sick. So I slumped over my bed and said, 'Hey Bertie, get a grip here. Do you really want to kill yourself over four measly pot plants? What are they going to do to you, anyway? Six months in the joint? It's not like I killed Mrs. Kilroy's barking dog, which I'd gladly do with a smile on my face.'

"I was woozy at that point, but I staggered to the door where it took all my remaining strength to slide the heavy furniture from it. Last thing I remember is falling into the sergeant's arms, scraping my nose against his badge. When I came-to three days later, the docs told me I was lucky to be alive."

"Holy Cheerios," Holly blurted, "talk about knock, knock, knocking on Heaven's door. That is one amazing story. But now Bertie, I hope you've learned a good lesson."

"You bet," he winked at Queen Bee, "Next year I'm gonna grow all my pot indoors!"

"Oh-kay, you Cuckoo Puffs, we've got one more story to tell, and it needs to be a good one to top Bertie's." Holly turned her smiling spotlight on Limey Bean, a 57-year-old bipolar with chronic kidney disease. He got his moniker after foolishly telling Sammy the Snit that the donor of his recent life-saving kidney transplant happened to be from England.

"After hearing Bert's story, I might as well share my own pot story. A story, I dare say, none of you here will ever forget."

Holly spread her winsome wings. "Wow, that's one ringing endorsement. Fire it up, Limey Bean!"

"This all happened back in the OPEC days of the late '70s, when Saudi Arabia was awash in cash and recruiting foreign staff for a new hospital in Jeddah. Both my darling wife and I were in the medical field at the time, and the Saudis were offering a sweet deal. We figured to bank enough in two years to return to Pittsfield and purchase a house outright. But I tell you one thing, Arabia was no picnic.

"The work itself was okay, but it was no fun living in a high-walled compound on a Saudi airbase. No booze, no fun places to go, and temperatures routinely above 100 degrees. Sheer boredom, and we might've lost our minds if not for a good bunch of ex-pats, especially from Ireland and Scotland. After our first eleven miserable months, we got a month's vacation and took it in Africa. The high point was Kenya."

"Did you go on safari?"

"Not exactly, but we did take a train from Mombasa to Nairobi that passed through a national park. So we got to see all kinds of animals and learn what they're called—herds of gazelles, prides of lions, parades of elephants, dazzles of zebras, rafts of hippos, towers of giraffes, even a crash of rhinos. What a relief it was from the barren desert in Arabia, with nothing but a stinking caravan of camels."

Penelope asked, "What do you think *our* group in the

courtyard should be called?"

Limey Bean studied Penny for a long moment, winked in my direction, and replied, "A bedlam of bobbleheads."

Leaving Penny sporting her signature bubby face, he continued, "One of the best things about Nairobi was the colorful outdoor marketplaces, and one day as I was strolling through the stalls, I heard a handsome white-coated vendor murmuring, 'Mango, papaya, guava, ganja.' That stopped me in my tracks, 'ganja.' Next thing, I was in a small tent and he was offering me a brick of marijuana the size of a bread loaf for twenty bucks American. Who could resist?"

"Not you, Limey Bean, I'm sure."

"Got that right. And it was fantastic stuff to boot. No way was I going to leave that block of pot behind when our vacation was over."

"Oh-oh," hummed Queen Bee. "You didn't try to take it back to Saudi Arabia with you. No buzz on earth could have been worth that risk."

"What can I say? I was young, foolish, and high, and that stifling desert was driving me stir crazy. Had to have some enjoyment, something to take me away from that everyday harsh reality."

"How'd you manage to smuggle it in?" asked Bertie.

"I really didn't think it would be so hard. The first time we landed in Jeddah, the customs agents were all sleepy-eyed and they just whistled us through. So I figured it'd be the same. My wife, Amy, had bought a satchel of native souvenirs, and unbeknown to her, I just wrapped the weed in a Swahili shawl and stashed it deep in her luggage."

"Ooh Limey Bean, you're giving me goosebumps here."

"Wait, it gets worse. I haven't told you we had our

four-year-old adopted daughter, Melody, with us."

"Please tell me you saw her sweet little face and thought better of it."

"I wish I could, honestly, but I didn't think it through. Only once airborne did I begin to realize the dire consequences, if caught. What an idiot I was! The movie *Midnight Express* had just come out, and I had to believe that Saudi prisons would be as bad as Turkish. And it wasn't just me who'd get thrown into their dungeons, but my lovely wife, Amy, as well, and our darling daughter, Melody, taken away from us, to God knows what ends of the earth. I wasn't airsick, but it was all I could do to keep from throwing up in the bag."

Limey Bean paused to take a deep drag from his cigarette; the decades-old event still rattling him to this day. His thrilling episode even piqued Big Wayne's interest, which is highly unusual for any Kodiak bear.

"Well, wouldn't you know, Jeddah airport was humming when we landed that morning. Annual inspection, I guess. Dozens of soldiers and religious guards swarmed the terminal like angry hornets, while customs officials blew their piercing whistles, herding us like goats to their stations.

"Amid the chaos, I began to shake so severely that I had to pick up Melody just to hide my nerves. One rat-faced inspector waved us to his station, but I pretended not to notice and moved on, searching for a compassionate face amongst a long row of hard asses.

"With time running out, I chose an elderly inspector, thinking he was my best bet. You know, a guy at the end of his career, not so eager to bust someone for a promotion. But, man, was I mistaken. He dug elbow-deep into my carry-on, even popped the head off my electric shaver, and squeezed out my tube of toothpaste.

"I stood before him dripping like candle wax, clutching Melody for dear life. Amy is staring at me the whole time, wondering what gives. Then he opened her bag, and the waft of sticky cannabis nearly bowled us over. Amy looked at me in horror, realizing my folly. Then the inspector dug toward the source like a rabid dog, until he held the massive block of Nairobian pot in his hands.

"Then everything went surreal, like a slo-mo movie. I watched helplessly as he brought the brass whistle to his lips and drew a deep breath. But just as he was about to give it one strident screech, little Melody reached out and knocked it clean from his lips, saying, 'Ooh, whistle! Can I blow, please?' "What happened next was nothing short of miraculous. He first looked at Melody, and at Amy, then me, and back to Melody. And somehow our princess had tapped a merciful vein in him, because he covered up the block of dope, zippered up the bag, stamped our custom cards, and pointed us through the terminal gates, pot and all."

A communal sigh of relief followed Limey Bean's riveting tale. Holly, clutching her right breast this time, gasped, "Oh Limey, you must've found your little Melody in a box of Lucky Charms. Then what happened?"

"When we got back to our airbase, I immediately buried the pot at the far end of our compound. A month later, while eating shish kabob and drinking 7-Up with our foreign mates, one homesick Scotsman said, 'What I'd do to catch meself a blaze right now.' So I slid off my hammock and said, 'Be right back to ya, laddie.' And I dare say, after I'd unearthed my stash and doled it out to all in attendance, you wouldn't find a happier bunch of ex-pats on the entire Arabian Peninsula."

Our bedlam of bobbleheads gave Limey Bean a rousing round of applause at the conclusion of his suspenseful tale.

"Now, I won't condone your poor judgment when you selfishly put you and your family in jeopardy," said Queen Bee, "but I must say that was a topper, no, a whopper of a story."

Holly stood atop the table, clapped her hands, and concluded, "In closing, I want to thank all you Fruit Loops for sharing your stupendous tales. Imagine, in less than an hour, we've gone from Reggie's Blue Highway to Limey Bean's Kenyan Plains."

"Wait a minute," said Bernice. "You haven't shared your story yet."

"I don't share stories. I'm the group leader, remember?"

Penny jumped in, toes first, "That's not fair. You should tell us one story, at least."

To everyone's surprise, Queen Bee gave in to the wishes of her workers and drones. "Okay, fair is fair, I suppose, as I do have a story that occurred one Christmas in my otherwise drab existence."

Holly sat back down on the table, drew a deep breath, and commenced, "I was twenty that Christmas, because my father was still alive. I wanted to buy him an electric razor because he was always nicking himself with his old Gillette. Not that he was clumsy, or a drunk or anything, but he was on a blood thinner due to his failing heart. But when I went shopping, I found that the cheapest one cost thirty dollars, and I only had seven dollars to my name.

"I walked home in the dumps that evening. Imagine, here I was, my daddy's only child, who didn't have enough money to buy him a decent gift. His last gift, it would turn out to be. So I said a prayer to the snowy stars above and, within a few blocks from my home, I heard this click-clacking sound coming from the bottom of my shoe. At first, I thought it was a pebble, but when I stopped to look, I found that a gold earring had stuck itself to my shoe, just like a thumbtack."

"Wow!" interrupted Penny, "That's a whole lot better than finding a quarter inside a bottle cap."

Holly smiled graciously at her worker bee and continued, "Next morning, I hurried to the antiques shop in town and asked the owner if I could trade it in for cash. 'Well, little lady,' he says to me, 'how much do you think your little trinket here is worth?' So I answered him straightaway, like I knew what I was talking about, 'Thirty dollars, sir.' He smiled back and said, 'If I gave you thirty dollars, what would you do with it?'

"So I told him how I'd buy my sick dad an electric razor, because he came down to breakfast every morning with bits of tissue dotted all over his face. Next thing I know, the man opens his cash register and hands me thirty dollars, saying, 'Here you go, young lady, and I suggest you buy your father a Remington. A very reliable brand, that.'"

"If he gave you thirty bucks right off the bat," interrupted Reggie, "I bet that earring was worth a whole lot more."

"Yeah," said Tommy, opening his big trap, "He probably saw you coming from a mile away."

"I might've thought that, too," Holly persevered, "but as I was leaving the shop, he called me back to the counter and handed me my earring, saying it wasn't worth a dime, but the smile those thirty dollars had brought to my face was worth a million bucks.

"Well, I just stood there, dumbfounded. I mean, really, who hands a nobody like me thirty dollars for a worthless trinket? When I tried to return the money, he just brushed my hand aside, saying he was simply casting bread upon the waters."

Big Wayne abruptly spouted, "'Cast thy bread upon the waters: for thou shalt find it after many days.' Ecclesiastes 11:1-2."

After acknowledging Wayne's contribution with a grateful nod, Holly resumed, "My Dad was thrilled with his Christmas gift, a Remington shaver in a snappy brown case. But Mom ruined the magical moment by demanding where I'd gotten the money to buy it. So I told her how I'd found an earring pinned to my shoe, and cashed it in at the antiques shop for thirty dollars.

"But Mom wasn't buying it, especially after I made the dumb mistake of running up to my room and returning with it to show them. By this time, my mother was fuming, saying this shop owner must have something up his sleeve."

"More like down his pants," snickered Tommy.

"That's what I'd think, too," agreed Bernice. "Nobody's that kind unless they have an *interior* motive."

Holly persisted. "Thankfully, my Dad saw things differently. He said he'd met people in his lifetime like that shop owner who performed 'random acts of kindness.' That was the big difference between my parents: Dad always saw the good in people, while Mom only saw the bad.

"Soon after my Dad died, I went back to the antiques shop and thanked the owner for his generosity. Then I handed him my father's Remington, saying I wanted him to have it. 'Definitely not,' he answered, telling me he'd consign it. But I answered him, 'No, it's yours, and yours to keep.' He then introduced himself as Russell, and surprised me by asking if I was looking for a job, and that he'd hire me for ten hours a week for ten dollars an hour, under the table. So for the past six years, when I'm not in here, or locked up in my dark hidey hole at home, I help Russell by polishing the furniture, running errands, and sometimes even wait on customers. That's where I met my good friend, Hapless Happy, who's been dead for three years now. He'd often come into the shop to play his mother's lovely piano, and he played it beautifully."

Holly looked out at her hive-mates. "Does anybody here remember Happy, besides me and Kevin and Charlie?"

Big Wayne lifted his large paw. "I was here the Christmas you won him a pair of gloves at Bingo."

"That's right, you were," gushed Holly in embarrassment. "Please forgive me. But you weren't a Kodiak bear back then, were you?"

"No, I was a bull moose from Maine."

"Oh, yes, another big boy!"

"Do you still have the earring?" asked Bernice.

"I sure do. And when I'm lonesome or blue, I just give it a rub, and it never fails to lift my spirits. That's because it always reminds me of three wonderful things: my loving dad, Russell's goodness, and the old expression that hope springs eternal. That's why it's important for all of us here never to abandon our dreams, despite our challenges. You never know when your luck is going to change, because it can show up at anytime, anywhere, or anyplace—even at the bottom of an old shoe."

Claps of appreciation filled the yard following Holly's inspirational tale. But rather than acknowledging their gratitude, she turned her back from the assembly and began to cry. No surprise, that. In her limited social orbit, I suppose it was the first time she had ever shared her story with anyone.

While Charlie led the others up the stairwell, Holly

remained at the table, blinking her eyes rapidly to hold back her tears. Once composed, she gave her nose a good honking, straightened her yellow and gold-striped jersey, pulled up her black tights that had bunched at the knees, and came shuffling toward me.

"Kevin," she sniffed, "can I run another Sharing Stories group tomorrow?"

"Sure, as long as you feel up to it."

She put on her best face. "Oh, I'll be fine by then. I just forgot to ask Reggie what kind of questions he asks God. That should be interesting, huh?"

"Most interesting," I agreed, "but don't press him too hard on it, okay."

She forced a wan smile, "Okay."

Holly then tucked her arm in mine, as I slowly led our spent queen up the steep stairwell to her honeyless hive.

*   *   *

Coming out of afternoon snoozes, Ollie and I were subject to various nursing treatments, as well as my twice-daily visits from Dr. DeMarco. Next came dinner, followed by my usual quota of visitors. When the operator announced that visiting hours were officially over, Fat Boy and I hopped back on our imaginary bus, loaded with homemade raisin oatmeal cookies brought in earlier by Belita.

"Hate to let you down, Kevlar, but here we are pulling into New Orleans, and I haven't the spunk to take you to Snug Harbor like I promised. Nor do I have an appetite for Cajun food. So is it okay if we just chill?"

"Sure, no problem. Anything wrong?"

"Naw," he replied in a belabored tone, "I just feel like I'm running on fumes."

"Okay," I agreed. "I really don't mind sitting in a dingy old depot, just minutes away from the French Quarter. But if it makes you feel any better, I wasn't looking too forward in strolling past all those strip joints on Bourbon Street, while swinging a catheter bag in my hand."

Ollie smiled. "Can't say I blame you there."

"But, speaking of road buddies reaching the Big Easy, we're quite a pair of Easy Riders, aren't we? Which one of us is Captain America, do you think?"

"That'd have to be me," Fat Boy cheered up. "After all, I'm the one named after a motorcycle. You're more the Billy type, good for companionship and comic relief."

"That's a role I've often played."

"Or like Pancho, the sidekick who rode a donkey alongside that crazy knight chasing windmills."

"Sancho," I corrected, "and his poky donkey, Dapple."

"Dapple! Damn, Kevlar, you certainly know your asses!"

I cast him a cold eye, but shared an amusing anecdote. "When I returned to Jones after my year-long donkey travels, I was greeted with great hullabaloo by staff and patients alike. But one old gent, in and out of confusion, and not knowing me from Adam, shouted, 'What's all the ruckus about?' So I told him how I'd just returned to Jones after walking a donkey around Ireland. He looked at me all teary-eyed and said, 'Don't worry, son. When I first came in here, I thought I was Teddy Roosevelt.'"

"Haa! That's a good one, Kevlar."

Shortly after Fat Boy and I pulled out of New Orleans, and settled in for a long night's journey into Texas, my road buddy took another satisfying bite of Belita's treat, and asked, "I've seen how your family has accepted Belita with open arms. But how did it go for you when you met her family?"

"No problem, except for one early blunder."

"Which was?"

"I might have told you that Belita's parents couldn't make our wedding due to martial law in the Philippines. But Belita's uncle, Dr. Jose Timbol, who gave Belita away, and her Aunt Yolanda, were able to attend the ceremony since they were living in Canada at the time. I made fast friends with the doctor, and had even charmed Belita's aunt until our wedding reception when I playfully snapped her bum with my cumberbund: a cultural no-no that sent tidal waves to Belita's distant archipelago."

"I bet! So when did you finally meet Belita's parents?"

"Two and a half years later: December, 1975. Upon our arrival at Manila Airport after an exhausting 16-hour flight, we recouped for three days with Belita's relations in nearby Quezon City before we headed south for Davao City in Mindanao, 600 miles away.

"During our three-day respite, we toured Belita's alma mater, the University of Santo Tomas, founded by the Jesuits in 1611. We also went 'shooting the rapids' at Pagsanjan Falls, an exhilarating whitewater ride beneath a canopy of screaming monkeys. It was like a scene out of *Apocalypse Now* which, by the way, was filmed in the Philippines."

"Any Vietnam flashbacks?"

"You kidding? It was like I was still in-country. Armed soldiers, hordes of poor kids, and that oppressive Equatorial sun. But despite all of that, I was more anxious about meeting Belita's parents, since her college friend was quick to inform me that Belita had dated the upper crust of Philippine society before following in the steps of her older sisters—Lynn and Cheryl—to enroll in our hospital's Med Tech program."

"Do her sisters still live around here?"

"Nope. They both married and eventually settled in San Diego. Fortunately, despite my modest status as a fledgling nurse, Belita's parents embraced me warmly upon our arrival at their impressive orchid farm outside Davao City. I also made fast friends with Belita's brother, Bob, my own age, and his wife, Dyels, who both lived at the farm. Belita's mom was an elegant woman of Chinese descent, but her dad, Rafael, was truly unforgettable."

"In what way?"

"Shortly after our arrival, he excused himself to go to his mountain retreat to pray for President Marcos, in hopes that the dictator would see the corruption of his ways. During his three-day absence, Bob told me a great deal about his father, who was born into a family of privileged Spanish plantation owners. Mr. Suarez had been inspired by the example of Mahatma Gandhi, and became a benefactor of the poor, and an outspoken critic of the Marcos regime. He donated large tracts of land to squatters, and would often arrive home barefoot, having given his shoes to some unfortunate along the roads. He was known in the surrounding villages as Lolo Paeng, which means Grandpa Rafael."

"Sounds like a saint. Is he still alive?"

"No, he passed on some years ago, near enough the same time as my dad. But we were able to visit the farm three more times, and even brought our sons along. In fact, I'm proud to say that our two boys have sat in the laps of both their maternal great-grandmothers—Rosario Timbol in Davao City, and

MaryAnn Kelly in County Roscommon."

"That's some global reach."

"After Mr. Suarez returned home from his three-day her-mitage, he asked if I'd like to go where no white man had ever gone before. Are you kidding? So I hopped on the back of his Harley and we rode toward Mount Apo, the highest peak in Mindanao. Once on foot, we hacked our way through the thick jungle with machetes, until we came to a tree-dwelling tribe; an isolated group that Lolo Paeng had stumbled upon on one of his many solitary expeditions.

"I tell you, Fat Boy, I felt like a 19th century explorer. I was the first European that the women and children of this prim-itive village had ever seen. During the excitement, the elders presented me with small clay pipes and bamboo spears, while the kids followed me around in awe, delighting themselves in pinching my exposed white legs, and seeing the pink rise from them. When leaving, one half-naked boy, high up in a durian tree, pointed to my white shanks and proclaimed, 'Johnson's Baby Powder!'"

"Wow," laughed Fat Boy, "talk about brand recognition to the ends of the Earth."

"I'll say! But this crazy, month-long sojourn was just begin-ning. A few days later, Lolo took me to the Lanang Golf Club, where 30 young caddies vied for the privilege of carrying his bag. Surprisingly, he accommodated them all by giving each caddy one of his 14 clubs to carry. Ditto, my clubs. Add two empty golf bags and, presto, 30 happy caddies followed us around like a Sunday gallery at St. Andrew's."

"I can see Gandhi doing the same thing if he played golf."

"Yeah, but here's the topper. Just before Christmas, I hopped back on Lolo's Harley, where he drove us to a desolate beach, to teach me how to meditate while bobbling on the ocean's surface."

Ollie chuckled, "Good luck with that."

"You think? I mean, talk about taking on a challenged student. First he instructed me how to float on my back, 'like the Phoenician sailors of old,' with my head tilted back, chest expanded, and my four limbs dangling freely by my sides. I soon got the knack of it, but found it difficult to fall into meditation while drifting dangerously out to sea."

"Can't say I blame you."

"I soon gave up, but Lolo didn't seem to mind, and pointing out my lunch, slipped back into the gentle waves, saying he'd be back in the course of time and tide. From a shady spot, I watched him float away, until he disappeared beyond the horizon. A full hour went by and I began to worry. How far could the tide carry him out? What about sharks? What if he never came back?

"I paced the pristine strand, fretting the whole time. Several hours passed, and dusk was coming on, when I spotted a faint speck in the distance. Could it be Lolo, or just a floating log? The incoming tide brought the flotsam in closer, but I still couldn't tell. I was staring intently when I saw a most wondrous thing: three shining fish leaping over the floating object in one glimmering silver arch. At that moment, the log stirred to life. It was Lolo, awakening from his oceanic trance, before swimming effortlessly to shore."

"That really happened?"

"Scout's honor! The most amazing thing I've seen in my life. Made me realize how little I know about anything.

"But here's the postscript: Midnight Mass at the Cathedral of San Pedro in Davao City. Upon leaving the church, Lolo was immediately swarmed by children; indigenous children from the mountains, Muslim children from the waterways, and street children from the barrios. Lolo was ready for them all, handing out three silver coins to each from a hefty cloth bag—their *pasalubong*—Christmas gift. The lively entourage continued to clamor around him, not for more coins, no, but simply to remain in his good company. Belita, Bob and I followed their festive parade that led to the coolness of the city's fountains. There the children of all faiths surrounded him and joyously chanted, 'Lo-Lo Pa-eng! Lo-lo Pa-eng!' I'll tell you, Fat Boy, you've never heard the likes, because their song was as sweet as any hymn from an angel's choir."

"Sounds like a lost paradise."

"In many ways, yes."

"Why didn't you just move there and begin your mission work as a nurse?"

"Sadly, not a chance. Martial law still had a stranglehold on the country, and Mr. Suarez was openly vocal against President Marcos. That's why Belita and her sisters moved to America in the first place. Also, the jungles of southern Mindanao teemed with desperate rebels who'd gladly kidnap any American for ransom."

While the story of my first visit to Belita's birthplace still lingered in the air, Fat Boy jumped to another topic. "Kevlar, you said something earlier about taking patients to visit your mother in her senior living apartment. Is that also true?"

"Oh, yeah, and definitely a win-win, both for the patients getting off the ward and my mom enjoying their company. Remember, my mother was a psych nurse back in the day, and took great interest in my patients. They, in turn, loved her tea and scones, and got a kick out of her lilting accent. On our way back to the hospital, they'd often tell me how lucky I was to have such a special mom."

"So you had two good parents?"

"You bet. Dad was a charmer, but Mom was practical-minded, and always gave me good advice. When Belita was pregnant with our first child, we put a bid on a house in Middlefield, twenty hilly miles from here. When I told my mother, she read me the riot act, saying I'd be a fool to buy a house way up on the Skyline Trail with a wife expecting her first child in the dead of winter. So I withdrew my offer, and bought the house we're still living in, about a mile from here."

"That's cozy. So she kept you close by."

"Yeah, but there's more. Come January, Belita broke water during a raging nor'easter, and we barely managed to get to the hospital from our short distance away. Once we arrived, x-rays showed that our son was breech, with the umbilical cord wrapped several times around his neck. Belita was rushed to the OR for an emergency cesarean. If we'd been stuck up on the Trail, I wouldn't want to think what might have happened. So I had good reason to thank both Mom as well as God.

"Actually, the nurse-anesthetist on duty that night was my good friend, Arthur Ruff who, you might recall, played a pivotal role in getting me through nursing school. When our obstetrician, Dr. Haling, expounded on the length of our son's umbilical cord, Arthur coolly replied, 'No surprise there, doctor. His father has always been partial to wearing long scarves.'"

Fat Boy pondered a minute: "But wasn't it risky taking patients to your mom's apartment?"

"No more a risk than any other day. My patients were also hand-picked, not hardened felons. The only problem I ever had was when Sammy the Snit unplugged her refrigerator without our knowing it."

"Why?"

"It was his M.O. He unplugged everything, except TV's."

"Not that, you buffoon! Of all people, why would you take Sammy to visit your mom?"

"He promised to drop his DMH complaint against me, if I took him for a visit."

"DMH complaint?"

"Department of Mental Health. He accused me of hiding the floor's TV remote control one Sunday afternoon, the only way you can change stations on our unit TV."

"Did you?"

"Yep."

"Why?"

"It was the final round of The Masters. Do you really think I was going to let him hog the TV for three hours to watch NASCAR?"

"Did he drop the complaint?"

"Like a gentleman. In fact, when my mom passed away, he sent flowers to the funeral home. He just hated her fridge, that's all."

"Must have been nerve-wracking when you brought them out on pass. What if one ran off, or jumped into traffic?"

"Again, our patients had to be pretty stable to get passes. That, or just about ready for discharge. I always found these passes therapeutic, since it allowed our patients to test the waters before being released. We recently had an unemployed woman who appeared to be cleared of her paranoia, but while on pass, some guy walked by us wearing a BUM sweatshirt. You know, the brand name. Next thing, she's crying, convinced he'd worn that sweatshirt just to mock her."

"Man, that's awfully concrete."

"We get a lot of that. Not long ago, I noticed a patient limping toward me, wearing his shoes on the opposite feet. I pointed it out to him, and he replied in a reasonable tone, 'Oh, I know. I'm just trying to see what it's like to find your shoe on the other foot.'"

"Haa, your loonies say the damndest things. But weren't you afraid some Crazy Annie might accuse you of molesting her or something?"

"Naw. You gotta remember, Fat Boy, I was Kevlar the Invincible. I'd gone so long without a blemish, I figured I could stand up to any accusation."

"Tell me more about your outings. What else did you do besides visit your mom?"

"Oh, we'd visit churches, hit the library, go to matinee movies, things like that. One Fourth of July stands out, when I made the announcement in our morning meeting, 'Who wants to go and see the famous parade that marches right by the hospital?' Four hands shot up like shoots of bamboo, five if you count Zippy. Did I tell you about Zippy?"

"Purple monkey, right? In the arms of—who again, begins with a Z, too, I think?"

"Zoe, right! Wow, you pass the test. Pretty *compos mentis* for a racked-up guy whacked out on drugs. Despite her problems, Zoe was a sandy-haired barrel of enthusiasm. So she and Zippy were the first to jump in, and were joined by three other young women eager for the excursion. Rosie was the youngest, and seemed younger still, since she had Down's Syndrome, and wound up with us after acting out at her group home. Stephanie was a pretty woman of thirty whose life had been derailed by severe epilepsy—no driving license, no college, no boy or girlfriend, no profession, and thus understandably depressed. Amelia was of a similar age and predicament, hers the lifelong result of a botched forceps delivery that left her face disfigured into a permanent grimace, like a smile turned upside-down, though her violet eyes were startling."

"You sure get a lot of different types for a lot of different reasons on Jones Three."

"True enough, but now that I think of it, this was back in 1985, so it must have been Jones Two, since Jones Three didn't open until 1988."

"So, how did that outing go?"

"Smashingly. The Fourth is always a big deal in Pittsfield, since the parade goes back to 1824, and USA *Today* recently cited it as one of the ten top parades in the country."

"Sounds like your classic hometown America."

"That's exactly what they called it, 'Your Hometown America Parade.' How'd you know?"

"Lucky guess, I guess. But get on with your story."

"It was a sunny, star-spangled morning, with the length of North Street festooned with flags and bunting, and thousands lined up along the parade route ten deep. My distinctive ensemble settled on a grassy knoll in front of the hospital which offered a fabulous view of the passing spectacle. Fife and drum bands played, baton twirlers kicked up their white-tasseled boots, and bozos in clown cars tossed out sweets to kiddies. Despite the passing pageantry, nearby spectators were more captivated by watching Zoe try to stuff gobs of pink cotton candy into Zippy's orange-stained mouth."

"Zippy must've been showing his age by then."

"Oh yeah, he was fairly bedraggled, having lost much of

his original stuffing. Anyway, as the cavalcade wound down, we returned to the courtyard for our noontime barbecue. Over hot dogs and burgers, we discussed the rest of the holiday's festivities. I had enough petty cash to pay for amusement park rides at the Fireman's Muster at nearby Wahconah Park, as well as admission to the baseball game that evening.

"Zoe, bursting at the seams, insisted that Zippy had been bugging her all week about riding the Dive Bomber. Rosie begged to go on the Ferris wheel, but only if I went with her. Stephanie wanted to take out her frustrations at not being able to drive by going on the bumper cars, and her roommate, Amelia, wanted to ride along with her."

Fat Boy had stopped interjecting, so I looked over to see him lying with his eyes closed. "Go on and finish your story. I'm nodding off, but I ain't gone yet."

"Well, that Independence Day turned out to be the rare occasion when each of these unfortunate women received her wish. At the entrance to the Dive Bomber, terrified screams from its riders stopped Zoe dead in her tracks, but a sharp poke from Zippy was all it took for them to board the white-knuckle thrill ride, from which the two emerged dazed and triumphant. Rosie took my hand in her pudgy little fingers as we boarded the Ferris wheel, and as we swooped up, around, and down in a dizzying circle, she squealed with delight, exclaiming how the throngs of people below looked just like ants. Meanwhile, Stephanie was Hell on Wheels, crashing into every bumper car with head-on collisions, while Amelia clung to her for dear life, wearing her perpetual frown, though her vibrant eyes blazed like solar flares."

Ollie's strident snoring told me he had slipped into the arms of Morpheus, which was just as well, since the story of that Fourth took a turn from the glorious to the inglorious, best not told to someone harboring thoughts of suicide. As I drifted back to that dark night, those unsettling memories came whooshing back to me like an incoming salvo of enemy rockets . . .

Many of our patients could be said to have a ticking time bomb in their brain, but for one it was frighteningly literal. Lou was one of the rare African-Americans to check himself into Jones Two. Grizzled and lanky, he was pushing forty, roughly my age at the time, and since we both had served in Vietnam, he took to calling me "Sarge." However, his tour had been horrific, and he clearly had a severe case of PTSD. The human reaction to war and other trauma has been around through the ages, but the diagnosis of Post-Traumatic Stress Disorder had just been introduced a few years before in the psychiatry bible, *DSM-III*.

Lou had a host of symptoms, but the most striking was a recurrent hallucination of three unwelcome visitors—Dobbs, Compton, and Slonski—every year on the Fourth of July, timed to the exact moment, 2235 hours—10:35 p.m.—when he lost three platoon mates to a single mortar round, during an airborne operation in the A Shau Valley. Lou survived the attack, much to his subsequent guilt, made worse, not better, by being awarded a Bronze Star and Purple Heart. The previous year's visit from his dead comrades had led him to a violent trashing of his home, and his wife Mae had pleaded with him to pass this Independence Day in a safe and secure environment, such as Jones.

At the family meeting with various staff at his intake, Lou assured us that his three visitors were not ghosts, but real presences, "as real as anyone in this room, 'cept you can stick your hands through 'em." He draped a lean arm over his wife's shoulder, "For a bunch of years, I was able to tough it out, so even Mae didn't know about their visits until two years ago."

"Maybe seven," Mae allowed, giving his hand a protective squeeze.

"Tell you the truth, doc. What I've done all these years is numb myself out with weed and booze. That's how I cope with these three jerks."

"And baseball, dear. Tell them how you follow the Red Sox."

Lou didn't reply, but just groaned as he stretched out his long legs. Mae turned to us and spoke for him, "Lou's a loyal Red Sox fan and knows everything about all the teams. Over the winter, he tends to coil up like a rattler, but when baseball returns, he's a new man. Twice we've driven down to Winter Haven for spring training, and during the season he listens to every game, even the late games from the West Coast. That, doctor, is sometimes a problem. He stays up late and drinks."

"What difference does it make?" Lou argued, "I can't sleep anyway."

"Drinking can exacerbate your sleeping problems," explained Dr. Robert Guerette, our top-notch psychiatrist at the time. "And the combination of the two can eventually lead to hallucinations."

"I'm just telling you what I see. They're right in my room every Fourth of July."

"So why did last year's visit set you off, when you were able to handle their previous apparitions?"

"They found me sleeping when they arrived and got all pissed off. Told me I was forgetting them, so they gave me something to remember them by."

"Which was?"

"A skull-bomb. They went planting it in my head like a ticking time bomb that they can set off at any time and put me to sleep for good."

"I begged Lou to sign in here for the three-day holiday weekend," said Mae. "I hope and pray you can see him through it safely."

Dr. Guerette assured Mae that we would do our best.

"It's not that my Louis is crazy, anything but. He's smart as a whip and very dependable at work. And, as far as baseball, he's picked the World Series winner on Opening Day two years in a row, and won three hundred dollars last year in the office pool."

"So Lou," Dr. Guerette inquired with a smile, "got any tips for this year?"

Lou's thoughts had drifted elsewhere, somewhere dark by the look of it. "Say what, doc?"

"Who'll win this year's World Series?"

Suddenly engaged, Lou answered eagerly, "I'd love to say the Sox, but I'm a realist, so I'm thinking Kansas City. The Royals have Bret Saberhagen, the best on the hill, a world-beater."

Lou's moods continued to be mercurial on the floor, but he and I became mates of sorts, and he told me a lot about himself. As if his tour of duty wasn't bad enough, his return home was worse. In Florida, he got busted for three joints, and spent three years on a chain gang.

"Didn't they take your service and your medals into consideration?"

"Sarge, that wouldn't mean jelly to them crackers. They'd just tell me to shove 'em up my ass."

He told me that his knees were shot by a score of night jumps in 'Nam, carrying a forty-pound pack and cradling an M-60. He likened the impact to jumping out of a second-story window, blindfolded.

After a thunderstorm rolled in on his first day, July 3rd, Lou needed a stat dose of Haldol. It wasn't the crack of thunder or flash of lightning that set him off, but the steamy heat that rose off the pavement after the storm. To him, the oppressive air reeked of the A Shau Valley.

On the floor and in the courtyard, Lou shunned groups and stood off by himself. He told me that any size group was just begging for a mortar round. So, on the Fourth, it was a surprise when his love of baseball overcame his cautious and solitary nature, and he asked to join our outing to historic Wahconah Park for the ballgame, after Rosie had opted out.

So, our evening group looked different from the morning's, with a tall, black man towering over my clutch of eager recruits, taking the place of a pooped-out Rosie. He hobbled alongside us, rangy but with a certain sinewy strength, and talked only of baseball. He told me about the games he made up around the game, something about how only foul balls count, but I couldn't really follow the game in his head. Finally, I interrupted him. "Hey Lou, you're such a big baseball fan, you wouldn't be named for Lou Gehrig, would you?"

"Hell no, I ain't named for no damn Yankee. I was named after Joe Louis, though I didn't exactly inherit his physique. Gehrig was a hell of a ballplayer though, gotta admit. Did you know he made his professional debut right here at Wahconah Park, and hit a towering home run into the Housatonic River? Before that, in a college game up at Williams, he pitched for Columbia and struck out 17, a school record that still stands."

"Wow, Mae sure told it right when she said you were a baseball expert."

We got to the park early enough to find a row of seats in the grandstand along the third base line. A capacity crowd of three thousand was expected, but many of those would arrive late for the after-game fireworks, more fans of pyrotechnics than baseball. Lou purchased a program from a passing vendor and led us down the long wooden bench, where he took up his post.

Amelia slid in next to him and asked, bright-eyed, "Who's playing tonight?"

"Albany Yankees versus Pittsfield Cubs," Lou said curtly, but not unkindly. "This is Double-A ball, so a few of these players have a chance of getting called up to the majors later this season."

The evening fell muggy and close, and the flag on its day of glory seemed to wrap itself around the centerfield pole as if trying to shimmy down. Lou stood for the *"Star-Spangled Banner,"* but begrudgingly, "only because I don't want to embarrass you guys."

During the final warm-ups, Lou excused himself to hit the latrine, giving me a wink. I suspected he was more interested in taking on fluids than releasing them, and likely to make a beeline for the beer concession. But, given his short-term voluntary status, I turned a blind eye. If I'd known what was in store for him later that night, I would've gladly bought him a six-pack.

Lou soon came back with a bit of a glow, plus bags of peanuts for the gang. "Play Ball!" he shouted, taking his seat and picking up his scorecard and pencil to record every pitch. He was all business, ready to take note of every bit of action, even foul balls. His demeanor betrayed no trace of trauma, past or present, as players in dazzling white sprinted across the midsummer green.

Midway through the fourth inning, a praying mantis alighted on the blue wooden rail in front of us. She was a pale-green beauty, big as my thumb, standing upright on four hind legs, with her spiked forelegs folded in front of her triangular head with big bug eyes. As a kid I'd been fascinated by these insects, and the way they'd stand, so still and patient, like a pious saint at prayer. But my three female charges reacted differently to the unknown, alien creature.

"What is it?" Stephanie retreated as far into her seat as she could.

Amelia clutched her roommate's hand, and giggled nervously, "Maybe it's a giant grasshopper."

"Or a tiny Martian," Zoe held Zippy out at arm's length for a closer look.

Delighted to have lore to impart, I explained, "It's called a praying mantis, from the way it holds its forelegs together like that. Gardeners love them because they eat insect pests. From ancient times, they've fascinated cultures around the world, and attracted folklore and myth in China, Greece, and Africa. Because they hold so still, and strike so fast, they're often taken as symbols of peace and quiet, or sometimes as a model for warfare or martial arts." I neglected to mention the female's fatal reputation for devouring her male companion after copulation.

Amelia leaned in bravely to examine the triangular face with its eerie oversized eyes and long antennae. "It really does look like a creature from outer space. Hey," she giggled, "if you're E.T., you better call home."

"There's a folktale in France that says the praying mantis grants wishes. Any of you like to make a wish?"

Amelia jumped at the opportunity, her violet eyes sparkling, "Praying mantis, I wish I could smile. And if I could smile, my first smile would be for you."

Stephanie caught her roommate's spirit, and bowing her head and crossing her arms across her chest in reverence, requested, "Praying mantis, I've had this childhood dream of skating at Rockefeller Center on Christmas Eve. If I could do that, I'd know my convulsions were finally under control."

Zoe chimed in, "Praying mantis, I wish Zippy could talk to me and tell me how much he loves me."

Full of enthusiasm, Amelia turned fearlessly to our saturnine odd man out, "How about you, Louis. What's your wish?"

Lou looked up from his program, "You girls don't wanta know."

The praying mantis stayed with us a full inning, more enthralling to my charges than any ballplayer on the diamond. Eventually, it hopped away along the railing, tilting its head back occasionally as if bidding us farewell. We followed its steady progress, and were horrified when a gruff man sitting in the aisle seat, swept the harmless insect off the rail and crushed it beneath his boot.

The girls screamed, as Lou leapt over the four of us and into action, bad knees and all. He grabbed the guy's shirtfront and lifted him clear off his seat. "Why'd you go killing that bug, you asshole!"

The ensuing ruckus spread throughout the grandstand, as fans rose from their seats and craned their necks toward the commotion. Lou continued to throttle the bug-killer, his underlying rage bursting through. I begged Lou to let him go, and he finally relented but insisted, "We need to leave before I bury this jerk-off. Now!"

I swiftly shepherded my confused and grief-stricken troops from the grandstand to the exit ramp, as a thousand eyes followed our erratic exodus. Lou led the way with hobbling strides, as the three girls followed, awash in tears.

"I thought we had plans to stop at O'boyski's Foodland for root beer," sobbed Stephanie, once she realized we were making a beeline back to the hospital.

I hurried my pace, fearing Lou would run off into the blackness. "Not tonight, I'm afraid."

When we'd returned safely to the floor, the girls shortly pacified themselves with thick slices of watermelon. Meanwhile, Lou hit the showers in an attempt to cool his jets.

Right around ten o'clock, the first battery of fireworks from Wahconah Park boomed above our heads, rattling the windows of the old Jones Wing. Most patients scurried to the Activities Room windows to view the fiery spectacle, but I accompanied a still-agitated Lou to the smoking room, where he flinched at every ear-splitting cannonade.

"I thought hospitals were supposed to be quiet zones," he grumbled. "I'd be better off at home."

His hands trembled as he rolled his first cigarette, glancing at the wall clock as it ticked toward 2235 hours, but saying nothing.

I broke through the fraught silence, "Lou, maybe they won't come back this year?"

He wiped his beaded brow with a fresh towel, as a long crackle of fireworks intruded on the scene. "Oh, they'll be back, Sarge. They've got nowhere else to go."

In normal practice we don't indulge a patient's

hallucinations, but in Lou's case, Dr. Guerette had backed me up in feeling it was better not to challenge his phantom visitations. It would only isolate him further and leave him to confront his nightmarish demons on his own. It was important to meet him within his own reality and offer him support in his trauma.

"I'll try to keep my cool, but these guys are persistent bastards. They don't let up until I snap. I'm already on edge, thanks to that jerko in the park."

"Would a little Ativan help to take the edge off?"

"No way! I've got to keep my wits about me." He smoked his cigarette in rapid puffs. "What's left of 'em, anyway."

"How long do they stick around?"

"Hard to say, by the clock. It ain't real time, the way you and me know it, but it feels like eternity. Same old bullshit, too. Slamming me for staying alive, and telling me I'd be better off dead. They're powerful, Sarge, and devious as hell. They tell me Mae's running around with a platoon of guys, and that I'm never gonna get it up again."

He field-stripped his first cig, as if still on patrol, and began to roll another. "Tonight I'll beg them to defuse the skull-bomb, but they'll just laugh it off like it's a big joke. 'What you talking 'bout, old buddy? Why'd we ever do something like that?' Shrinks tell me I've got survivor guilt. That's a laugh. Ain't my fault they croaked. I just wish those honky bastards would stay dead."

Lou took a hard pull from his cigarette, creating an angry ring down its length. "They want me to join the L.W.D. Ever hear of it?"

"No, I'm afraid not."

"Stands for Legion of the War-Damned. They want me

back doing night jumps with them and patrolling the Laotian border just like old times, the Four Amigos. Here's the kick, we were great friends, closer than family under fire. We'd talk for hours about the reunions we'd have stateside, making the rounds, with Dobbs in Sandusky, Compton in Seattle, Slonski in Galveston, and me up here. I've never been tighter with any group of guys, black or white."

Louis snuffed out his second cig between thumb and fore-finger, and looked up warily at the clock: 2220 hours—15 minutes to go.

"Compton is the big talker, which is weird because he carries his head in his hands. Gets even weirder when he throws it into my lap, to laugh up in my face."

He started to roll a third cig, but threw it aside. "I covered their sorry asses for ten months. Ten months before a 122 rocket blew them sky-high. I saw them blown to bits, but never saw them die. I was deafened by the blast, but could still see them standing there plain as day, wiping blood from their faces, and clowning around like it was a big joke."

Lou stretched out his aching legs. "I don't want to believe in their L.W.D bullshit, but they do look like they're coming straight out of hell, yellow stinking fog and sulfur. They're stuck in some crazy space between life and death. They can't get out, but they want me in."

Fireworks continued to reverberate from Wahconah Park, as Lou continued to stare balefully at the wall clock. He stood up slowly and told me it was time to leave him be. "Walk me to my room, Sarge, and keep everyone away from my door. I need to face these mothers alone, and if they do detonate my skull-bomb, I don't want there to be any collateral damage. And please, when and if I get through this, don't come in and start asking me questions. That's what set me off with Mae last year."

"You have my word," I promised him.

Our somber walk down the hall toward his room felt like a *Green Mile* indeed, to a life-or-death confrontation. Lou fiddled with his lights until deciding to keep only his nightlight on, and then took a seat facing the window, as if it were a portal between worlds. I said I'd stand guard at a distance, but within earshot if he needed any help. Cubs program in hand, he gave me a ragged salute as I closed the door behind me.

Taking a seat in the darkened hallway, I half-joked to myself on whether I should have requisitioned a helmet and flak vest for such hazardous duty. But then again, what good is armor against phantoms who can pass through walls? To compound my sense of the uncanny, the flash and boom of fireworks continued to penetrate our walls.

At 2235 sharp, Dobbs, Compton, and Slonski must have arrived on the scene, since just then I heard Lou begin to speak. At first the conversation seemed cordial enough, but the loud fireworks drowned out much of it, so I left my chair and edged closer to his door to eavesdrop. I heard Lou laugh once or twice, and for a while it sounded like a lively back and forth among old friends. But in all my years of working with patients suffering from either visual or auditory hallucinations, I rarely recall anyone ever reporting pleasant visions or sooth-ing words. Typically the apparitions are monstrous, and the voices tormenting.

Suddenly, Lou began to sing. Not like someone happily lending his voice to the choir, but rather as someone coerced into joining a mob in a sing-a-long around a raging bonfire.

A-10 flying high

Drop that napalm from the sky
See them kids down by the river
Drop that napalm and watch 'em shiver.

Things went rapidly south from there; Lou lashed out with accusations against his old mates, and pleaded with them to defuse the skull-bomb in his head. Clearly, he was gaining no ground with his persecutors, and became more and more agitated.

A fusillade of fireworks—the grand finale—rocked our floor, and sent eerie flashes of light ricocheting around the corridor. In the clamor, I peeked through the small window in Lou's door to view what was happening. I could see him kneeling at the window, arms raised and fingers splayed against the panes, seeming to implore his ghostly tribunal for release from the terrible ticking in his head—his desperate silhouette flickering madly off the walls. Soon it became apparent that his plea had been denied, for he crawled weakly into bed, cradled his head in both hands, and wept like a child.

True to my word, I let him be, since the worst was over and he didn't seem likely to do damage to himself or anything else. My shift ended at 2330—11:30 p.m.—so I had to leave his care to others. I walked home, worn out, wondering about Lou's condition and fate. However unreal the visions, his pain was palpably real.

Along Wahconah Street, a thick haze of smoke hung heavily under the street lamps, along with the sulfurous stench of spent gunpowder. Cherry bombs continued to rock the neighborhood, and it was easy to imagine Lou's platoon mates slogging through such a landscape, forever in the thick of it, with never an Independence Day to free them from the Legion of the War-Damned. And Lou neither.

Next morning, however, I found Lou chowing down breakfast, looking no worse for wear. "Hey Sarge, looks like I'm good to go for another year."

At his midmorning discharge meeting, Lou was quick to minimize the previous night's events, although he knew that we knew otherwise, and that nothing had really changed.

"I just sent 'em packing like I always do," he told Dr. Guerette with bravado, taking Mae by the hand. "I feel good, doc, real good, and my three days with you are up. Still got the skull-bomb, sure, but the best thing for me is to get back to work and not lose any more vacation time."

Upon leaving, Lou thanked me for pulling night patrol. "Sarge, you would've made a helluva point man."

That October, the Kansas City Royals made it into the World Series, just as Lou had predicted. During the match-up against the Cardinals, I could imagine him at home, alternating chugs of beer and tokes on a doobie, while keeping track of every pitch, like a team statistician. I could also picture his lovely wife, Mae, looking in at him from the kitchen, happy to see him content, with no crazy talk for a change. Not during the Fall Classic, anyway.

When Bret Saberhagen clinched the decisive seventh game for the Royals, I wanted to call and congratulate Lou on his third straight World Series prediction, no small feat. But it was late, and after all, we weren't really friends, despite the intimate experience I had shared with him. That was in here, but didn't carry over into out there. Let him enjoy his rare night of peace and tranquility, I decided, without a reminder of sadder times.

Perhaps I should have called. In December, Lou's obituary appeared in *The Berkshire Eagle*. It didn't say how he died, or even that he was a decorated Vietnam veteran. Only that he passed away at home. Eventually word got back to our floor, as it often does, that Lou's body had been found by hunters in the woods near his house. The coroner report showed that Lou had died from a self-inflicted gunshot wound—the loud, ticking skull-bomb had finally gone off in his head.

SATURDAY: CONFESSIONS AND REVELATIONS

Next morning, I woke to Ollie's grumbling. "What's that, Fat Boy?"

"I *said* Occupational Therapy stopped by. They told me I'll be stuck taking bed baths for another three months."

I rubbed the drugged sleep from my eyes. "That's not so bad. I once went a month without a bath during my donkey travels. Didn't bother me much."

"You must've been pretty ripe."

"If I was, my donkey never complained."

Ollie forced a smile, "True love, that. But this bedbath business just adds salt to the wound. Come Christmas, I'm gonna smell like an ungodly mix of baby powder and vegetable soup."

He switched off his bedside radio, in no mood to listen to U2's *"Beautiful Day."*

"If it gives you any comfort," I offered, "we once had a patient who went ten years without bathing, and he didn't smell at all."

"Ten years! C'mon, you're pulling my bad leg again."

"Scout's honor."

Ollie let out a lung-crackling sigh. "Great, that's something to hang on to. But how could anyone go ten years? Was he afraid of water?"

"No, but he had his reasons. His name was Stan."

"Stan the stinking man," Ollie chuckled. "Tell me about him sometime, but right now I'm in need of some serious shut-eye. Just wake me when we arrive in Houston. By the way, we'll be traveling the I-10 all the way from here to Tucson. Didn't I tell you I knew this country as well as Pencil Man?"

"You certainly did."

Ollie drifted off as I fell into a reverie about one of my most memorable patients of all time. This tiny mystery man, Stan, came to us several years ago, but the story was as vivid to me as yesterday . . .

The nurses' station fax machine was churning out multiple pages, signaling a new admission.

"We have a nursing home patient coming our way." Ceil read the incoming report to her day crew. "Stanislaw, let me say, Crystal-o-witch, age 80."

I looked over her shoulder and saw the name, Krzysztalowicz, "Wow, his surname has gotta be worth a thousand points in Scrabble."

"They're sending him to us because he hasn't taken a bath since he got there, three months ago."

Nurse Hatchet spun around angrily in her swivel chair, "That's the lamest excuse I've heard for a psych admission since that idiot Joe Parker threatened suicide after he got the short end of a wishbone last Thanksgiving! Why don't they just give the stinker a shot of Haldol, and hose him down while he's sedated?"

"Nursing homes aren't allowed to chemically restrain residents any longer," Ceil reminded her chief nemesis. "You know that."

Nurse Hatchet bit her lower lip and pondered, "Okay, then, when he gets to our ED, let our docs medicate him, have a house orderly scrub him down, and send him back all spic and span. Besides, why on earth now, after three months?"

"It seems that other residents complained, and their families got wind of it."

"Probably got wind of him, too," our clinician Rob Mickle remarked.

Ceil continued to summarize the intake, "His previous caretakers believe he hasn't taken a bath or a shower in ten years, maybe longer."

"Holy cow! Should we open the windows?"

"They say he isn't malodorous, but let's play it safe and put him in Room 76."

Nurse Hatchet rammed her chair up against the chart rack, like a bumper car at Six Flags. "If we're actually going to accept this stink bomb, why give him a single room? Stick him in with Sammy the Snit, give that joker a reason to get his lumbering ass out of here. And what do those nursing home knuckleheads think we can do that they can't?"

Ceil whispered a prayer to the nursing gods for patience. "They're hoping a change of scenery might do the trick."

Nurse Hatchet snapped her pencil in two. "Change of scenery? Oh, yes, like he's going to fall in love with our floral shower curtains. Give me a break. He's a classic dump!"

Ceil persevered, "Stan was born in Warsaw, Poland in 1919. He's Jewish, and very small. Only four foot-seven, and weighs 85 pounds."

"Tom Thumb's little brother," ribbed Rob. "Why don't they just give him a bird bath?"

"He's so small," I chimed in, "if he played golf, he'd yell Two instead of Fore!"

"Yeah," added fellow-staffer Sean Jennings, "but he'd probably have a hell of a short game."

Ceil stilled our flapping tongues with an icy stare. "The nursing home is giving him a ten-day bed hold, meaning if we can't plop him into the tub during that time, they won't take him back."

"Can nursing homes do that?"

"This one can, it seems."

Ceil reached for the assignment board, as I tried to wrap a cloak of invisibility around me. I failed.

"Kevin, you'll be primary nurse, and Sean, therapist."

"Ceil, you know I'm no good with a bar of soap," I objected. "I'm the donkeyman, remember? Pasture pal to every bucking bronco in your paddock."

Ceil brushed away my self-serving plea, and wagged a warning finger at me, "And don't even try to pull your 'Irish shower' stunt again."

The whole crew chortled at Ceil's jab, recalling how she'd busted me a month earlier. I'd been assigned to an elderly gent, but didn't find the time to give him a sorely needed morning bath. Just before lunch, I got word that his family was unexpectedly on their way for a visit.

Under the gun, I had to take a shortcut with his hygiene—not the first, I confess—by foregoing a time-consuming bath for what I called an Irish shower. This entailed soaking a patient's hair over the sink, combing his hair, giving him a quick shave, a clean shirt and, presto, ready for his close-up! On that day, however, Ceil happened into the bathroom where the miraculous transformation had taken place, and discovered that the porcelain tub was bone dry. Her reaction was somewhat damper, shall we say.

Now that the incident had come up again, Rob needled me, "Kev, you should've been a mortician. Your specialty is making people look good from the neck up."

Sean, our eager-beaver therapist and former Golden Glove boxer, had already shot from his chair and returned from the linen closet with towels, latex gloves, and enough soap to scrub down a regiment. He rolled up his sleeves, exclaiming, "Leave the ambulance parked outside! We can do this, Kev, we just gotta believe!"

Ceil rolled her eyes. "Let's let him have lunch first, okay, fellas?"

She handed me Stanislaw's fax sheets so I could set up his chart. "Boys, you have ten days to pull off what hasn't been accomplished in ten years. If you don't succeed, this little stinker could be ours for keeps."

"Consider it done," I affirmed with foolhardy confidence.

The hospital gurney rolled through our doors at high noon, carrying a grizzled, toothless little gent who peeked out from beneath a blanket like a frightened sparrow. His skin was stained the color of mahogany, and dark layers of grime circled his neck and painted his forehead and cheekbones. His right eyelid drooped like a broken window blind, and his nose bulged like a potato. His thin arms, bare to the elbows, looked like strips of beef jerky.

Once we got him off the stretcher, he walked with a wobble, as if punch-drunk, or maybe he had rickets as a kid.

He had little body odor, true enough, but his worn shirt and stained pants stank of urine and mildew. All told, Stanislaw Crystal-o-witch was the strangest little dude who ever graced our unit, and that's saying a mouthful.

Sammy the Snit came charging toward us, his flip-flops slapping wildly against his bare soles. "Kev, please don't make that pygmy my roomie. Please, please, pretty please! I'll do anything, wash floors, scrub toilets . . . "

"Cool it, Sam. He's going into a single room."

Sammy raised his arms to the heavens, proclaiming "Hallelujah" as he flip-flopped away.

Wrong-Leg Levi was next to approach, eyeballing our newcomer as if he were a specimen under glass at the Smithsonian. "What we got ourselves here, the wild man from Borneo?"

"His name is Stan," I said firmly, looking down to find the man in question tugging at my pant loops.

Wrong-Leg balanced on his one leg and a single crutch. "He looks like that 5,000-year old Iceman they recently found in the Alps."

Wrong-Leg Levi was a tough old bird who'd stick in anyone's craw. After his left leg had been amputated from a bad mix of diabetes and alcoholism, he'd bought himself a new pair of Levi's jeans. Anxious to wear them, he failed to check twice before cutting once, and snipped off the right pant leg rather than the left. Only when he put the jeans on did he realize his mistake. To his misfortune, Sammy was present and immediately laid the moniker on him—Wrong-Leg Levi.

Of course, his only recourse was to chop off the left pant leg as well, so he ended up with a pair of rough-cut shorts. Whenever he'd wear them, Sammy would sing, "Who wears short shorts? Levi wears short shorts," and then scurry away.

Levi was aching to give him a swift boot, but that would have taken some clever acrobatics on his part.

At lunch, Sean and I sat on either side of Stan as he studied his tray as if it were an abstruse mathematical equation. When I lifted the lid from his steaming soup, he calculated a minute. Then his eyes lit up, and he raised the bowl to his lips, slurping noisily.

"Damn, this cretin ain't even housebroke," muttered Levi, turning away in disgust.

When the one o'clock courtyard break was announced, Sean asked our new resident if he'd like a cigarette. Getting a blank stare in return, Sean reloaded, "Stan. Cigarette. You want? We have! No? Yes?"

I laughed at Sean's futile attempt. "C'mon, Sean, you're confusing him. Here, let a real linguist give it a go." I stood in front of our little man. "Stanza, you wanta smoka?"

Stan's confusion only intensified, his half-masted eyelid fluttering in bewilderment.

Levi joined in, "Watch, you idiots." He lifted two fingers to his mouth and pretended to inhale. Stan immediately banged both fists on the table and rasped, "Yah! Yah!"

Levi pivoted on his heel, as if to prove he had a leg to stand on. "How much do you bozos make an hour, anyway?"

Both Sean and I escorted Stan, with his rickety gait, to the elevator and down to the courtyard. At the entrance gate, he scanned the iron-barred enclosure and threw on the brakes.

After we'd finally coaxed Stan inside the confines and secured the gate, Rob came over and observed, "Classic sign of an ex-con."

"Remember Hynes from Leavenworth?" added Sean. "He'd always balk at the threshold, flashing back to that old prison yard."

I recalled the likable felon, who somehow went from a federal prison to our establishment through little fault of his own. "What a clever jailbird he was! Remember the cake he made using only our kitchen condiments—milk, cocoa mix, graham crackers, and instant coffee packs. It could have done for a wedding!"

"Probably did, a time or two in the joint."

Sean helped Stan sit in one of our plastic Adirondack chairs, where he squirmed about and looked around nervously. I gave him a cig and lit it, but his deep inhalation brought on such a hacking seizure, I didn't know whether to call a pulmonologist or a chimney sweep. I anxiously patted his frail back, "Clearing the flue, are we?"

After his paroxysms subsided, he relaxed and sank deeper into the oversized chair. He definitely enjoyed his smoke, possibly his first in years. Say what you will about nicotine, but within moments Stan had gone from frightened hare to meditative monk. He reached up and pulled again at my pant loops, in gratitude, I suppose.

Sean sidled over, "A captivating gnome, isn't he?"

Sammy shortly flip-flopped across the yard, dressed in his old high-school football garb, and continued to be his usual, irksome self. "Gee, Kev, it's one thing to be Irish, but do you always have to hang out with the Little People?"

"Cool it, Sammy."

He paid me no mind and squatted in front of Stan, giving a light tap on his mahogany forehead. "Knock, knock, anybody home? No, I didn't think so."

"Knock it off, Sammy, or I'll send you upstairs."

"Gee, Kev, why so touchy?"

After Sammy flitted away, I scanned the yard to check on the rest of our charges, ten in number, smokers and nonsmokers alike, enjoying their sunny break off the unit.

At the picnic table sat three young men—let's call them Huey, Dewey and Louie—rolling in laughter and undoubtedly swapping favorite tales of "getting high." Three middle-aged women—April, May and June—were admiring the morning glories that crept up our high metal bars. They were anticipating the return of our ruby-throated hummingbirds, who seldom disappointed. Sammy had joined Poker Face in a game of hoops, and Levi, wearing his infamous short shorts, was tanning his arms and leg. Meanwhile, Stan seemed entranced by the blue contrails of smoke escaping his lips, as I wondered what stories this strange little man must have bottled up inside.

Sean broke through my musings. "Should we give Stan a shower once we get him upstairs?"

"What's the rush? We've got ten days," I replied. "Besides, he looks like he could use a little R and R."

"Nurse Hatchet will shit a canary."

"She'll shit one any which way."

Rob sauntered over, walkie-talkie in hand. "Why don't we ask Poker Face what card Stan's playing?"

"Good idea. Hey, Poke!"

Poke came trotting across the yard. A nice guy, but bedeviled by gambling. He'd been known to take his weekly paycheck and buy a book of lottery tickets, 300 in all, and still lose! His recently assigned rep payee—the guy who handles his money—said he'd lost so much money to the Mass Lottery that the Commonwealth ought to compensate him with a furnished bungalow overlooking Nantucket Sound. Good luck with that.

Poker Face believed that everyone was dealt a defining playing card at birth, and that Poke alone could read the card and its attributes, just from the person's appearance. For example, he told me I'd been dealt the Jack of Hearts, symbolizing a benevolent goofball. Not so bad, I suppose. In turn, Nurse Hatchet had been dealt the Queen of Spades, which signified "the monarch of all reigning a-holes." Another apt appraisal. Poker was very proud of his gift, saying he'd had it since he was a kid.

"Poke," I asked, "what card do you think Stan here has been dealt?"

Poke pulled up a chair and assessed Stan as if across a green felt table. He took note of his diminutive stature, his leathery skin, and his faraway eyes, before muttering, "This guy's played a lot of losing hands. Not with a full deck, either."

Following his close and thorough inspection, Poke fell back in his chair in exhaustion, as though his strength had been drained by the higher power he'd called upon. Pure theater, but most convincing. He finally roused from his weakened state and pronounced, "He ain't the last boxcar on the train, but he's sure got himself a good view of the caboose."

"But what card is he?"

"The lowest card I've ever seen in the flesh."

"Which is?"

"Three of Clubs!"

"Oooh," we whistled in unison.

"Yep, my friends. Not gonna win many hands with that card. The man's an unlucky dude, I'm afraid. Big time in a small package."

"That bad, huh?" I gazed down upon our forlorn refugee, who had ultimately found refuge with us.

Poker stood up with exaggerated effort. "Yeah, but don't blame me. As I told you all before, I don't deal the cards, I just read 'em."

At Treatment Planning that afternoon, Sean and I laid out our timetable before a dozen staff members from both the day and evening shifts.

"After much deliberation in the yard," I said, as I glanced warily at Nurse Hatchet, "Sean and I have decided to let Stan settle in for a few days. The plan is to gain his trust, and then drop him into the tub on Thursday."

Nurse Hatchet shat her prescribed canary, "Trust? What does trust have to do with anything? The little stink bomb needs a hot bath, period!"

Dr. David Raskin, our affable supervising doctor, gave us a favorable nod. "Sounds reasonable enough. How's his English?"

"Little to none, unless he's playing possum."

"Did you do a mental status mini-exam?"

"Yes, doctor. He scored three of ten."

"Yippee!" Nurse Hatchet cheered cynically, "Not only is he dirty, but he's a dirty dunce."

Dr. Raskin's intake that afternoon shed little light on our newest mystery man. Nor did subsequent phone calls to the nursing home. It was apparent, even taking a language barrier into account, that Stan was mentally challenged. A recent CT scan of his brain showed a history of blunt trauma, as well as gross deterioration over the years.

Sean and I made few inroads with Stan those next two days. His appetite did improve, however, and he never failed to enjoy his time out in the courtyard. He also recognized Sean and me as his go-to guys, and would often pull at our pant

291 • O'Hara

loops like a toddler at his mother's apron.

Come Thursday, Ceil laid down the law, "Boys, this is scrub-a-dub day, right?"

Sean pulled a few cakes of Dial from his pockets. "Ceil, we're loaded for bear!"

Our day started well enough, with Stan enjoying a full breakfast. Next stop was the courtyard, where I opened a fresh pack of Marlboros in front of his fluttering eyes, suggesting the promise of more in the near future. Back upstairs, we walked him to the bathroom, where a perfectly-drawn bath was waiting for his little brown body.

I swirled my arm elbow-deep through the steaming pool. "Stan, let's hop in for a quick bath, shall we? By the time we finish, it'll be lunch and then time for another courtyard. Whaddya say?"

Stan seemed receptive at first, allowing Sean to unbutton his shirt. At the same time, I removed his slippers, revealing leathery feet with curling yellow toenails that looked like stale corn chips. But as soon as we sprinkled Stan with a splash of water, he scratched, clawed, and screamed bloody murder. We backed off and approached again, but this time the feisty bantamweight landed a stinging blow to the side of Sean's head, which left his boxed ear ringing like *The Bells of St. Mary's*.

"Damn," said Sean, "this little guy can pack a wallop!"

We gave up hope of accomplishing our task, and Sean and I soon found ourselves in our own hot water, as we reported back to our disappointed crew at Treatment Planning.

"I thought we were first and goal," I explained, "but we ended up third and long."

Nurse Hatchet hissed like an old steam iron. "Will you please stop with your tedious football metaphors, and give it straight."

Sean picked up the ball, "Guys, it was unreal. We just dabbed him with a little water, and he went berserk like it was sulfuric acid."

Our hatchet-faced nemesis listened, unmoved, to our story. "Since you two can't work your promised healing magic, I say we zonk him with Haldol, plop him in the tub, and be done with it. Do I need to remind the team that he's taking up a precious bed, and eating up valuable tax dollars?"

Dr. Raskin, no fan of the Queen of Spades, eyed her disapprovingly. "I'm not keen on chemical restraints. There has to be another way."

"The little guy probably doesn't want to go back to that nursing home," voiced John Lavalley, an evening staffer. "Mr. Stokes came from there, remember, and woke up that first morning convinced he was in a dog kennel. True story. All he heard from behind his curtains were nursing aides shouting, 'Sit up! Lie down! Roll over!'"

Nurse Hatchet tapped her long red nails in witchy contemplation. "I hear he enjoys his smokes. So let's hold his courtyard privileges until he takes a bath?"

She scanned the room, searching for allies. "It's our only leverage. Let's use it."

Fearful that her proposal might sway a few like-minded staffers, I played my last card. "Once our bath attempt failed, I called Irma, who works in Dietary and speaks fluent Polish. She's agreed to talk to Stan, but she's afraid to come up to the floor. So Doctor, I wonder if we could take Stan to the cafeteria. Maybe Irma could help us communicate and shed light on his behaviors. It can't hurt."

"We should've thought of this earlier," Dr. Raskin frowned.

"But if you and Sean fail in giving him a bath tomorrow, we'll have to revisit this smoking strategy. Now, let's move on, we have fourteen other patients to discuss."

Like many hospital employees, Irma viewed our unit as the proverbial Snake Pit, filled with unimaginable creatures, from gargoyles to zombies. These legends often spread from workers who visited our floor, lab techs, dietary aides, and the like, who might witness something outlandish, and then make an exaggerated tale of it back at the Main House.

There was also a certain type of patient who enjoyed perpetuating those fears. Sammy, of course, was one who liked to play crazy for all its kicks. He'd shout out a high window at unsuspecting employees below, yapping annoyingly at everyone within earshot. "Help, there's a nurse in my room swinging a ten-gallon enema bag! Help, my wife ran off with my psychiatrist, and I miss him!"

Others preyed willfully on visiting young females. One male patient enjoyed covering his privates with a coffee cup, shouting, "Monkey in a cup! Monkey in a cup!" Another joker would pop out his glass eye and roll it around on a soup spoon. A third would stop every female visitor in the hall and shout, "Rectum? Rectum? Damn near killed 'em!"

On Day Five, I wheeled Stan to meet Irma in the cafeteria. Over bagels, I gave her a script of questions to ask him. Stan began to stir once he heard his native tongue, and commenced to tug at my pant loops beneath the table. After their back and forth in a language incomprehensible to me, Irma gave me encouraging news.

"Stan has agreed to take a bath, but only a bed bath in his room, not the bathroom. He also wants to smoke while it's happening."

I shook her hand, and then Stan's. "Tell him we've got ourselves a deal! By the way, did he say why he hates taking baths?"

"He says he's clean enough."

"What about his Polish? Does he speak well, or not so good?"

"He talks like a 1st-grader, if that's what you mean."

"Okay. How about hobbies or interests?"

"He says he likes to play draughts—checkers."

"Checkers? Well, that's good to know. Thank you for all your help."

Irma hurried back to the kitchen, where she was met eagerly by her culinary mates, all dying to know the latest strange and scary story from our locked ward.

Next morning, the Bed Bath Brigade was ready for battle.

"Man your stations!" shouted Sean.

"Fire in the hole!" Rob sloshed into Stan's room with a basin of steaming water.

"Yee-Haw!" I brayed at the top of my lungs.

Stan got a kick out of our clowning but remained nervous, slipping his first cig from hand to mouth like a man in front of a firing squad. He wanted to remain standing during his scrub down, so we removed his ratty old clothes, including the yellow long johns that peeled off his thin shanks like banana skins.

"This guy's in serious need of Three-in-One oil," uttered Sean, hearing Stan's bones crack when pulling off his shirt.

Once Stan was naked, I took inventory of his misshapen body. "Poke was right, this little fella has truly been dealt a bad hand. From the looks of it, he's been through a world of hard knocks. You don't need to be an orthopod to know his ribs have been busted up a time or two."

We decided to start with a shave, but despite our cafeteria treaty, he resisted with flailing arms, showing more strength than we could have guessed.

I called our efforts to a halt. "Damn, if only he'd take a little Ativan."

"Or a shot of Stoly." Sean looked warily at Stan's clenched fists.

Rob sat at the edge of his bed. "I bet you ten-to-one that someone tried to drown him as a kid."

I offered Stan another smoke, which he took readily. In his contentment, I mimed what we were about to do with shaving cream and razor, then scissors for a haircut. Remarkably he allowed us to commence, but squeezed his eyes shut so tightly that tears leaked out during the procedure. In short order, a surprisingly presentable face emerged from under the dirt and stubble.

"Boy, Stan, you're as handsome as Cary Grant."

We continued to make slow but steady progress, working our way down his body, shoulder to finger, hip to toe.

"Sure glad Stan is no Free Willie." Sean recalled an obese patient from a month before. "Or we'd be at this job for three days."

At length, Stan forsook his defensive position and lay down on the bed, spread-eagled, motioning us to continue. With easier access, we took up our task in earnest.

"It's like scrubbing off a tan," panted Rob.

"Or peeling bark off a tree," puffed Sean.

I worked around his head and neck. "Stan, old boy, you're slowly emerging from your dark cocoon."

"Hey, who's going to do dingleberry patrol?"

"Not me," I laughed. "I'm gonna pull rank here, fellas."

"Hey, we lucked out, no hanging onions!"

We dashed in and out of the room for fresh basins of water, like a firefighting bucket brigade.

Ceil peeked in for a look-see. "How's it going?"

"Going, but never-ending," Rob reported, rubbing his shirt sleeve across his brow. "It's like stripping furniture."

"Have you got down to bare skin yet?"

"Some," I replied, "but we'll have to revisit a few areas, where I swear he's grown vegetation."

Ceil handed me a bag of clothes. "Here's an outfit I picked up in the boy's department at Target. Hope it fits."

Sean stood back to marvel at the pink patches emerging from Stan's brown shell. "Amazing to discover an actual body under there, isn't it?"

Rob abruptly stopped scrubbing Stan's arm. "Guys, you gotta see this. Probably why he's not wild about showers."

He lifted Stan's arm to show five numerals in black tattooed onto his forearm.

"What's this? Was he a POW?" I guessed.

Sean smacked his forehead with an open palm. "Guys, how stupid! Stan was born in Warsaw in 1919, right? He must have been in a German concentration camp during the war."

Sean held up Stan's arm and pointed to the numbers, "Stan, where'd you get this?"

Stan rubbed the spot and mumbled, "Auschwitz."

"My God, he's a Holocaust survivor. From Poland, no less. How did he ever live through all that?"

Imagine our surprise when Stan pointed to his broken nose, and muttered in barely intelligible English, "Nazis make me box."

Thus Stan started to emerge from his shell, figuratively as

well as literally. When we'd finished our arduous labors, we escorted him, freshly groomed and dressed, to a belated lunch. A few patients didn't recognize him, such was the metamorphosis from pitiable homunculus to a dapper little man. Those who did, applauded the transformation.

"My, look at you!" exclaimed Ceil, holding Stan at arm's length. "Aren't you a handsome one?" She also gave me a gratifying hug, "This makes up for all your Irish showers."

Stan must've liked the way he looked, too. All that day, he never passed a mirror without stopping to admire his new threads: white chinos and sneakers, with a red sweatshirt.

"He looks like a walking Polish flag," Sean commented.

"Clean as a whistle, too." I pointed out. "Take a picture, boys, because in ten years time, he'll be back to his old self." It occurred to me that, for now at least, Stan looked more like a Heart or Diamond than a lowly Club.

Later that afternoon, Dr. Raskin painted a vivid picture of what life must have been like for Stan in a Nazi concentration camp, and speculated that he survived as a featherweight boxer for the amusement of the guards.

On the seventh day, I called Stan's nursing home to report that our mission was accomplished, but was shocked to hear that they were blocking his readmission.

"You people did a fine job," the administrator allowed, "but our social worker informed us that you bribed him with cigarettes to give him a bath. Since our facility is smoke-free, we don't believe he'll be as cooperative here. That's the way it is. I'm sorry." *Click.*

I couldn't believe my ears. Nurse Hatchet had been right all along. Stanislaw Crystal-o-witch was a straight-up dump.

As Stan's primary caregiver, my next task was to assist our

skilled social worker, Mark Keller, in getting him into another nursing home. Otherwise he'd be sent to the shoddy, state-run facility, notoriously known as the "Last Nursing Home on the Left," a horror movie in itself. With Stan's health, hygiene history, and lack of insurance, the cards were stacked high against him. Yes, another low draw for the Three of Clubs.

In the ensuing weeks, a dozen nursing home screeners came to our floor to evaluate our little man. But, however we spruced him up, nobody wanted our little doggy in the window. Our last hope was Mapleview, in nearby Hinsdale, a small, 20-bed operation staffed by St. Luke's nurses. They agreed to accept Stan when a male bed became available.

Meanwhile, Stan had become a fixture at our place. Free from his carapace of grime, he sat in on groups—"making funnies," as he called his unintelligible jokes—and never missed a courtyard. Whatever his history of brain damage, he whipped everyone at checkers. All in all, he became a tiny, walking advertisement for the indomitable human spirit.

After weeks without a callback from Mapleview, the inevitable bureaucratic word came down: Stan was to be transferred the next day to the "Last Nursing Home on the Left."

Hearing the news, Sean and I marched Stan into Dr. Raskin's office to plead his case.

"Doc, a Cabulance is scheduled to pick up Stan tomorrow for you know where. But we just called Mapleview again, and they have a guy about to check out as we speak—Last Rites and all. Please, doc," I pleaded, "could you give him one more day, repeat a blood test, or something?"

Dr. Raskin looked up wearily from his desk. "Guys, what do you want me to do, make Stan our floor mascot? He's been here for seven weeks, and Administration has been on my ass about it."

He took a deep breath, and looked at the diminutive figure standing between Sean and me, with his fingers hooked into our pant loops. "What is it about this little guy? I know just how you feel. He's touched my heart more than a thousand other patients who've come through our doors; something about surviving against all odds, battling through the sort of life that's just a dim, grim report to us. Imagine what he's seen? What he's endured? And who would ever think such a tooth-less grin could be so charming?"

He glanced at the wall calendar. "One more day, boys. But if Mapleview doesn't come through, Stan's next bout might be the knockout. And please, find a way to keep our resident scold from storming my office."

"Yes, doctor! Thank you, doctor!" We scurried out of the room before he could change his mind.

For once, Stan's low card won a trick, and a bed opened up at Mapleview the very next morning.

Dr. Raskin gave Sean and me special permission to trans-port Stan to Mapleview in the hospital's station wagon. A real treat for each of us, a day on the loose. That morning we took a circuitous route to Hinsdale and enjoyed the outing on hos-pital time. I drove, with Stan sitting shotgun, and Sean behind. It was early November, but the graying hills were still flecked with muted colors, looking like gigantic pots of fading mums in the distance. Stan rolled down his window and took in great gulps of country air.

At Mapleview, two warmhearted fellow grads of St. Luke's, Beth and Sally, greeted Stan like a long-lost family. You couldn't ask for better attendants to check-in your final board-ing pass, so to speak.

"Perfect timing," Sally smiled, "we've just made up your bed." She took Stan by the hand, "Your roommates are dying to meet you." As the kindly nurses led us down the narrow hallway toward the last bedroom on the left, Sean and I exchanged an ironic glance.

"Look Stan, here come your new roommates, Bart and Darby, to greet you."

The odd pair that shuffled toward us seemed eager to make Stan feel right at home. Bart was a dwarf and former circus clown, and Darby was an ancient war veteran with an alarming head wound; shrapnel had cleaved his bald skull so it looked like a peeled orange with a slice missing. I worried that Stan would make a run for it, but he embraced the pair like old pals.

Sean and I stood flabbergasted, but neither Beth nor Sally seemed surprised by their immediate bond. "God makes 'em and matches 'em," Beth affirmed with delight. "I could write a book about the friendships I've seen at the end of one's living days."

When we entered their room, Bart shouted, "Stan, watch!" and proceeded to somersault down the length of his bed. Darby chuckled indulgently, "Bart's a real barrel of laughs. You'll love it here."

Sally cranked up the head of Stan's middle bed, which offered a pleasant view of sugar maples outside his window. Sean and I shortly waved goodbye and turned to leave, with a gratifying last image of Stan looking out at a world of beauty at the end of a life of pain.

Stan's absence was palpable back on Jones Three. The short fellow with bowed legs and toothless smile had left a lasting mark on us, more indelible than the dirt we stripped from him. Even Nurse Hatchet had softened, if stone can soften. It became a thing for staff to tug at each other's belt loops, in memory of the "Bantam Champ" who had touched each of us in some special way. We all had a sense of a mission fulfilled in easing the final stage of a difficult life. We had helped the Three of Clubs win a hand at last.

Sean and I continued to call Mapleview every weekend to check on Stan. He'd never come to the phone, but Agnieszka, a Polish-speaking aide, would report that he appreciated our calls, as well as the *Chrusciki* she'd bake for him at home, better known as angel wings. He was undefeated at checkers, she added, but still not crazy about bed baths.

Agnieszka also tried to solve a mystery for us, "Do you know how he always tugs at belt loops? One evening he told me how he escaped through Europe by riding on a train, standing up on a crate for days on end. He showed me by raising his hand as if to grasp a railcar strap, and I just thought, well, maybe?"

At any rate, it was clearly a gesture of holding on for dear life. We were sad to get word the following April that Stan had passed away, playing out his lowly card from the cradle to the grave, from war-torn Poland to the bucolic Berkshires, and beyond.

* * *

Ollie wasn't the same cat when he woke from his midmorning nap. He grumpily refused his light rehab, pushed away his lunch tray, and snapped uncharacteristically at the nurses. Nor was he inclined to play his role as Fat Boy, or even respond when I mentioned how we'd be changing buses in Houston.

He looked cold and detached, like a Viking warrior preparing for battle, with a grim and faraway look in his eyes. He must have looked something like that while staring down that lone oak the past Sunday. I tried to pull him out of his funk, but every attempt was answered by an irritable grunt or groan.

Perhaps the opiates were getting to him, or his still-mysterious bleed was troubling him, or maybe the consequences of his "accident" and the lengthy rehabilitation required may have finally hit him head-on. Yesterday he'd vented out his frustration to Dr. Carter, "Doc, if I end up disabled, I ain't long for this world."

After we received our 2 o'clock meds, I took another stab at reviving his spirits. And what better way, I thought, to pull a hot-blooded male from the doldrums than with a bawdy tale?

"Fat Boy, you know, halfway between Houston and San Antonio, barely ten miles off the I-10, there's a place from my past that I'd take you if we could detour the bus. I've got a juicy story about it, X-rated, or maybe a hard R. Want to hear it?"

He turned off the TV he wasn't watching, "Do I have a choice?"

"Well, I guess not, but it's a captivating tale of titillation that I'm bursting to tell, a confession I'm dying to make, and you happen to be the only available ear. You ever hear of the Chicken Ranch in La Grange, made famous by the movie, *Best Little Whorehouse in Texas?*"

"Oh yeah, La Grange." Fat Boy began to stir alive again. "Wasn't there a ZZ Top song about it?"

"Yep." I began to growl in my deepest voice: *'Rumor*

spreading round in that Texas town/'bout that shack outside La Grange/ and you know what I'm talkin' about . . . '"

"Indeed, I do." Ollie continued to show interest. "But what was a good Catholic boy like you doing in a Texas cathouse?"

"I had no choice. Part of our initiation as firefighters at Bergstrom Air Force Base, just outside Austin."

"Likely story."

"I'm serious. Our crew chief, Sgt. Kilfeather believed that having a 'cherry boy' in the firehouse was bad luck, so he made sure every new recruit lost whatever remained of his innocence with a La Grange girl. He even commandeered these junkets personally, to make sure no rookie weaseled out."

"Easy duty for him."

"You bet. But in the bunkhouse on the eve of our trip, I pleaded with him, saying I wanted to remain faithful to my girlfriend, Lily, back home. He mocked me in front of the whole crew, saying, 'Tell you what, Housefly, if you want out of La Grange, I need a note from your family doctor saying how he treated you for the clap. That, and a crisp Polaroid of your girly-girl in the nude. And I want 'em by tomorrow.'"

"Sounds like a real jerk. Why did he call you Housefly?"

"He complained that I was always buzzing around the firehouse."

Fat Boy broke into a warm smile, "I can certainly believe that."

"The next evening, I found myself wedged in the back of a station wagon with three other newbies, Parsons, Smith, and Willis, while Kilfeather drove up front with his two side-kicks who kept heaving empty cans of Pearl beer at jackrabbits along the way.

"Driving the hour down Route 71, Sgt. Kil kept praising

La Grange like it was the cradle of civilization. 'Boys,' he drawled, 'the Chicken Ranch is true Americana, dating back to the 1840s when Texas was still a republic. Pity Miss Jessie didn't keep herself a log book back then,'cause dozens of famous gunslingers took comfort there. By golly, boys, if bedsprings could talk what tales would be sprung.'

"He spat a wad of tobacco juice out the window. 'Now, I've been driving cherry boys like yerselves to La Grange for nine years without a dab of trouble, so I don't want you four mucking up my good standing. And whatever you do, don't go asking one of these gals to become your pen pal, like that whack job, Owens, did a year back, when he invited Rosie O'Day up to Tulsa to meet his parents over the Christmas holidays. Boys, these gals are professional, not inclined to romancing notions. So don't get it in your hat-rack you're anything special, because to them you're nothing but a deli number waiting to pound some ham.'"

"Your sarge sounds like quite a character. How about the other newbies? Were they balking like you were?"

"Hardly! They'd been counting down the days since Sarge first mentioned it. But I hated the thought of cheating on Lily. In addition, after seeing all those graphic military films about venereal disease, I figured my penis would be speckled with canker sores for all eternity, whether I wore protection, or not."

"Couldn't the Air Force intervene or anything?"

"You kidding! The Chicken Ranch was practically a military institution. We got ourselves a 10 percent discount just by showing our dog tags! When we pulled off Route 71 toward La Grange, we traveled up a dusty road to a rambling old farmhouse, with turret, gables, porch, and a picket fence all painted white. No signs, just a few overgrown gardens, cottonwood trees, and a couple of empty chicken coops. At the back screen door, we were greeted by a buxom black woman who checked our I.D's. When it was my turn, she looked from my picture to my face and declared, 'Damn, son, you don't look a day over 14.'"

"Just like the Boy Scout you were pretending to be." Fat Boy was really enjoying himself by now.

"Once inside the joint, we were led to a red-carpeted sitting room where ten or twelve scantily clad girls were draped over red velour settees. Supposedly they were college girls, Aggies and Longhorns, but I doubted it. There was a smaller room across the hall where guys drank soda and played pool. Waiting on a double header, I guess."

"Wait a minute. Drank soda? In a cathouse?"

"House rules. The madam, Miss Edna, didn't allow any liquor in the house, just soft drinks."

"Were the girls pretty?"

"Pretty enough. Certainly my mates had no trouble choosing them. Parsons, Smith, and Willis hooked up to their gals like nails to magnets, and disappeared up the old creaking staircase. But I kept stalling, hoping that Kilfeather and his cronies would go in first, so I could claim I went in after them but came out before them. Sarge, however, was bouncing a busty blonde on each knee, and keeping a rattler's eye on me.

"'Hey, Housefly,' he yelled across the room, 'who you waiting on, Cinderella?'

"I hemmed and hawed, 'No, Sarge, I'm waiting on that pretty brunette who just went in with the Hoover salesman.'

"He wasn't buying it. 'Best hurry it up,' he says to me, 'because I'm not going in 'til you come out, and right now I'm hornier than a snot-snorting bull in a field of throbbing heifers. So move it, or you'll be walking back to Austin with my chukka boot lodged up your ass!'"

Fat Boy smirked, "Poor Kevlar, what a dilemma."

"Painted into a corner, I looked around and finally decided upon the girl least attractive to me; a pimply, redheaded dumpling, figuring I could survive her charms in private. Kilfeather split a gut when he saw me following her through the swinging doors. Once in her chamber, she introduced herself as Ruby and asked if I'd buy her a Coke. I agreed, but she asked for a dollar. 'A dollar?' I questioned, knowing that a Coke only cost a dime in their soda machines. 'Yes, a dollar, honey. You got a Q-Tip stuck in your ear?'"

"From where I lie," quipped Ollie, "I'd gladly buy her a case of Coke, pimply or not. What was your total bill?"

"Eight bucks with my military discount. Plus the Coke and a dollar tip. A tenner, all told."

Ollie coughed and sputtered, "Then what happened?"

"Ruby placed the unopened soda on her night stand and dropped her fingers on my thigh, playing itsy-bitsy spider. But I told her I wouldn't . . . no, I couldn't, because I was saving it up for my girlfriend back home.

"She let out this wild cackle, 'Why, cut me off at the knees and call me Shorty! I do believe that's the sweetest thing I ever did hear. Saving it up for your hometown sweetie, as if a young buck like yourself needs to be minding his emissions.'

"Then, trying a different tactic, Ruby stepped back and started to dance, undulating seductively in her sheer red lingerie. On the verge of succumbing, I spluttered, 'And I don't want to bring home any, you know, weird diseases.'

"She stopped her dance and slapped me playfully on my bum. 'Why, honey child, I'm checked out by a certified doctor once a week in town.'

"But tell me, Fat Boy, what's so reassuring about a weekly check-up when her door has been swinging off its hinges for six straight days? Then she kissed me, a little buttercup kiss."

" A buttercup kiss?"

"Yep, that's what I called it, because I melted like butter, and was up and off of her quicker than a greenhorn on a bucking bronco."

Ollie laughed so hard that his Pleur-evac set off its alarm. "Ha, no wonder Ruby never opened her Coke. She knew all along she wasn't going to work up a thirst!"

I gave my roomie a withering glance. "Wow, that's rich, Fat Boy. Real rich."

Fat Boy couldn't rein in his amusement. "So, how was it?"

"It wasn't, even at my randy age."

"C'mon, Kevlar, there must have been some pleasure in it."

"Joyless, Fat Boy. Like I fired a blank."

"Were your efforts good enough to please your sergeant?"

"Oh yeah, though he made me the laughing stock of the firehouse for the next two weeks, telling the whole crew how Housefly had picked the only dandelion from a bouquet of yellow roses."

* * *

Unfortunately, Ollie's interest faded quickly, and his mood pancaked through the rest of the day and evening. It was only after he'd received his nighttime meds that his gloominess broke like a child's fever.

"Kevlar, you know, this road we're on right now, Interstate

10, is really my life. I was thinking about it when we went through San Antonio earlier. A week ago, I seemed sure to meet my Alamo, reach the end of the road, but here I am, still on the damn highway, headed back to where I came from. We'll be in El Paso by morning, and like the song says, *'Back in El Paso my life would be worthless/Everything's gone in life; nothing is left.'*"

"Hey Fat Boy, we'll just stay clear of Rosa's cantina."

"Doesn't matter. Soon after that, we'll be in Arizona. Then I'll be re-traveling roads I know awfully well and am trying to forget, first Tucson and then Yuma. Places I meant to leave behind for good."

"I'll tell you, Fat Boy, I'm a firm believer that you can go home again. If you ask me, my life is living proof. The Air Force sent me to the other side of the world, but I came back, and for all these years, I've lived a stone's throw from my child-hood home, less than a mile from here."

"Fine for you. I've seen your happy family traipsing through this room, all of 'em. Me, I've destroyed every rela-tionship I ever had."

"Relationships can be repaired."

"Only by death, I'm afraid."

"C'mon, Ollie, that's dark. I'm more hopeful for light at the end of the tunnel."

"You can use that term after Vietnam?"

"Well, I'm also thinking about near-death experiences, you know, being drawn toward the light."

"So you believe in all that?"

"I have no reason not to."

"But do you have any hard evidence?"

"Evidence, no. Hints of immortality, yes."

"Such as?"

This was a turn in the conversation that I was uncomfortable with, for my own reasons as well as for Ollie's sake. Plus, I was not comfortable, period, nor in good humor, despite the opiates coursing through my veins. After six days in bed, my urine remained red, my lower back still twanged like a tuning fork, and my ribs felt like caved-in rafters. Mortality was not a topic I was eager to discuss. Or any sort of life beyond. But I had dumbly brought it up, and Ollie was determined.

"Well, Kevlar, do you got any hereafter stories to share? Or are you going to take 'em to your own grave?"

"Okay, per your request," I reluctantly resumed. "I have a close friend, Rick, whose story is a double dose of the incomprehensible. He had Crohn's disease and was hospitalized with severe inflammation of the bowel, and due for surgery the next morning. On the toilet that night, he suddenly began to bleed out, and collapsed while trying to reach the call button. When he recovered, he reported the same type of thing as many people do in near-death situations. He found himself out of body, floating around the room, and being drawn to a tunnel of white light."

"Pretty standard stuff," Fat Boy grumbled.

"For sure, but there's more. A few days later, while he was recuperating in ICU, a nurse he'd never actually met came to visit, and before she could introduce herself, Rick reached out his hand and thanked her for saving his life. She asked, 'How could you know that? You were unconscious when I found you.' My friend replied, 'I was far gone for sure, fighting against that pulling white light, but I watched you enter the room and call a Mayday.'

"The nurse was amazed, then added her own uncanny

experience. 'You know, it was pure luck I looked into your room that night. I was working another floor, and for some reason, when I took my break, I was drawn to your room, which has always held a special significance for me.'"

"Hey, just like the room that burned woman had for you."

"What? Yes! Julie Potter, Room 404. How do you know about that?"

"You were raving about it one night."

"Really? I can't believe I was actually talking about that." In this through-the-looking-glass world I'd entered, nurse-turned-patient, drug-dispenser-turned-drug-taker, I hardly knew where my mind or my mouth was taking me.

Fat Boy wheezed. "Got any more oh-wow stories?"

"I do remember another patient's story, a Korean veteran, whose tale was just as incredible. Helping him to bed one night, I noticed severe scarring down his left leg, and asked how it happened. His reply was rational, even though his story was horrific. He'd been walking home one blustery winter's evening, when a passing car caught his raincoat in its fender, and dragged him for a hundred yards."

"I'm amazed he survived."

"Yeah, plus, the driver fled, leaving him for dead. He was picked up by a sanitation truck, of all things, and taken to the hospital. There, the on-call surgeon told him he was going to lose his leg, but surgery had to be put off for a few days until the swelling went down. That night, the veteran was visited by his deceased father, who walked into his room, plain as day. There he told his son that he wasn't going to lose the leg, and he'd recover nicely. Sure enough, a couple of days later the surgeon came in, saw that the swelling was down, and decided not to amputate."

Ollie shifted his burly body in his puny bed. "But this Korean vet was a resident of your ward, who probably suffered a head injury while being dragged. Why would you believe him?"

"You'd have to meet him to understand. He was so matter of fact, not delusional at all, and he told his story in the most convincing manner. He just struck me as a reliable witness."

"I'll take your word for it, Kevlar, but I don't find either of those stories totally convincing. Got any others?"

"A few more, but here's a funny one. My longtime plumber, Bill, slipped into a week-long coma after being involved in a head-on car collision. When he came to, he told his wife how her departed mom had visited him every night, assuring him that he'd be okay. But here's the kick—Bill had hated the sight of his mother-in-law when she was alive."

Fat Boy snickered, "Talk about a recurring nightmare! Now, tell me one more, the best in your bag. Because if you do, I'm inclined to tell you my own."

"Really? I'd love to hear that. So I'll make my story the most personal, the cream of the crop."

"Great. Time we both swap our finest,'cause it's going to be an awful long night across West Texas, I'm afraid."

"Okay, this is recent, and made a tremendous impression on me. My Mom passed away a year ago at age 92. She'd developed a brain tumor, a glioma. She lived for seven months after her diagnosis, without pain, thankfully, but with partial paralysis that took away her speech. Still, we found ways to communicate, and I was grateful for how close we were, at the beginning as well as the end. One evening, sitting peacefully together, I asked her, after she died, if she'd give me a sign from the other side, if allowed. I figured if there were an afterlife, my mother would surely have earned a golden pass through Heaven's Gates. She smiled as best she could, and nodded that she would.

"Shortly after her death, I was writing a remembrance of her for my annual Christmas story for our local newspaper. As I often do, I was priming my emotions by listening to a single song. In this case, the tune was from Meg Hutchinson's album, *The Crossing*. Meg, by the way, is a brilliant poet and folk musician, as well as an advocate for the mentally ill.

"The song I was repeatedly listening to was *'As the Crow Flies,'* and the words that kept me going were, *'Let me open this heart again/Wider than the sky/To all the pain and wonder/Of being in this life/Let me go.'* The haunting lament urged me on, and allowed me to memorialize my mother at the same time. But once I finished, I was never able to find that CD again, and the empty case just nagged at me. I looked high and low, and kept looking, until I came to the conclusion that this was the message from my mother, to *'Let me go'* and return to the *'pain and wonder of being in this life.'* And I haven't found that CD since, nor do I believe I ever will."

"That's touching, Kevlar, but still sketchy about proving the hereafter. Everybody loses or misplaces CDs."

"Well, Fat Boy, it's not so much what something means, as the meaning you invest in it. And that mysterious disappearance made me feel an intimate connection with my departed mother. That's my story, and I'm sticking to it."

"Fair enough, Kevlar, but I think my story might even top your own."

"That's great. I'm all ears. Out with it."

Ollie raised the head of his bed as high as his suffering body could bear, and turned his ravaged Viking visage toward me. "Ahem, here goes. My story, Kevlar, is all about the price you pay for a glimpse of paradise. Are you ready for that?"

"I've been waiting all week to hear your story, hoping to find out how Ollie became Fat Boy."

"I'm going to have to take you way back, right to the beginning, to tell how I both found and lost the love of my life. It was back in the '80s, sort of a nothing time. I was a young man working at the tire center in Tucson, and tending bar part-time at a local joint called the Mirage. The extra money was nice, but I really did it to meet women, or at least to have a friendly chat with them.

"One night in walks this out-of-place girl, probably too young, but the Mirage wasn't the sort of bar that carded minors. She wasn't a looker by any means, sort of plump and pimply like your gal at the Chicken Ranch. But she had these deep brown eyes that you could drown in, and a smile that could light up a football stadium. Her name was Betsy and she was from Georgia, on the run by the looks of it. I didn't snoop, and she didn't tell. But all night, and for some nights after, I'd keep gravitating back to her, standing her drinks and being charmed by her Georgia drawl, talking about nothing at all. She was a real peach, but seemed lost with no place to go. Soon she stopped coming round, and to be honest, I forgot all about her."

"I'm guessing that's not the end of the story."

"You guess right, just the start. Four years later, I'm still at the Mirage when this knockout walks through the door. A hush fell over the joint, except for the squeaks of barstools swiveling to follow her progress. She walked up to me, leaned across the bar, and asked, 'Remember me?' For a few seconds, I couldn't place her, but how could I forget those brown eyes? Then she smiled and, damn my eyes, it was Betsy! Her teenage acne had cleared up, and she'd lost her baby fat."

"The ugly duckling turns into a swan."

"You can say that again! She told me that four years ago she'd decided to return home to Marietta, to face facts and change her life, and that the way I listened to her talk about anything at all, like she was *somebody*, had made a big impression on her. Now she was passing through Tucson again, in a much different place in her life, and she stopped at the Mirage in hopes of thanking me for my kindness.

"I was stunned on many levels, but managed to say, 'Yep, here I am, standing behind the same bar, pouring the same drinks to the same drunks, sure haven't changed as much as you have.' She took a seat in her old spot, and was impressed that I still remembered her favorite drink, Captain and Coke.

"There was a carnival going on that night, not far from the bar. You could actually see the Ferris wheel from our front window. So when I clocked out as barback at 10, I asked Betsy if she'd like to walk over to the fairground, maybe go for a ride. 'I'd love that,' she smiled back. I couldn't believe my luck. You know that Tom Petty song, *'Even the losers get lucky some time'?*"

"I sure do. What a great song."

"Yeah, but I ought to have paid attention to the last verse: *'Should have known right then it was too good to last.'* But don't let me get ahead of myself. Let me enjoy those fleeting moments at the fairground."

"By all means, Ollie. Tell me the whole story, just as it happened."

"When we get to the fair, she picks the merry-go-round, of all things. So we squeeze into a golden chariot led by a unicorn, and I'm embarrassed as hell. But after our first ride, we're so darn silly, we jump back into the chariot for a second go-round.

"Soon, we were walking around the park, holding hands. As we passed a booth, we were stopped by a barker, 'Hey bud, win your honey a honey bear! Three shots for a dollar!' He was spinning a basketball in his hand, and pointing to a hoop way up in the bright lights. I walked right on by, but Betsy tugged at my sleeve, and said, 'C'mon, Oliver. I'm here to bring you luck.'

"I was never a jock growing up, more into fishing and motorcycles. But I gave the carny a dollar, and took a heave. No one was more surprised than me when the ball went straight through the hoop. Bulls-eye! I thought I'd won Betsy the big plush bear with a goofy grin. But instead of the bear, the barker hands me another ball that weighs three times as much as the first one, and tells me I have to sink three in a row to win his dumb bear.

"One basket was sort of a miracle, so what does that make three in a row? I was set to walk away in disgust, but Betsy encouraged me with a surprise kiss, 'It's time you start believing in yourself.' I looked into her beautiful brown eyes, and the light of her smile flipped a switch in me. Who was this mystery woman who'd just walked into my drab life mere hours ago? So I took up the medicine ball, reared back, and launched it into the lights—swish, two in a row!

"A crowd had begun to gather, and the barker played to them, touting my chances to take home that stupid looking bear. I bet none had been won all night, least of all by a guy throwing a basketball overhand like a baseball. This time he handed me a lopsided ball with a big bubble on it. If it were a tire, I'd have thrown it into the rubbish heap. 'C'mon man, that ain't fair,' I say to him. 'Take it or leave it,' he snarls back.

So I grab Betsy and I kiss her this time, take the ball out of the carny's hand, and toss it high into the night."

"Let me guess. You made like Larry Bird, and sank it again."

"Yep, three in a row! Everyone went crazy, knowing it was a one-in-a-million shot. Even the barker got caught up in the moment, presenting Betsy with the honey bear, and sticking a big fat cigar in my mouth. 'Son,' he says, 'you've got yourself a keeper there. And I ain't talking about my bear.' So I walk out of the fairgrounds with one arm around a big stuffed animal, and the other 'round my newfound Georgia peach. And everyone is looking at me, like I'm a hero or celebrity. It was the greatest moment of my life up to that point."

"You paint a vivid picture, Fat Boy. I can almost smell the cotton candy and fried dough. Do go on."

"I used to tell the guys in the shop that if I were a car, I'd be a rusty old Pinto in need of a valve job. But that night, with my arm around Betsy, I felt like a Cadillac Eldorado. On our way back to the Mirage for a nightcap, we passed a small park, empty at that hour, and found a secluded spot under a wide-spreading velvet mesquite tree. As such things go, one thing led to another, and under those rippling leaves, we soon pressed that big plush bear into service as a cushion. Came in handy, huh?"

"I'll say."

"Between the bear's arms and mine, Betsy was totally enfolded, and the two of us became one. And it was no giddy-up, like you call it, but a magical carpet ride through the cosmos. We stayed there till dawn, curled up in the chill, and came to know each other in so many other ways. She told me how she first came to Tucson, on the run from an abusive stepfather, and the big difference I made by just being kind and listening to her. I told her about my dreams and my search for the girl who would help make those dreams come true."

Fat Boy paused to catch his breath.

"Kevlar, it was the most amazing night of my life. From that time on, we were inseparable. Why we even kept the goofy bear that Betsy named Chopper, and that became our code for making love, 'Care to take a hop on Chop?'"

"That's cute."

"Cute, yeah, but also transformational. Betsy was the new set of spark plugs I desperately needed. During our first month together, I quit smoking, cut back on drinking, and even bought a new rack of clothes. She was truly a lifesaver, and at a time in my life that definitely needed saving. Alcohol had finally killed off my dad, and Mom was losing her battle with ovarian cancer. I don't think I'd have gotten through that year without Betsy.

"I just turned 27 and Betsy 21 when we got married that October. Betsy was carrying our little Davy at the time, so it was a wedding of the shotgun persuasion, you know, though I sure didn't need any persuading. Mom lived long enough to attend our small ceremony, and got to meet Betsy's mom. Clara was a true Southern belle, full of class and sass, and Mom really liked her."

Ollie paused as his Pleur-evac kicked in, the racket as loud as any blender at his old bar.

"My working buddy, Brad, had his band play at our reception as a wedding gift. For our first dance, they played Van Morrison's *'Tupelo Honey.'* Do you know it?"

"Know it? It's one of my favorite Van the Man songs."

"Well, that tune certainly led to a few months of *'wild nights'* and *'sweet as Tupelo honey'* days. Things changed some after little

Davy was born, but it was a good change. Davy was a cute little kid with his mother's big brown eyes. No couple could be happier than us that first year, even though we were living in a stifling hotbox, and just scrimping by. Hell, Chinese takeout was fine dining to us. All the while, Clara kept asking us to move into her big house in Marietta, but I was Mr. Macho Man. You know, wanting to provide for my own family."

Ollie lifted his hand to signal a pause as he tried to catch his wind, his one healthy lung working overtime on his uncharacteristically lengthy speech.

"A year later," he continued, "I was offered an assistant manager's position at a tire franchise in Yuma. So we moved out into the desert, 240 miles west of Tucson. I figured, why not? With my parents gone, Tucson was nothing but tombstones. Time to stake a new claim. The job in Yuma paid a little more, and the rent was cheaper. A no-brainer.

"So we moved into a well-kept trailer park on Yuma's outskirts. No Beverly Hills, but an upgrade from our hotbox back in Tucson. Good neighbors, too, mostly military retirees. They liked me because I was an Army brat whose dad had served in 'Nam. And, of course, everyone loved Betsy.

"As Davy became a toddler, Chopper became his favorite plaything. He'd wake up in the morning, and chatter away with his goofy stuffed companion, letting out little happy squeals. We'd listen from our bedroom, and Betsy would snuggle up to me and say, 'Didn't I say I came back to bring you luck?' My, did she ever.

"After a while, we started thinking about how we could afford to have another kid. Opportunities were scarce, and we were both growing tired of Yuma. Then, a week before our fifth anniversary, my musician friend, Brad, called out of the blue, inviting us to hear his new band play at the Mirage that Saturday night. Thrilled to get the invite, we got ourselves a sitter, and hightailed it four hours to Tucson.

"Turns out we were walking into our own surprise party, which Brad had organized, with cake, champagne, and old friends. Time came for the band to play and Brad called Betsy and me out to the dance floor, and kicked into *'Tupelo Honey.'"*

Ollie suddenly choked up, "I wish that dance had lasted forever."

He took another pause, longer this time, so long that I didn't think he'd continue. I surmised the back end of his tale carried all the weight. I was surprised when he resumed.

"What a night that was, Kevlar! Everything seemed so fresh and hopeful. Brad had even hooked me up with a guy who was opening an auto parts store in Tucson, and told him that I'd be just the ticket for his new manager. The owner and I hit it off right away, and I raced to tell Betsy all about the offer that I was expecting to get. It made the evening all the more festive, and we toasted each other on the new life opening up in front of us. Yep, there was plenty of toasting going on."

Again Ollie halted, before steeling himself to push on. "When we were getting ready to leave, Brad invited us to crash at his place, but he had a new girl wrapped around him like cellophane. So Betsy egged me to drive home, even though we'd paid the sitter for an overnight. I'd had my fill of drink, but kept my wits about me, and I figured an extra-large coffee would see me through. Betsy had more to drink than she was accustomed to, so I buckled her into the car seat, gave her a kiss, and promised to have us home before the pink sky spread itself over the desert floor.

"Before Betsy dozed off, we talked about moving back to

Tucson. She was thrilled, figuring the schools would be better there for Davy, and it'd be easier for Clara to visit us when we had our second child. By the time we turned off the I-10 onto I-8, we'd decided to make the move if I got the job. As Betsy slept, I sipped my coffee, with my mind racing into the future. It had been hours since my last drink, and my Malibu was humming sweetly down the deserted highway.

"We were only 10 miles from our exit, when I looked in the rear view mirror and saw the first sliver of sun appearing over the foothills. Then suddenly, without a warning, my car spun out of control, round and round, before slamming into a concrete barrier.

"When I came to, I found my steaming V-6 engine where the foot pedals ought to be, but somehow the radio was still working, blaring out Glen Campbell. I looked over at Betsy and found her looking back at me, but the light had gone out of her beautiful brown eyes, and her neck was at an odd angle—like a puppet with broken strings. I reached out for her, but found my arms were pinned down by the steering wheel. Behind Betsy, I saw the pink light climbing into the desert sky and embraced the two of us like a giant rose. And that's all I remember till I woke up in a hospital bed twelve days later."

"You were in a coma for twelve days?"

"Yep, but I sure wasn't counting. Come to find out, we'd been airlifted to Phoenix. Betsy had a broken neck, and a rib that tore through her heart. I had a skull fracture and a smashed pelvis. You've never seen me walk, have you? I walk like a goddamn duck."

Ollie wheezed again, "You know what would help me get through this story? A bottle of Skol."

"Take your time, Ols. There's no rush."

"Naw, I have to speed up, or I'll never get to the end of the story. I remember what you said about Pencil Man comparing time to an accordion: how it fans out and squeezes right back in again. That's how it is with me and that accident. It's been over seventeen years, and sometimes it feels way, way in the past, and other times like it happened yesterday. Right now, it's very present, so I'm going to tell you something that might strike you as being crazy."

"You're many things, Fat Boy, but crazy isn't one of them. I bet whatever you say to me will make sense, so let it fly."

"Did you ever wonder where people go when they're in a deep coma? Well, I can't say, but at least I can tell what I saw when I was there. It's a vision as vivid as any memory I have. Betsy appeared to me, clear as day. She was standing beneath an arch of flowers, like a gateway to a radiant garden. I tried my damnedest to join her, but found myself pinned down, like I was still trapped in my Malibu. Betsy held up her hand and said tenderly, 'Oliver, please stay, it's not your time. You must take care of our little Davy. I love you forever.' Then she blew me a kiss, and disappeared into the garden."

"That's a beautiful vision, Ollie, and if I were you, I'd take it to heart."

"Yeah, but then I woke up, and the news wasn't so good. It was a nurse who broke it to me, a young woman about Betsy's age. She was trembling and fighting back tears, trying to find the right words to say, when her eyes had already spoken the ugly truth. Even then, I resented that some high-and-mighty doctor made that poor nurse tell me the terrible news, because he or she didn't want to waste their precious time telling a drunkard how he'd killed his wife in a car crash.

"But that sweet nurse made it up to me, by giving me the

best care possible. Nor did she or the rest of her nursing crew ever judge me. Not that I saw, anyway. That's why I respect and admire your profession so much."

"Glad to hear it."

"Well, it's deserved. She also told me that Betsy's bed had been directly across from mine in their ICU, and that she had died three days after our admission. She had never regained consciousness."

Ollie adjusted his burly body as best he could within his constraints and entanglements, and continued, "After more than a month of hell-on-earth days, lying there thinking about Davy growing up without his mother and Clara losing her only child, I was discharged. But not before a highway patrolman came in and slapped me with a charge of Vehicular Homicide. He would put me under arrest unless I could post bail. I was looking at four to seven years in the state pen. Now, ain't that a swell way to get on with the grieving process?

"Clara was a saint about everything. She took care of Davy in Marietta and posted my bail, and even hired me a high-powered lawyer. It only took him a few days to discover a report of an oil slick that was never cleaned up at the site of my accident, but the case still went on for months of legal wrangling. Eventually, I got off with no time in the slammer, but two years probation, two hundred hours of community service, and mandatory attendance at AA meetings. Best of all, Clara forgave me, and returned Davy to my custody. I can't tell you what that meant to me."

"I can imagine it was a real lifeline. So you could now do what Betsy asked you to do."

"Exactly. And the AA meetings might have helped too, given my dad's history and my own. But despite all their talk about reliance on a Higher Power, whenever I tried to talk about my vivid visitation from Betsy as she passed into paradise, there was always a scoffer who'd chalk it up to an hallucination, or me trying to impress the chicks in attendance. Boy, did that ever piss me off. In due course, I stopped telling my story, maybe because I stopped believing it myself. And as soon as I was allowed, I stopped going to AA.

"About a year after, I was at home trying to get my head into a book. You know, trying to fill the big black hole that Betsy's death had left behind. Turning a page, I looked down and saw a black widow spider crawling between my bare feet. I calmly closed the book and dropped it. Splat! When I picked the book back up, the markings of the spider's red hourglass was perfectly tattooed to its cover.

"Funny, but that hourglass began to play crazy tricks on me. Before I knew it, I'd gotten Davy a sitter, and was high-tailing it north to Phoenix to look up my old medical records. The Coroner's Report stated that Betsy died on a Tuesday at 3:33 a.m. So when I got to the hospital's Record Room, I skipped through my own chart's mumbo-jumbo, and went straight for that time and date. Sure as Shinola, at 3:33 a.m. on the morning of Betsy's death, my wrists and ankles had to be restrained, and I was given a 'stat dose' of IV sedatives for 'agitated behavior' and 'seizure-like activity.'

"Kevlar, without a doubt, those entries proved to me that I hadn't dreamt Betsy's vision. Think about it! I was twelve days in a coma, and the only time I needed to be restrained and medicated was at the exact moment of Betsy's death. Are you with me here? Or have I been blowing smoke rings up my ass for the past seventeen years?"

"Pretty convincing, Fat Boy. As you know, you're preaching

to the choir here, and I'm a big believer in the power of belief. There are many things we can never know or understand, so we have to take them on faith. Only you know the reality of what you saw that morning, and your faith seems well-founded to me. The surest proof would be in how you lived out the truth of your vision."

"Thank you!" He paused and reached an aching arm for his water.

"When I got back to Yuma, I hung on to Betsy's words about taking care of Davy, and that became my primary mission. And he grew up fine, despite the early tragedy of his life. Davy became an honors student and a helluva soccer player, a good kid all around. I even had people coming up and telling me that I was a model single-parent. Me, a first-class loser. But it all went south during his freshman year of high school. Davy came home crying, and I finally pried it out of him that some bully classmate had been spreading it around that his drunken father had killed his mom in a car crash."

"What had you told him when Betsy died?"

"We'd gone to a family counselor right after, and told him as much of the truth as we thought he needed to hear, but left out my legal problems and any mention of alcohol. He was only five at the time, remember. So now I told him that I definitely wasn't drunk, had nothing but coffee in the previous four hours, and took the plea deal rather than risk a trial, with the threat of a prison sentence if I lost."

"Did Davy understand?"

"Well, he was a teenager, and destined to drift away from me anyway. But from that point on, he lost all confidence in me. I could take that, maybe I deserved it, but other signs of his pain bothered me. His grades dropped and he quit the soccer team. He also insisted on spending every school vacation with his grandmother in Georgia, and when he was home, all he did was hole up in his room and play video games."

Ollie's voice cracked at the memory, and his breath faltered again. "When I tried to talk to him, he'd turn his back and crank up his music. If I'd done that to my dad, he would've wrung my sorry neck. Looking back, I think all he needed was a good kick in the ass. Then I'd let him kick me in the ass, and we would have been done with it.

"It was bad when Davy was with me, but even worse when he was away with Clara. I soon went back to drinking, and chewing Vicodin. Not surprisingly, after the accident with Betsy and three less-than-successful back surgeries, I was living with chronic pain. But until the break with Davy, I'd pretty much stayed clear of beer and painkillers.

"Once Davy graduated from high school and moved to Georgia for good, I had nothing to hold me back, and sure enough, temptation came calling. I was moonlighting a brake job, and the guy had no money to pay me, so he offered me an eightball of cocaine instead—three and a half grams. In dollar value, it was probably a good deal, but I handed back the baggy and told him I really needed the cash. He said that by the looks of me, I needed the magic powder more, and pressed it back into my hand. Like a sap, I took it.

"I'd dabbled with coke a time or two at the Mirage, but I never had such a huge amount to myself. I drew up a line to give it a taste and, whammo, sign me up for the endless march to Bolivia. I don't know if you've ever tried coke, but once you start, it's not like you twist up the bag after a few lines and say, 'That was pleasant. I think I'll save the rest for Saturday night.' No, it doesn't work that way. Believe me, you'll be chasing the

White Lady until you're licking the inside of the bag.

"That same night, I started snorting rails like there was no tomorrow. Maybe that was my intention all along—no tomorrow. Soon my heart was pounding, and the left side of my brain was sizzling like the egg in that anti-drug, frying-pan commercial. It was a race to see what would give out first, my head or my heart. But I didn't give a damn, and I still had half a bag to go. I kept snorting one fat line after another. On and on. The high-wired rush, the beastly fall, the rush again."

"I don't like where this is going, Fat Boy."

"That's the thing, Kevlar. It was going just where I intended. And I'd just drawn up a line the length of a night-crawler when the pink sunrise filtered through my window blinds. In my coked-out, hijacked state of mind, I took it as an invitation from Betsy, to join her in paradise—at last! So I added another inch to the long rail for my last hurrah. But just as I was bringing the straw to my bleeding nostril for the grand finale, I heard music. Not just any music, but Brad's memorable rendition of 'Tupelo Honey,' clear as day. Tell me, Kevlar, of all the songs ever sung, how did that special tune pop into my head at that very moment?"

"Another message from Betsy."

"Yes, maybe. But however it happened, I dumped the mirror, tossed the bag, crawled into bed, and wept like a child."

"Dodged one there, my friend."

"When I recouped a couple of days later, I was bursting to tell someone. I called Brad, whom I hadn't spoken to since Betsy's memorial years earlier. But when I called the tire center, my old boss told me that Brad had died a year back from an aneurysm after shooting up a speedball—coke and heroin. When I hung up, I was more confused than ever. Had Betsy and Brad teamed up in the afterlife to save my sorry ass? Or had Brad done it on his own, not wanting me to make the same fatal mistake he did?"

"Fat Boy, I got to admit, you sure have good reason to believe in messages from beyond."

"Don't I know it!"

He reached out for another sip of water, and carried on. "Now my story jumps ahead to just a few weeks ago. At this point, it'd been three years since I'd last heard from Davy. Three long years of filling the lonesome gap with opiates and alcohol. Smart choice, huh? I was so messed up I wouldn't even return Clara's phone calls, even though she was the woman who saved me from incarceration, and was my only link to my son. Hell, I didn't even send Davy a card for his 21st birthday."

"Sounds like a bad stretch, Fat Boy."

"So I sat home alone, on another thankless Thanksgiving, waiting on Davy's call, a call I knew wasn't coming. Instead, I set my mind on a mindless journey, to get as far away from Yuma as I could. On Black Friday, appropriately enough, I saddled up my Harley Fat Boy, and hightailed it down Highway 8 toward Gila Bend, headed north for the Maine Woods, or somewhere deeper and darker.

"Two weeks into my senseless journey, I was higher than a giraffe's ass, much like Pencil Man's drug-induced runs from coast to coast. My face was wind-chafed, my eyes red and dry, and my hands, like my brain, totally numb. I was at the end of my tether and something had to snap. I no longer had thoughts of a final destination, but only that I'd meet Betsy at the end of it.

"Come Sunday, I was so crazed and beaten-up that I started searching for a passage that would lead me to her. A flowered bridge or a radiant gateway. Then, in your Berkshires, I spotted a lone oak tree just off the road, with its two remaining brown leaves winking at me in the low morning sunlight. I was certain it was a sign from Betsy, so I backed up, slung off my helmet, pulled a wheelie, and gunned my Fat Boy straight for that tree's massive trunk."

"And yet here you are. Do you know exactly what happened?"

"Your docs in the ED, who didn't know my true intention, told me I lost control on black ice. Now ain't that a kick in the ass? Oil slick or ice slick, I survived them both. And instead of finding myself wrapped in Betsy's loving arms, I woke up beside a banged-up psych nurse. Now, what am I supposed to make of that?"

"Well, if you're asking my off-duty opinion, I'd say you ought to believe in what Betsy told you long ago, and that's to take care of Davy. Reach out to your son and make amends, in the name of the woman you both love. To start with, sign a damn HIPAA release, so our nurses can contact him. I bet Davy and Carla are worried sick about you."

"I seriously doubt that," Ollie scoffed. "Three years have passed, and they probably think I'm still drinking and drugging back in Yuma."

"Never assume anything, Fat Boy. You know, over the years, I've seen all sorts of family estrangements: kids who went bad, parents who went sour, siblings who went south. Whether it's guilt or shame or pride, I haven't a clue, but people seem to cut themselves off from the ones they love most. Remember, there's plenty of time to turn your rig around, as Pencil Man often told our patients."

"But the kid hates me."

"Maybe now, but he loved you for what, 15 years? There's a history to build on, and you've got to start by communicating. Count on Betsy's enduring memory and her last request to rebuild the bond between you two."

"There may be something to what you say, so I'll sleep on it."

"C'mon, Ols, just sign the damn release. Hell, I'll even call Davy and hand you the phone. Believe me, you'll never be happy until you reclaim your relationship with your son."

Ollie went silent, but piped up after long moments. "If something crazy goes wrong with me tonight, could you share my story with Dr. Carter? He's a great guy who's been trying his utmost to pry open my can of worms. And if you ever do get a hold of Davy, tell him I love him."

"Gladly, but I think you should tell him that yourself."

"Maybe I will, if I'm able. But right now I feel I'm on my last leg. The end of our journey."

I looked across at Fat Boy, and found him very pale. "You don't look too hot. Should I call a nurse?"

"Naw, Kevlar, I'm just strung out after spilling my heart. It's been bottled up for years, you know."

He turned his whole, aching body in my direction as if to reassure me. "Just wake me when we change buses in El Paso," he winked. "We should be in Tucson by noonday tomorrow, and Yuma before dark."

"Remember, you can go home again, and you can get your son back."

Following his heartrending tale, and before I could say anything more, my redheaded Viking had fallen asleep, his lone, healthy lung languishing like a bagpipe after playing its mournful dirge.

SUNDAY: COMMUNION
OF SAINTS

My eyes opened to a tranquil stillness, as if all the clamor of the world had subsided. I turned to ask Ollie if he was basking in the same silence, but found an empty bed instead. Then I realized the reason for the quiet—his noisy Gomco had been unplugged from the wall, and Ollie was gone. Alarmed, I hit my call bell, and hit it again.

A night aide was first to respond. She told me that Ollie's blood pressure had plummeted in the wee hours, the result of severe internal bleeding, and he had been rushed to Surgery. A ruptured spleen was suspected, but he was still in the OR.

I struggled to sit up. "I didn't hear a thing. Didn't they call a Mayday?"

"No, the MET team just whisked him out of here. It's touch and go, I'm afraid."

I looked out at the wintry dawn, my mind in a tailspin. "Damn, I should've alerted the nurses last night. Ollie was so fatalistic, I just knew something was wrong."

The aide tried her best to console me, "Kevin, you're getting way ahead of yourself. Oliver's not dead, and you're definitely not to blame. These things happen when you're as banged up as he was."

"Yeah, but I was the nurse on the scene. I should've recognized something was up."

"No, Kevin, you're a patient, and not your roommate's keeper," she reminded me. "You should stay focused on your own recovery."

I was surprised that Dr. DeMarco was next through the door, neither confirming nor denying what the aide had willingly told me, due to the oftentimes senseless HIPAA regulations. I sensed, though, that the good doctor wanted to divulge all. After he went over my recent labs and overall condition, he informed me that I was to be transferred to a single room.

"A single room? Thanks, but why?"

"Tell me," he joked, "who wants to bunk with a roommate who never shuts up? Besides, our nursing director, Diane Kelly, thinks it's only proper that you should have a private room after your recent heroics."

"Heroics? I just got in the guy's way!"

Shortly after breakfast, Maria from Housekeeping came in to strip and sanitize Ollie's bed. Always cheerful and outgoing, she asked, "Where's your roommate? Don't tell me the insurance companies booted him out in his condition?"

"No, Maria. He's in the OR having emergency surgery."

"Good Lord, I'm sorry to hear that. You two were great pals."

"I hope we still are," I answered apprehensively.

She looked down at her work pad. "I see they're transferring you up to Four East."

"Four East. Does it say what room?"

"404."

My heart did a somersault. "That room and I have quite

the history."

"Well, I hope it's a good history."

Early that afternoon, after settling into my storied room, I got word from a passing orderly that Ollie was out of the OR, and in ICU. His condition remained critical and, as suspected, his spleen had been the culprit.

Not long after, an old friend and coworker dropped by. Joanne Hessler was what we called a nurse's nurse and the mother of a nurse to boot. I'd always found her a congenial colleague on our unit, reasonable and reliable. She was carrying a large bundle in her hands.

"I come as the bearer of gifts. This came for you this morning. Can you guess what it is?"

"I don't know—a parachute? I've been looking for a way out of here."

"No, silly, but you'll recognize who it's from right away. It'll also bring back a flood of memories, as it did me." Joanne unwrapped the package and handed me a red and green woolen shawl.

"My God," I gasped, looking at the knitted fabric in my hands, "it's the prayer shawl that Grace knitted for Angela way back when."

"Exactly. Guess how many years ago?"

"Ten?"

"Try seventeen."

"Seventeen, no way! But how did Angela know I was hospitalized?"

"Oh, you know how word gets around in those group homes."

A note was attached to the blanket with a safety pin. Joanne insisted I read it aloud:

Dear Kevin, When I heard about your accident, I called Joanne to see if I could send you my Christmas shawl. You might remember how it helped me with Margaret's birth, and now I hope it helps you. I know Grace would want you to have it, too.

You're in my daily prayers, Angela.

P.S. My little Margaret is now a senior in high school. Can you believe it? She visits me twice a week, and takes me out to lunch every Sunday, when I'm able.

P.P.S. Once you get better, please pass the shawl along to another patient who needs it. As you know, every stitch holds a special prayer from a very special person, and it's been boxed away for far too long.

"This note is well written," I commented, "Angela must be doing pretty well for herself."

"She was always a smart girl," Joanne reminded me. "She would've been a college grad if her illness hadn't intervened."

I took a closer look at the woolen shawl and found it in remarkable condition despite its age. "Funny, Spencer and I were just talking about Grace last Sunday. And now, exactly a week later, the Christmas shawl she knit for Angela appears out of the blue. Talk about coincidence."

"C'mon, Kevin," Joanne playfully scolded, "you know coincidence is just one of God's little miracles. Remember how Father Decker thought Grace was a traveling saint, a mysterious stranger with the gift of healing miracles?"

Joanne spread the shawl over me before leaving. "Now do as Angela says, get well and pass it along to someone else in need."

"I've got just the person in mind," I said, kissing my long-time friend goodbye.

Left to my own musings, I pulled the shawl to my chin and thought about Angela and Grace, two strikingly attractive young women, both diagnosed with schizophrenia, but polar opposites in many ways. Both had wound up on our unit at the same time. All due credit goes to Angela for her grit and determination, but Grace was truly the angelic presence on our ward.

You wouldn't have known it at first, when the police brought her to the hospital for her own protection. They'd found Grace wandering around our city's bus depot on a bitter Thanksgiving night, not wearing a coat or hat. An officer asked if she needed help, and she stared at him blankly. She remained mute when he asked if she had an ID or money. After letting her warm up in the patrol car, he still got nothing out of her, so he brought her in for a psych screening.

During the intake interview, with a warm blanket around her shoulders and coffee in her hands, the frail young woman would only give her name as "Grace of Krakow." Her reason for being in Pittsfield was simply to serve Pope John Paul II, who had been born in Krakow, Poland. When pressed, she explained that she had devoted her life to the Pope's mission after she saw how his humble prayers helped bring down the Berlin Wall.

Grace's appearance showed more than she was willing to say. It looked like she'd been traveling a long, hard highway, what staff called "road rash." She was wearing a ragged, buttonless sweater for a topcoat, laceless shoes without socks, and stained pants with torn and muddy cuffs. She carried a flip-top wicker picnic basket, with virtually no belongings except a prayer book stuffed with holy pictures, and a pair of knitting needles stuck through numerous balls of colored yarn. Her preliminary diagnosis was "schizophrenia with religious delusions," and she came willingly to our floor on a "voluntary" basis for observation.

Assigned to a single room, she promptly pasted her prayer cards to the bed's headboard: Teresa of Avila, Elizabeth of Hungary, Catherine of Siena. Only then did she eat, and did so ravenously.

During her first week, Grace remained isolated in her room for the most part, coming out only for meals and mandatory groups. All she requested was to knit in the privacy of her own room. Since sharp objects such as knitting needles weren't allowed on the unit without supervision, staff, when available, had to sit with her, and I was quick to volunteer for such easy duty.

Grace would sit by the light of the window, and murmur prayers as she worked away. When I asked what she was making, she would say only that it was "a prayer shawl." When I tried to press her for more information, she shushed me, "Can't you see I'm doing God's work?"

Who was this enchanting drifter, our staff wondered. And why had she fallen into our company?

When Grace completed a prayer shawl, roughly the size of a woman's scarf, she'd ask to see our hospital chaplain. Father Neil Decker, an affable priest who had a comforting word for everyone, would arrive promptly and comply with her request to bless the shawl. Then Grace would walk through the common areas of the ward, looking for the patient in the most distress. She would approach gently, and wrap her shawl around the person while she whispered a fervent prayer.

Every few days she would repeat this process, and soon the ward was dotted with her shawls of robin's egg blue with ivory trim. She seemed to have an intuitive understanding of who was most in need. And her handiwork, loosely but lovingly knit, always seemed to offer comfort, even to the most troubled patients.

After her second week, Grace began to emerge from her shell and spent more time in the milieu. Finally, she agreed to take a much-needed shower. What a surprise when she came forth, clean and freshly dressed. She had seemed frail and stooped before, but now looked slender and tall. Her ratty hair was a blond halo around her flawlessly sculpted face, where her blue eyes shone. Krakow nothing. She looked more like Grace of Monaco!

When a male patient complimented her on her enchanting beauty, she quickly dismissed his comment. "My supposed good looks have brought me nothing but pain. I'd rather be a shrinking violet than a so-called rose."

On December 8th, Our Lady's feast day, I was allowed to take Grace to nearby Holy Family Church, a Polish parish with an outdoor grotto. Grace's clothing had been transformed as much as her appearance. She was dressed semi-stylishly in a hand-me-down winter coat, boots, and gloves provided by our weekend nurse, Ruth. At the shrine, Grace knelt before a statue of the Blessed Mother, and, despite the ruckus of passing traffic, she prayed as ardently as a cloistered nun in her cell.

After finishing her prayers, she turned to me with great urgency, "I need to knit a prayer shawl for that young pregnant girl, Angela, our forlorn Madonna. But I'll need a few skeins of yarn, berry red and holly green, because it needs to be a Christmas shawl. Can you do that for me?"

"Consider it done." I would have promised the world to this ethereal beauty who had such an aura of sanctity about her. I began to understand why so many would follow a Joan of Arc into the fray.

Angela, in contrast, had dark brown eyes and a mop of curly brown hair. She'd been admitted in her sixth month of pregnancy, the day after her husband, Todd, had been admitted to Medicine with Stage IV pancreatic cancer. As is often the case, she'd had her first schizophrenic break in her late teens, when she was a sophomore in college and already in love with Todd. He had stuck by her thick and thin, and married her for better or worse.

The expected baby was the best, but now the worst had come for Todd, and it was far more than Angela could endure. Whatever her symptoms—and they were severe—it was hard to call it a psychotic break, and not simply a natural reaction to a woe too great to bear?

Joanne and I had been assigned to Angela, and twice daily, we'd take her to visit Todd in the Main House. The ill-fated couple would sit for extended spells in his darkened, single room, talking about what might have been, but also what was to be. Todd arranged for his mother, Margaret, to adopt the baby, so there was no chance of it being taken away from Angela. It would also allow her as much of a role in the child's upbringing as she could handle.

Todd's death was not long in coming, and soon after, Angela made a startling announcement to staff, "I've decided to have a natural childbirth, and breastfeed my baby. So I need to stop taking all my crazy pills as of today."

Her proclamation upended all our plans for a controlled delivery by cesarean. We'd now have to wean Angela off her hefty dose of Haldol and deal with the consequences, as well as work out a sane battle plan for the actual delivery.

You can be certain Nurse Hatchet had a few choice

words to say about the decision to accommodate Angela's wishes. "This is beyond ludicrous," she ranted to the visiting Maternity staff. "You've never witnessed her primitive behavior firsthand. Add a few painful contractions and you've got yourself a pregnant woman bouncing off the walls. And breast feed? Ha! The poor girl can hardly feed herself at times."

But Joanne, never one to let anyone step on her toes, made a heartfelt appeal to the natal nurses, "The birth of Angela's child may well be the most joyous moment of her life. Who are we to deprive her of this singular joy?"

Besides tending to Angela's predictable outbursts and wild behaviors, Joanne and I worked with Maternity staff to allay their concerns, and volunteered to be present at the birth. In the prenatal weeks, during intervals when Angela was lucid and manageable, we'd be on hand so Maternity nurses could take a fetal heartbeat and perform a pelvic exam. Joanne also tutored Angela in Lamaze, and we both took hope from the cases we'd witnessed when patients rose to a physical challenge and managed to put their mental problems on hold for the duration.

But things could also turn ugly. Angela would sometimes literally run mad with grief, racing around the ward in a frenzied state, screaming Todd's name until she was hoarse, and bewailing his abandonment of her. She'd often search for him in all the places he couldn't be; she'd crawl beneath beds, fling open closets, and rip away shower curtains. Eventually she'd collapse in a sobbing heap. Without Haldol to ease her illness, Angela was a kite without a string, flailing wildly in the winds of fate.

Sometimes her ravings were so prolonged and violent that they posed a hazard to the baby, and we had little choice but to put her in a body net and four-point restraints. This necessary intervention was agonizing for all. A small dose of Ativan sometimes helped, allowing her an interval of sleep, but it was a harrowing experience all around.

Grace, of course, was witness to many of these goings-on, but would have been attuned to Angela's distress in any event. As soon as I brought in the red and green yarn she requested, Grace set to work in earnest. I sat with her for hours as Angela's Christmas shawl took shape. Knit and purl, row by row, prayer by prayer, Grace's lips mumbled in tandem with her clacking needles.

I was startled one day when she broke into speech and addressed me, "Kevin, is it true that you made a pilgrimage around Ireland with a donkey?"

"Yes, a lifetime ago. Though the experience has certainly stuck with me."

"Ireland is such a holy place. You must have had visions, revelations, epiphanies."

"Oh, I don't know about that, but I did see and hear and feel many things that changed me, made me the person I became. I met so many generous people along the roads that some of their kindnesses had to rub off."

She stopped knitting and looked at me appraisingly for a long while. "I suspect it did. Probably made you a better nurse, too."

"I'd like to think so."

Grace set her needles down on her lap, and mused aloud, "It must have been wonderful to have walked the outer edge of that spiritual island with a blessed donkey as your only companion. You were brave to cast yourself to the four winds like that."

"Me? Seems like you do it all the time."

"Yes, but God is my safe harbor, my protection." She caught herself and blushed, "Forgive me, Kevin, I'm not suggesting that God doesn't protect you, too. Or everyone else, for that matter."

"No offense taken," I assured her.

She leaned toward me and whispered, "Sometimes I feel God's presence so strongly that I'm certain no harm can come to me. Why, I believe I could throw myself into the deepest lake, and I'd skip over it like a flat stone."

"I don't suggest you try it," I answered.

"And sometimes I find myself walking down the middle of a frozen river in the dead of a winter's night, with the blue ice creaking beneath my feet."

"Why would you ever do that?"

"That's when I feel closest to Jesus. I do it in imitation of Christ, you know, walking on water."

When a snow squall suddenly rattled the window, Grace turned as pale as the flurry itself, and went silent for a long moment. Finally, she managed to speak, "I tried to take my life once. A foolish and selfish enterprise, as I hated God as much as myself. When I came out of my coma in the hospital, the first thing I saw was snow tapping at my window, just like this. I turned to my nurse and said, 'What do you do, when you think you were finally out of this troublesome place, only to wake to a fresh fall of snow?'"

I remained quiet, not wanting to break the spell, as Grace was verbalizing her thoughts and inner reality in a way she never had before.

"That nurse was very kind to me, a healer such as yourself and your team. She said God must have other plans for me.

I thought it was cliché, you know, just something to say, but she didn't leave it at that. The next day she brought me a copy of *Lives of the Saints,* and that book became my ever-faithful companion and inspiration. I took those saints as my teachers, and one, in particular, stirred my dying embers into life again, igniting a flame of spirit. That was Elizabeth of Hungary."

"That's a saint I don't know," I confessed.

She pointed to the prayer card of Elizabeth attached to the headboard of her bed. "Elizabeth was a princess who became a follower of St. Francis. When she was widowed at a young age, she used her dowry to establish a hospital and spent her life caring for the sick. She's often depicted spinning wool for the poor, and that became my revelation, to knit my prayer shawls as a way to help heal the souls of the sick. Little as it is, it's all I have to give."

"Little as it is?" I said. "Just look around the ward and you'll see all the people you have helped. Each of them cling to your shawls, which offers much more than warmth. The prayers you put into them are as essential as the wool."

"You're very kind to say so. If I didn't think my prayer shawls had any meaning, I'd be lonelier than the loneliest star."

"Well, you needn't worry your head. Your shawls are beyond gifts. They're treasures."

Angela's shawl was a treasure far more elaborate than the others. It was larger and more meticulously knit. Grace had even embroidered a Nativity scene onto the design— Madonna and Child with Donkey.

After Father Decker had blessed the shawl and compli- mented its exquisite beauty, I accompanied Grace to Angela's room where we found the expectant mother lying in bed on her back, hands rubbing her round belly. Grace approached Angela meekly, more like a shepherd than a Magi, though her gift seemed as precious as gold. She held her offering in out-stretched hands, "Angela, I've knitted this Christmas shawl for you and your baby. I pray that it may be a source of warmth and protection for you both."

Angela was in one of her difficult moods. She turned away and said nothing, but motioned for Grace to leave her offering at the foot of her bed. I almost urged Angela to thank Grace, but her misery and exhaustion were palpable; the tragedy and struggle of her life had worn her down. I knew she was embarrassed by her own behavior, and wanted to be left alone. Grace, with a mix of understanding and humility, took her leave, with no offense.

At breakfast the next morning, Angela came into the kitchen wearing the shawl over her shoulders, nodding to Grace in mute acknowledgment. She continued to wrap it around herself whenever she could, and her outlook and behavior seemed to improve.

Just before Christmas we discharged Grace, at her request, and set her up in a residential treatment home. To no one's surprise, she skipped out that same night to a destination as mysterious as wherever she came from. We never learned where that was, nor even her real name.

I'll always remember Grace's departure from the ward. I watched from her doorway as she packed her few belongings into her wicker basket, took down her prayer cards and put them back into her book of saints in a well-practiced manner. She seemed healthy and radiant, ready for the next station on her enigmatic pilgrimage. She buttoned up her fashion-able coat, and reluctantly accepted the few dollars staff had collected for her.

As she took her leave, everyone gathered to bid her farewell. Angela, in particular, was moved, even though she had exchanged few words with Grace, they seemed to have formed a special bond. She watched Grace's departure from her own doorway, wiping away tears with her shawl.

When I went to unlock the outer door, I asked Grace if there was anything more she needed. She took my hand in hers and warmly replied, "Yes, Kevin, enough yarn to cloak the world."

With Grace gone to parts unknown, Angela clung to her Christmas shawl like a life vest. Unfortunately, it did not exempt her from her fits of derangement when she would turn antagonistic toward everyone and everything around her. She'd curse the shawl, spit on it, even try to rip it apart. But never once did she abandon it.

On January 6th, the Feast of the Epiphany, or Little Christmas, Angela's water broke, and Joanne and I were pulled from our warm beds at an early hour. Once on the ward, we strapped Angela safely onto a gurney and set off for Labor and Delivery. At the elevator, she lifted her head and shouted, "You've forgotten my shawl!"

Once prepped and gowned in the Labor Room, Angela surveyed the bright lights, masked attendants, and glistening instruments. Gripping Joanne's hand, she whispered, "This is when I have to shine, isn't it?" To all the assembled doctors and nurses, she announced, "My husband, Todd, will help me through this. He's dead, you know, but that doesn't mean he still can't help." Then she instructed me to drape the Christmas shawl over a nearby rocking chair, so it could be her 'focal point' during her delivery.

A sudden spasm lifted Angela clear off the delivery table. "Holy Toledo!" she gasped, her face flushed crimson and her brown eyes bugging out. "One more of those and I'll be turned inside out!"

As another contraction came on, Angela bit her lip in determination, but again she couldn't find the rhythm, much like a surfer mistiming a wave. When the pain subsided, she looked around the room sheepishly, and quipped, "I've got to be more like the Big Bad Wolf and learn how to huff and puff, or this little piggy of mine will never come out of its house."

Hearing this playful comment, Joanne gave me a wink, signaling that everything was going to be just fine. Yes, our Angela was at her best, the woman Todd had fallen in love with—a witty, charming, and comical cherub.

Coached tirelessly by Joanne, Angela soon fell into the proper breathing rhythm when her contractions came. Despite all her life's disappointments, she was determined this wasn't going to be one of them. All those in attendance sensed it as well, and settled into their roles with confidence in the outcome. Yes, this fragile young widow, with an agonizing past, had the fortitude to perform the miracle of birth.

And so it went. Angela was able to keep her demons in check, and soon produced a bouncing, bonnie girl, through sheer strength of will. No drama, no uproar, no psychosis. Just doing what comes naturally.

Amid the celebration, Joanne and I embraced Angela as if she were our daughter, and soon the healthy baby was brought to the Madonna's breast. For a moment, it was possible to believe all was right with the world.

Flushed and glowing with joy, Angela caught her breath, and announced. "Todd and I never had a chance to pick out a name, so I'm going to call our baby Margaret Grace, after Todd's mother, Margaret, who's going to help me take care of my little bundle. And that saintly woman named Grace, who pretended to be sick like me."

I turned to Joanne and whispered, "If only we could let Grace know."

"Believe me, Kevin, she already does."

With that memory swimming fondly in my head, I snuggled beneath my newly-acquired Christmas shawl, and fell into a sound sleep.

*   *   *

I felt a tug at my toes—it was Dr. DeMarco. "Great news, Kev. I just got Ollie's permission to inform you that he's regained consciousness, and his condition is stable. Furthermore, the first words out of his mouth were, 'Where the hell's Kevlar?' You'll also be happy to hear that he signed a HIPAA release, and the ICU nurses are trying to get hold of his son as we speak."

"That's wonderful news! All of it! Fat Boy rides again!"

"Hold on, that's not the half of it. Have you checked your catheter bag lately?"

"Not since it was emptied last night. Too depressing to keep checking it."

"Well, better take a look."

I leaned over and peeked. "Wow, it's a whole lot clearer."

"Kev, I'm glad to report that your urine has gone full circle—cabernet to rosé to chardonnay—and your morning labs confirm that. So, you're almost good to go, my man. You ready to be discharged tomorrow?"

"How about this afternoon?"

"Only if you want to go home with your catheter in place. Let's discontinue it, and see how your plumbing is working. If everything runs smoothly, we'll discharge you first thing in the morning. By that time, I'll have your outpatient physical therapy all set up."

"Thanks, Doc. Any idea how long I'll be on the DL, when I'll be able to return to work?"

"Can't say for certain, maybe six months."

"Aw, shucks, I was hoping for a year. I really could use a sabbatical."

"Just be glad you'll be swinging a golf club by the time the course is greening up."

"Okay, then." I shook Dr. DeMarco's hand. "Next pint's on me at Patrick's Pub."

"I'll hold you to that."

He cast a smile over his shoulder as he walked out the door.

Later that afternoon, I took my first unfettered stroll, tube-free. Though the nurses' station was a mere twenty yards away, it felt as big a challenge as through-hiking the Appalachian Trail. I made it, even though I'd passed up my afternoon dose of Dilaudid, hoping to wean off the opiates before their effects became insidious.

After Visiting Hours with my relieved and delighted family, I decided to take my last shot of Dilaudid, to ensure a good night's sleep before my release. After receiving the injection, I prepared to fall into a deep snooze with Angela's Grace-given shawl spread over me as a counterpane.

However, rather than nodding off, I felt I was being pulled toward the room's large picture window, the same window where, forty years earlier, I had gazed pityingly upon the suffering reflection of Julie Potter. Rising from my bed, broken back and all, I draped the Christmas shawl over my shoulders and hobbled to the window that continued to draw me. But on this night—the winter's solstice—the glass mirrored back no pain of the disturbing scene, but a vibrant image of a living Miss Julie joyously hoisting sails with a handsome sailor on the Finger Lakes.

Batting my eyes in disbelief, this wondrous display was followed by a hundred more—a kaleidoscopic parade of ever-changing images depicting scores of my patients over the years. As I recognized each of them, I saw a flash of their dreams realized, their heaven attained. I watched Diesel Dan climbing effortlessly into Pencil Man's cab. I saw Timothy Quail chasing Audrey Nolan across St. Michael's Green, and witnessed Happy picnicking happily with Holly on the Tanglewood lawn. There were Lou and Mae cheering on the Red Sox at Fenway Park, Stephanie circling the ice rink at Rockefeller Center, and Amelia smiling broadly at her dinner date. I heard Zippy whispering into Zoe's ear, telling her how much he loved her. And there was Stan the Man winning a checkers tournament, and Mic-Mac being named honorary chief of Pequot Tribal Nation. And, lastly, my dear old dad chatting happily with his loving bride.

After the breathtaking phantasmagoria dissolved, I turned from the window, exhausted but also exhilarated. Before I stumbled into bed, I was beckoned again to the window for a curtain call. And there, the most welcoming scene illuminated from the pane—a smiling Tanya and Toby waving to me as they walked their Yorkshire terrier through a honeyed glade. A vision that filled me with a profound sense of absolution and even redemption.

I remained at the window a long while, thinking of Grace, and all that she had wrought in my life and that of so many unknown others. I had always believed there was a fine line between the mad and the sane, but now I realized there was also a fine line between the mad and the saints. We often speak of the insane as "touched," but the question remains whether they are touched by madness, or by God. Either way, they deserve our deepest sympathy and attention.

Wrapping the shawl more tightly around me, I called out to this enigmatic woman in silent devotion, "Where are you tonight, Grace of Krakow? Are you checking yourself into some psych facility in Morgantown, Boise, or Escondido? I know that you're still working your Christmas miracles, because I witnessed one at this window tonight. At last, I realize just who you are. You're a mender of hearts, a stitcher of souls, a saint woven into the fabric of humankind."

MONDAY: MORNING OF DISCHARGE

After a week as a hospital patient, my day of release finally came. But before I was sprung from the joint that morning, I pushed my four-wheel walker down the long hallway to ICU. I was going to look in on Ollie, and I had Angela's Christmas shawl draped over my rollator bar.

Fortunately, my longtime friend Michelle Franklin was the charge nurse on duty, and she had no qualms about allowing me to visit that early. When she pulled back Ollie's curtain, I recoiled a step in shock. While his hair remained flame-red, his skin was whiter than porcelain, as if my dear Norseman had just been pulled from an icy fjord. Michelle nodded me forward, and I gently nudged my road buddy awake, "Hey, Fat Boy, are we in Yuma yet?"

Ollie slowly opened his eyes; his lids looked as heavy as boulders in a Viking weightlifting contest. When he got his bearings and recognized his erstwhile roommate, the first thing he noticed was that I was dressed in civvies. "Hey," he mumbled, "how'd you get out of here before me?"

"Connections, what else? How you doing, mate?"

"I'm doing, that's about it." He drew a raspy breath.

"Funny thing, a week ago I wanted to die. Now here I am, fighting for my life."

"Often the case."

"You'll be happy to hear a nurse stuck a phone in my ear last night, and it was my kid, Davy. Yep, Davy! He said he had a feeling something was awfully wrong, and when he got the news, he wished things between us could be like they were way back when. Then he tells me he's married. Got a kid, too. Named him Oliver James! How's that for a shocker?"

"That's terrific, Ols. All of it. Congratulations!"

He paused again to catch his breath, "Imagine, Kevlar, I've gone from graveyard to grandpa in 24 hours. Davy's even planning to visit me after his first Christmas with his new family. He hopes we can get a fresh start in the New Year."

A smile spread slowly across Ollie's cracked lips, which reactivated the nurse in me. I reached for the cup of ice chips on his bedstand, and fed him a heaping spoonful. "Great stuff, Fat Boy. I'll be sure to meet him then."

Ollie savored the ice as it melted over his parched tongue, and then smiled more broadly. "You know, Kev, docs tell me I was close to checking out. But I didn't see any of those tunnels of white light we were talking about. Can't say I was looking, either."

"A good thing, Ols, since you've got a promising journey ahead of you right here. Speaking of which, I brought you something to help your recovery."

I unfurled Angela's shawl before him like a flag.

"What's this?"

"You could call it a Christmas comforter, but it's more of a prayer shawl, knit by one unforgettable patient for another nearly two decades ago. Now it's come down to me, and I can vouch for its curative powers. I mean, look, I'm out the door after one night under it."

Ollie reached out and fingered the wool dubiously. "Do I have to pray underneath this relic or anything?"

"That wouldn't hurt, but I think prayers are part of its fabric. It's not magic, but it's certainly spiritual. Use it as long as necessary, then pass it on to someone else in need."

"I'll do my damnedest to hurry that up."

I pointed out the shawl's embroidered design. "See the Nativity scene? The Madonna and Child will remind you of the daughter-in-law and grandson you'll soon meet. And the donkey, Trottemenu, will remind you of me."

"Thanks, Kevlar, but you're certainly one jackass I'll never forget."

Still a pooped-out patient myself, I took a seat on the handy bench of my walker. I felt a newfound appreciation of mobility as the foundation of health, both physical and mental. "Got to say, Fat Boy, it was great to spend a week on the road with you, going places and seeing things, telling our stories. Made my hospital stay almost enjoyable at times."

"Same here, Kevlar. You gave me plenty to laugh about but, more importantly, you got me to share my own story, which helped me look at things differently. Connecting with you has led me back to my son. And my grandson, Oliver James—I still can't believe it!"

"Happy to help, and happy with the result, but now all the work of healing is up to you. Give yourself credit, have faith in yourself, and you'll find yourself in the best possible situation."

"Now that you mention finding myself, Davy and I even talked about my possibly moving to Georgia when I get out of here, for rehab and maybe longer. He says Clara is willing to set me up, and I can be closer to my new family. Lots of options when you're still on the sunny side of the grass."

"Ain't that the truth."

Ollie halted out of sheer exhaustion, and motioned for more ice chips. Then, refreshed, he gazed into the future, "As long as I don't drive them, or myself, crazy, maybe I'll even get to stay. There's nothing for me in Yuma anymore. It's just as well that Fat Boy and Kevlar never reached the old hometown. As they say, it's the journey not the destination that matters."

"We certainly had ourselves a great road trip."

"Yeah, but now our road splits in two. I'm still a patient, and you're back to being a nurse."

"Not quite yet. I'm looking forward to a nice extended leave. But you know I do feel a lot better about being a nurse than I did a week ago. Took one last ride on the Dilaudid train last night, and had some wild visions. Turned into a strange celebration of nursing, and a vindication of my vocation. It made me feel as though I still have something left to give as a nurse."

"Oh, you do. I can swear to that. I'd say you're a born nurse, able to connect with people, and connect people with their own better selves. You do it all through your heartfelt tales."

Ollie took my hand and held it, saying, "You know, I've been thinking about it ever since Kevlar and Fat Boy's road trip, the healing power of stories. You've seen a lot of things, and encountered all sorts of people in the small space of this hospital. You should write another book and share your tales with the world. Hell, if you've got to, consider me your muse."

"That's good advice, Ols, and I'll certainly keep it in mind."

With that, my burly, redheaded road buddy turned his head and drifted away, but not in the burning boat of a Viking funeral, and thankfully, not toward Valhalla. I took Angela's Christmas shawl and tucked it beneath his bearded chin, then drew the curtain half-closed.

* * *

Belita and our two sons, Eamonn and Brendan, were anxiously waiting for me as I hobbled my way back to Four East. So was Maria from Housekeeping.

"What are we going to do with all these flowers?" She swept her arm around the room, which was lined with pots and vases.

Belita stepped in and sorted matters out. "We'll take some of them home." She chose a pink orchid and a few others. "The rest should be sent to other units. They're too beautiful to be thrown away."

Maria gave me a nudge, "You're lucky to be going home with such a good caretaker like Belita. She'll keep things just so."

"Did you know I was an orderly and Belita a lab student when we first met? She's stood by me ever since, definitely for better and for worse, and now for sure, in sickness as in health." I reached gingerly around Belita's waist and pulled her toward me in a hug of solidarity and gratitude.

I spotted a Christmas cactus in full bloom, and had an inspiration. I crossed out the card's inscription and wrote beneath it, then asked Maria to deliver it to my old roomie: "To Oliver, Get Well Soon! Your dearest desert flower, Betsy."

Our procession moved slowly through the familiar

corridors, with me in the lead. I set the pace with a halting gait and pushed my walker forward, as my glittery "Get Well" balloons bobbed with every lurch. Close behind, Belita carried her orchid like a royal orb, and behind her the boys shuffled along with as many plants and vases as they could carry.

We were greeted in the main lobby by a contingent of well-wishers led by Chris Doyle, my nursing manager, and a hodgepodge of buddies from various departments.

"You sure you're ready to go home? You don't look so hot to me," Ceil Roosa cast a clinical eye over my stooped form.

Brian Plouffe from Security walked up to me sporting a grin, as he tugged at his clip-on tie. "You're Kevlar, right? Invincible, I understand? Or did I get the name wrong?"

Marianne from Admitting waved a pamphlet in my face. "You're not going anywhere until you fill out a Patient Survey!"

I took the form from her. "I'll mail it in, I promise. But I sure learned one thing this past week—I'd much rather be a nurse than a patient."

I braced myself for the long hike to our car, a mere thirty yards. Amid cheers from my hospital friends, I aimed my walker straight through the exit door, and piped over my shoulder in my best Tiny Tim voice, "Merry Christmas to all. God bless us, every one!"

About the Author

Kevin O'Hara, a retired RN following a 30-year career at Berkshire Medical Center in Pittsfield, Massachusetts, is the proud recipient of the 2012 John Fitzgerald Kennedy National Award, for his first two books, *Last of the Donkey Pilgrims*, and *A Lucky Irish Lad*. In addition, Kevin is a longtime contributor to *The Berkshire Eagle*, and the 2020 Writer-in-Residence at Herman Melville's farmhouse, Arrowhead.

Kevin and his wife, Belita, live in Pittsfield, Massachusetts. They have two grown sons, Eamonn and Brendan.

Visit his website at www.thedonkeyman.com

Acknowledgments

When you've worked at the same hospital as an RN for over 30 years, it's impossible to thank all the people who have enriched one's nursing career. Therefore, before I begin, I apologize tenfold for the numerous folks that I've failed to mention below.

Fortunately, there are a number of colleagues who come readily to mind. They are Vicki Robare, Randy Wallingford, Rick Glaesner, Pete Francoeur, Jan O'Brien, Janet Mickle, Cathy Plakun, Alyce Kaplan, Colleen Rossi, Helen Stewart, Kathy Gideon, Jeannie Stasiewski, Takayo Minami, Jeannine Tonetti, Anita Pierce, Judy Fitzgerald, Gina Doyle, Jonathan Meehan, Michele Perrier, and Jessica Farr.

Furthermore, Mark Keller, Lyance Littlejohn, Gary Quadrozzi, Debbie Krebs, Mike Fitzgerald, Chris Symanowicz, Jim Vanasse, Kathy Aherne, Sue Spiewak, Steve Young, Betty Ann Walak, Val Trela, Dan Sadlowski, Erin D'Avella, Sherril Guinan, Rob Kirkman, Mark Massaconi, and Jonathan Weinstein.

In addition, Beatrice Selig, Marjorie St. John, Linda Patterson, Dominic Bondini, Brys Cabiles, Jana McKnight, Debi Orlando, Sally Green, Joe and Sharon Choon, Sue Reeves, Nancy Wyman, Jamie Greenlaw, Ned Minifie, Bill

Moser, Pam Morehouse, Carol O'Brien, Michelle Perrier, Mike and Ellen Greer, Brenda Bahnson, Marc Simon, Juliana Reiss, Lynn Ellis, Trish Sweeney, Cindy Dumas, Don Scherling, Derek Murphy, Tom Cole, Andy Mickle, Annmarie Cicchetti, John Bassi, Kevin Kelly, and all my coworkers who kindly allowed me to use their names in this memoir.

I also wish to thank the psychiatrists and physicians with whom I've had the privilege to work with over the long years. They include the late Samuel Tarnower, James Cattell, David Raskin, Stuart Bartle, and Gary Donovan. Other doctors are Alex Sabo, Rob Guerette, Carlos Sluzki, William Knight, Liza Donlon, Bob Tabakin, Richard Culley, Linda Smothers, Michael Ende, Leslie Fishbein, Emil Kayatekin, Richard Berlin, Phil Pryjma, Roger Pumphrey, Lara Aillon-Soules, Charles Wohl, Richard Rosenfeld, John Kearns, Barry Lobovitz, Carlos Carrera, Jennifer Michaels, John Miner, and the current Department Chair of Psychiatry, Liliana Markovic.

I'd be amiss not to mention our hospital security, aka The Blue Coats, who promptly responded to our units in time of need. They are Kevin Jester, and his valiant band of brave men, namely Jim Yeaman, Caleb Appleton and Ed Bertoldi.

Those who assisted in editing this book are Paula Dunn of Kenai, Alaska, Marc and Vivienne Jaffe of Williamstown, MA, Gene Christy of Pittsfield, MA, Martin Langeveld of Vermont and, most importantly, my longtime friend Steve Satullo of Lanesboro, MA, whose writing skills have enriched this memoir immensely.

I'd also like to thank my agent and publicist, Mary Bisbee-Beek, who found "Ins and Outs" a home at Apprentice House Press, along with its publisher, Kevin Atticks, and his talented bunch of students at Loyola University in Baltimore—namely

Elle White, Mik Fallon, Sam Dickson, and Tyler Zorn—for putting together such a handsome book.

I conclude by thanking my seven brothers and sisters—Mike, Mary, Jimmy, Dermot, Eileen, Anne Marie and Kieran—for their tireless encouragement throughout the years. Lastly, my dear wife, Belita, and our two sons, Eamonn and Brendan, who remain at the heart of my writing.

Apprentice
House Press
Loyola University Maryland

Apprentice House is the country's only campus-based, student-staffed book publishing company. Directed by professors and industry professionals, it is a nonprofit activity of the Communication Department at Loyola University Maryland.

Using state-of-the-art technology and an experiential learning model of education, Apprentice House publishes books in untraditional ways. This dual responsibility as publishers and educators creates an unprecedented collaborative environment among faculty and students, while teaching tomorrow's editors, designers, and marketers.

Outside of class, progress on book projects is carried forth by the AH Book Publishing Club, a co-curricular campus organization supported by Loyola University Maryland's Office of Student Activities.

Eclectic and provocative, Apprentice House titles intend to entertain as well as spark dialogue on a variety of topics. Financial contributions to sustain the press's work are welcomed. Contributions are tax deductible to the fullest extent allowed by the IRS.

To learn more about Apprentice House books or to obtain submission guidelines, please visit www.apprenticehouse.com.

Apprentice House
Communication Department
Loyola University Maryland
4501 N. Charles Street
Baltimore, MD 21210
410-617-5265
info@apprenticehouse.com
www.apprenticehouse.com

9 781627 203968